THE RED LAND TO THE SOUTH

The Red Land to the South

· · · ·

American Indian Writers and Indigenous Mexico

James H. Cox

Indigenous Americas

University of Minnesota Press
Minneapolis
London

An earlier version of chapter 1 first appeared as "Mexican Indigenismo, Choctaw Self-Determination, and Todd Downing's Detective Novels," *American Quarterly* 62, no. 3 (September 2010): 639–61; copyright 2010 by The American Studies Association; reprinted with permission of The Johns Hopkins University Press. Chapter 3 first appeared as "Indigenous Nationhood and Intertribal Kinship in Todd Downing's 'The Mexican Earth,'" *MELUS: Journal of the Society for the Study of the Multi-Ethnic Literature of the United States* 33, no. 1 (Spring 2008): 75–92.

Published by the University of Minnesota Press
111 Third Avenue South, Suite 290
Minneapolis, MN 55401-2520
http://www.upress.umn.edu

Library of Congress Cataloging-in-Publication Data

Cox, James H. (James Howard).
The red land to the south : American Indian writers and indigenous Mexico / James H. Cox.
    (Indigenous Americas)
    Includes bibliographical references and index.
    ISBN 978-0-8166-7597-5 (hc : acid-free paper)—ISBN 978-0-8166-7598-2 (pb : acid-free paper)
    1. American literature—Indian authors—History and criticism. 2. Indians in literature. 3. Mexico—In literature. I. Title.

PS153.I52C69 2012
810.9'897—dc23   2012020997

Printed in the United States of America on acid-free paper

The University of Minnesota is an equal-opportunity educator and employer.

20 19 18 17 16 15 14 13 12   10 9 8 7 6 5 4 3 2 1

For John Kavanaugh Cox, Caroline Ruth Schafer Cox,
and John Lewis Cox

James Alfred Greer

and Domino and Ewan, as always

Contents

Acknowledgments

M Y MOST SINCERE GRATITUDE BELONGS to Robert Warrior and Jace Weaver for their support of this book. I owe Jace Weaver additional thanks, as well as José Limón and Chadwick Allen, for writing grant letters on my behalf. Many thanks as well to Jason Weidemann, a patient, flexible, and generous editor, and the wonderful staff at the University of Minnesota Press.

The insightful observations of many other people appear in this book. Chadwick Allen read chapter 1 and reviewed multiple drafts of grant proposals. Eric Gary Anderson, Susan Kalter, Paul McKenzie-Jones, John Purdy, Carter Revard, and Matt Sparke kindly and quickly answered questions. Daniel Justice and Chris Teuton responded to a plea for help with an early version of the introduction. *Miigwetch* to Meg Noori for a last second explanation and picture of the *mide* stones.

An extra special thank you to Charles Rzepka, a fellow admirer of Todd Downing, for generously sharing his Downing materials, meeting me at odd hours during MLA conventions to talk, and writing *Detective Fiction.*

Thanks, also, to Sallie Andrews of the Wyandotte Nation, for sending her materials on Jane Zane Gordon; Frederick Boling; Lou Brock of the Osage Tribal Museum; Milissa Burkart, Library Paraprofessional, and Marc Carlson, Librarian of Special Collections and University Archives, University of Tulsa's McFarlin Library; Katy Young Evans, for finding "Encounter in Guerrero" in the Beinecke; Roy E. Goodman, Assistant Librarian and Curator of Printed Materials at the American Philosophical Society; Johannah Hochhalter; Maria Hynson, Executive Secretary to the Provost and Dean, Washington College, Chestertown, Maryland; Justin Kerr and Barbara Kerr; Hillebrand Komrij, for sending images of Todd Downing's books published in Dutch; translators Crystal Kurzen (Portuguese), Nantinee Nualnim (Thai), and Alex Pettit (Italian); David Rettig, Curator, and Belinda Trujillo, Curator Assistant and Image Archivist, Allan Houser Inc.; Sylvie Rollason-Cass, Special Collections Library

Assistant at the D'Arcy McNickle Center; Graham Sherriff, Public Services Assistant, Beinecke Rare Books and Manuscripts Library; Jacquelyn Slater, Assistant Professor of Bibliography and Librarian, Western History Collection, University of Oklahoma; and Lori Styler, Permissions Director at the Barbara Hogenson Agency.

The supportive community at the University of Texas includes research assistants Kirby Brown, Lacey Donohue, and Colleen Eils. Kirby and Colleen read the entire manuscript and provided invaluable suggestions. My deepest thanks to you both. Thank you, too, to the graduate students in my courses "American Indian Writers and Indigenous Mexico" and "Contemporary American Indian Fiction" and the members of the Native American Reading Group. The Department of English, the Center for Mexican American Studies, and the College of Liberal Arts provided support for travel, research, and relief from other duties. ¡Mil gracias a todos!

Finally, a thank you without bounds to Helen Greer Cox, who saved the day by helping check quotations.

American Indian Literature and Indigenous Mexico

T HE PUBLICATION OF CHOCTAW AUTHOR Todd Downing's *The Mexican Earth* in late March 1940 inaugurated an exciting few weeks in American Indian literary history. Fans of Downing's detective novels set in Mexico could read Philip Ainsworth Means's lavish praise of his first book-length work of nonfiction in the *New York Times* March 31 issue, and a week later theater aficionados could attend the premiere of a new play from Cherokee dramatist Lynn Riggs. *A World Elsewhere*, a drama set in Mexico and completed by Riggs while there in 1937, opened April 8 at the San Diego Community Theater. One week later, Confederated Salish and Kootenai author D'Arcy McNickle, the most celebrated American Indian writer of the mid-twentieth century, traveled to Patzcuaro, Michoacan, Mexico, for the first Inter-American Congress on Indian Life / Congreso Indígenista Interamericano from April 14 to 24.[1] Though Osage writer John Joseph Mathews is not a major figure in this study, he attended the conference as well. He had been in Mexico since October 1939, when he arrived on a Guggenheim fellowship awarded for the project that became the memoir *Talking to the Moon* (1945).[2] During this brief moment in the early spring of 1940, the three American Indian authors at the center of this study and one of their prominent contemporaries all had their eyes on Mexico.

The Red Land to the South takes as its primary focus American Indian literature between 1920 and 1960, particularly novels, histories, and plays about Mexico and indigenous Mexican peoples, cultures, and histories. The forty years under consideration here remain underexamined in the field of American Indian studies and elusive of clear definition for scholars of American Indian writing. These four decades are part of a longer era of Native writing from 1900 to 1967 defined, in the words of Jace Weaver (Cherokee), by assimilation, apocalypticism, and reform and by Daniel Heath Justice (Cherokee) as "the hyperassimilative post-allotment years."[3] Robert Warrior (Osage) describes a shorter period from 1925 to 1961 as "marked by a lack of associative cohesion," or a lack of shared political commitment, among American Indian writers.[4] These writers constitute, Warrior concludes, "a generation of free agents."[5] According to Sean Teuton (Cherokee), these free agents were writing during "a somewhat arid period for Native intellectuals."[6] Craig Womack (Muskogee Creek and Cherokee) includes "the Native novelists of the 1920s and 1930s" in a group of "earlier writers [that] were uncertain or hesitant about whether a Native voice, Native viewpoint, the narration of tribal life, or even a Native future was possible."[7] Leech Lake Ojibwe scholar Scott Richard Lyons asserts, "From the assimilation era until the civil rights movement, Native nationalism was basically dormant."[8] *The Red Land to the South* joins the conversation initiated by these scholars and others such as Chadwick Allen (2002), Louis Owens (1992), and Robert Dale Parker (2003) in an effort to define with precision and clarity the American Indian literary history of this era. By recovering Downing's entire corpus, the two plays about Mexico by Riggs, and the place of indigenous Mexico in American Indian literary history, and in its attention to many other American Indian writers from the twentieth century's middle decades, *The Red Land to the South* situates this era more securely in American Indian literary history.

The main organizing principle of *The Red Land to the South* is the political affinity for and historical interest in indigenous Mexico shared by some of the American Indian writers of this period. Mexico was a common destination and topic for American Indian as well as U.S. and British writers in the middle of the twentieth century.[9] Indeed, Cecil Robinson argues that in U.S. literary history, "[Mexico] is an unavoidable presence, and as such it has been reflected in our literature from the earliest days of border contact."[10] Downing, Riggs, and McNickle, as well as Mathews, John Milton Oskison (Cherokee), and Will Rogers (Cherokee), all visited Mexico and wrote about it. The writing of Downing, Riggs, and McNickle, in particular, coheres in its contemplation of the revolutionary potential of the indigenous peoples of the settler-colonial nation on the other side of the United States' almost two-thousand-mile-long southern border. Warrior observes of the early twentieth-century Society of American Indian generation of intellectuals that "their various writings are connected in content and context through their associations with one another."[11] The writings of Downing, McNickle, Oskison, Riggs, and Rogers are also connected in content and context through their focus on Mexico. Mexico is, for Downing, McNickle, and Riggs, a landscape resonant with exciting anticolonial possibilities that were to them much less visible, or nonexistent, in the United States.

These literary revolutions share an optimism about but map different paths to a more self-determined indigenous future. Downing sees indigenous Mexican revolution as a continuous process of patient vigilance punctuated by eras of violence, while Riggs represents it as an outburst of long-repressed indigenous anger. McNickle's revolution is local but requires for success a journey into the heart of urban Mesoamerica. Within the reindigenized territory of an American Indian imaginary, McNickle asserts a direct correlation between intertribal diplomacy and the political and cultural health of American Indian communities. Oskison and Rogers share an explicitly politicized interest in Mexico with their contemporaries, but they do not incorporate indigenous people into the Mexico they represent. The literary and political vision of indigenous Mexico produced by Downing, Riggs, and McNickle, therefore, more clearly anticipates the literature and politics of the civil rights era, as well as the alliances during that era between American Indians and Chicana/os. In quincentennial novels by Leslie Marmon Silko and Gerald Vizenor, this vision of Mexico as a shared homeland in which indigenous peoples could assert themselves far more forcefully than they could in the United States makes a dramatic return to American Indian literary history.

Comparative Indigeneities

The indigenous peoples of Mexico, who have been continuously fighting foreign occupation since May 1520 according to Downing, are the main actors in these literary revolutions, and Downing and other American Indian authors imagine them from the perspective of their own positions in indigenous spaces defined by tribal and U.S. national contexts. Definitions of indigeneity vary dramatically in the United States and Mexico and change from era to era and census to census. Many Native people in the United States, for example, have a legal indigenous identity. Discussions of this issue in the United States, such as Cherokee sociologist Eva Garroutte's *Real Indians* (2003), often begin with a consideration of these legal definitions. Garroutte explains, "Both federal and state governments formally classify certain groups as 'recognized' or 'acknowledged' Indian tribes and invest them with specific rights and responsibilities not shared by other groups."[12] She observes that while the United States grants de facto recognition to many tribal nations, such as large ones with which it signed treaties, it forces other groups, such as many small ones in the east, to navigate the arcane federal recognition process. When the United States counts individual indigenous people, it does not always or exclusively use its own tribal-nation recognition process as a factor. Historian Nancy Shoemaker reports that in the United States "budgetary constraints on the 1920 census collection meant that the Census Bureau took no special care to enumerate Indians as it had with the 1890 through 1910 censuses and the 1930 census."[13] The result was an apparent decline in the American Indian population. When the federal government actually attempted to count American Indians, its methods changed throughout the twentieth century:

> The most common standard applied today is some degree of "Indian blood." Most government programs and services use one-quarter "Indian blood" to judge eligibility, and many Indian tribes have blood-quantum requirements for tribal enrollment. Before 1960 census enumerators classified race based on observation. When in doubt, the enumerator could fall back on a list of criteria: enrollment in a tribe or at an agency, community recognition as Indian, and the "degree of Indian blood." Individuals of mixed parentage were to be classified as the race of the nonwhite parent. Since 1960 the Census Bureau has employed self-identification as the sole criterion: anyone who says they are Indian is Indian.[14]

The shift by the U.S. federal government to self-identification from either blood calculus or recognition by tribal nation and community has contributed significantly to an astonishing rise in the official American Indian population.

While budget anxiety, phenotype, and blood quantum documentation informed the number of American Indians counted in the United States in 1920, the 1921 census in Mexico asked people to identify as one of the following: "indígena pura," "indígena mezclada con blanca," "blanca," or "extranjeros sin distinción de razas."[15] Mexico took this census during the early years of postrevolutionary indigenismo, an official discourse that shaped national definitions of indigeneity in Mexico throughout the mid-twentieth century, which, along with the related discourse of mestizaje, receives a fully developed treatment in chapter 1. The 1921 census allowed the Mexican state to document two distinct populations: indigenous and mestizo, the people of both indigenous and Spanish ancestry that form the majority in Mexico. Sociologist Natividad Gutiérrez describes a perpetually antagonistic relationship between these two populations: "The mestizo culture is the cultural and linguistic model of national integration to be embraced by all indigenous peoples. Official encouragement to overcome Indian-ness and to adopt mestizaje is a source of the permanent tension and mutual distrust characterizing interethnic relations between the dominant majority and the Indian groups, the latter being exposed to every possible disadvantage derived from their marginalized situation. Indigenous sentiments of cultural rejection are intensified by the fact that mestizo culture benefits from the usurping of selected elements of the indigenous past."[16] Indigenous people in this context are defined by "low socio-economic status, subordination, inferiority, oppression, and cultural and linguistic dissimilarities vis-à-vis the mestizo," while mestizos are defined by "the overcoming of the Indians' sociocultural situation."[17] Mestizaje in the Mexican context, therefore, is a rejection of the indigenous. While this division between indigenous and mestizo was a dominant social force before and after the 1921 census, the Mexican government stopped counting mestizos after 1921.

Instead, until the year 2000, people could officially identify as indigenous in Mexico only if they spoke an indigenous language. The federal government did not account for ancestry or blood. Thus in 1940, when McNickle attended the Congreso Indígenista Interamericano and Downing published *The Mexican Earth*, about 3 million or 15 percent of the 20 million people in Mexico spoke an indigenous language.[18] Mexico, therefore, was 15 percent indigenous. In the United States, the 1940 census had a category for "color or race." Using the criteria outlined by Shoemaker, census employees counted 333,969 American Indians of a total of 132 million.[19] The United States was officially in 1940 a quarter of 1 percent indigenous. Though McNickle, Riggs, and Downing did not simply draw their perception of Mexico from these numbers, the official statistics help to explain why indigenous Mexico represented for them indigenous strength, cultural cohesion, and potentially transformative political power.

Indigenous self-identification in both Mexico and the United States varies widely within and among tribal communities and nations. Gutiér-rez sees evidence in Mexico for what she calls "microethnic identification," intensely local identification with pueblos and their patron saints, as the norm for self-identified indigenous people throughout the twentieth century.[20] "Indians identify and designate themselves," she asserts, "in a variety of ways expressing their place of origin and labor relationships. There exists a large vocabulary used by these individuals in order to avoid the word *Indio* as a source of identification. References are first to the place of origin—the coast, the highlands, the lowlands—which implies the linguistic region, and then concrete references are made to the town or pueblo of origin."[21] She adds that *paisano* and *compita*, indicating either a peasant or a relative, are common. One of her informants, the Nahua historian Luis Reyes García, says the people of his pueblo call themselves *macehual*, or "people who belong to the pueblo." Non-Indians are *coyotl*, and indigenous people from other pueblos are *pilume*.[22]

By comparison, anthropologist Circe Sturm, in *Blood Politics* (2002), and Garroutte, in *Real Indians*, take Cherokee Nation–specific and mul-titribal approaches, respectively, to documenting how American Indians define indigenous identities within or against U.S. national definitions. Following a successful petition for federal recognition, the burden of defining "Indian" shifts to the tribal nation. Garroutte explains, "Tribes have the exclusive right to create their own legal definitions of identity and to do so in any way they choose. [. . .] About two-thirds of all federally rec-ognized tribes of the coterminous United States specify a minimum blood quantum in their legal citizenship criteria, with one-quarter blood degree being the most frequent minimum requirement."[23] "However," she adds, "many Indian people cannot meet the definitions of identity imposed by the federal government or even by their own tribes."[24] In addition to blood quantum, some tribal nations base citizenship requirements on patrilineal or matrilineal descent or direct descent from an ancestor on a tribal roll. Garroutte describes the vagaries of these citizenship rules, including one particularly confounding legacy of the tribal rolls. Perhaps thousands of non-Indians found illegal ways to get their names recorded as citizens of a tribal nation. The descendants of these "non-Indian 'Indians'" are also, legally, Indians.[25] After she outlines the role of federal and tribal-nation law in establishing legal indigenous identities, Garroutte describes contem-porary American Indian views of how indigeneity is defined biologically (especially as measured by blood quantum), culturally (shared thoughts and behaviors, for example, that manifest in a person's connection to the land, participation in ceremonies, and fluency in an indigenous language), and personally (especially as invented by "ethnic switchers" and Indian recruitment organizations).

Sturm examines the political implications of these identity contexts in her Cherokee Nation–specific work. In the twentieth century, the era under consideration in this study, "blood became central to Cherokee identity," Sturm explains, "not just as a racial, social, and cultural metaphor but as a documented biological possession."[26] Citizenship in the Cherokee Nation requires this documented possession of Cherokee blood quantum or what Sturm calls "blood belonging."[27] She adds, "Even though the Cherokee Nation requires some blood connection to an ancestor listed on the Dawes Rolls, it sets no minimum blood quantum for tribal membership, unlike most other Native-American nations."[28] In contrast to this Cherokee national definition of citizenship, "local systems of social classification are still shaped to a significant extent by criteria other than blood ancestry, causing Cherokees to question the almost exclusively blood-based definition of tribal identity."[29] Sturm discusses "five indexical markers of Cherokee identity other than blood ancestry: phenotype, social behavior, language, religious knowledge and participation, and community residence and participation."[30] These Cherokee local rather than Cherokee national markers of identity, especially language and community residence, correspond with several of the categories of identity at work in indigenous communities in Mexico.

Thus local community definitions of indigeneity in the United States and Mexico affirm but also frequently challenge indigeneity as it is defined by American Indian tribal-national, U.S., and Mexican governments. There are, however, regardless of the definition, many more indigenous people in Mexico than in the United States. According to the Mexican federal government, indigenous people comprised at least 10 percent of Mexico's approximately 110 million people in 2010. Half of these eleven million indigenous people speak an indigenous language. In comparison, according to the U.S. federal government, there are approximately five million American Indians and Alaska Natives in the United States or 1.5 percent of the total population of 308 million. Approximately 1 percent of the five million people who identify as American Indian speak an indigenous language. According to these numbers, Mexico has twice as many indigenous people and at least ten times the number of indigenous language speakers as the United States, and the indigenous population of Mexico represents a much larger percentage of the nation's total number of people. Indigenous Mexicans also represent a significant percentage of Mexican migrants to the United States, such as Mixtecs and Zapotecs from Oaxaca who began in the 1940s to build, explains anthropologist Lynn Stephen, "migration networks" throughout the United States but primarily in the West.[31]

When American Indian writers in the mid-twentieth century visited Mexico, they likely saw "Indians" where indigenous Mexicans, mestiza/os, or nonindigenous Mexicans did not. Key components of the historical context might even have predisposed some American Indian writers to perceive an overflow of indigeneity in Mexico: the much higher percentage of indigenous people as part of the total Mexican population, the central role of indigenismo in the construction of a unified postrevolutionary Mexican national identity, the reform of Mexican federal Indian policy in the 1920s and 1930s, and the prominence in Mexico of mestiza/os who might have identified or have been identified as American Indian in the United States. These authors then optimistically, but at times inaccurately, represented this overflow of indigeneity to a U.S. audience as a powerful cultural and political force in Mexico. This lack of correspondence among textual and lived Mexicos, however, did not diminish the potential political value of these representations and narratives of revolution.

Indigenous Mexico in American Indian Histories

These representations and narratives of indigenous Mexico were, in fact, already part of some American Indian tribal-nation histories. Downing, Riggs, and McNickle reconstruct these already present cultural and historical bonds among indigenous people in Mexico and the United States, which Spanish, French, and English colonial and independent Mexican and U.S. settler-colonial literatures and histories obscure. These bonds are recorded in the oral and written histories of the Mexicas (Aztecs), Cherokees, and Choctaws, for example, and also delineated by many nonindigenous historians and anthropologists. Despite the borders established by settler-colonial nations in North America, many indigenous peoples in the United States continue to view Mexico as part of a large shared homeland. Some American Indian writers in the middle of the twentieth century draw upon and perpetuate this history for the next generation of indigenous American people when they imagine Mexico as a space in which to contemplate the futures of their own tribal nations and, more broadly, all American Indians.[32]

The Chicana/o civil rights movement gave the story of Mexica origins in Aztlán some prominence in U.S. social and political contexts.[33] In her study of Chicana/o indigenism, Sheila Marie Contreras observes, "Most scholars of the Mexica believe Aztlán, if an actual geographic space, was located in Mesoamerica, somewhere north of Mexico City. [. . .] For many others, the term has more mythical than geographic significance and is understood as symbol or metaphor, as an Edenic—to use a familiar Judeo-Christian term—place of origins."[34] Anthropologist Carroll L. Riley identifies the entire region north and west of Mexico as Colhuacan and describes Aztlán, "The Place of Herons," as an island, "a central place, containing seven magical caves, the natal place, the womb so to speak, of the Aztec people."[35] As a cultural area, however, Riley argues that Aztlán encompasses much of the U.S. Southwest and the Mexican Northwest.[36] For information about the location of Aztlán, anthropologist Martha Menchaca looks to the first accounts of the Mexica homeland documented by Spanish chroniclers: "When the Aztec transmitted their accounts of Aztlán, they conceived it as reality and acknowledged it as their ancient past. They claimed that Aztlán was the place of their birth as a people. No one knew where Aztlán was located; they merely indicated to sixteenth-century cartographers that it was to the north of the Valley of Mexico."[37] Historians Michael C. Meyer and William L. Sherman offer a more specific suggestion: "The origins of the Aztecs are apparently found on an island off the coast of the state of Nayarit, at Aztatlán or Aztlán, from which many tribes wandered southward."[38] Accounts of Aztlán by Chicana/o writers of the civil rights era situate it in Arizona, New Mexico, Colorado, and/or California.[39]

The indeterminate location of Aztlán gives the site part of its political currency; American Indian as well as Chicana/o writers have some liberty to choose its location based on specific political goals. In *The Mexican Earth*, his history of indigenous Mexico, Downing situates Aztlán in the southwestern United States as part of his project of making legible a kinship among American Indians and, in Downing's figuration, the more culturally and politically cohesive indigenous Mexicans: "Aztlan has been located in Canada, California, up and down the Rockies. While it is too nebulous a place ever to be identified with certainty, there is reason to believe that the Aztecs crossed the Colorado and Gila Rivers and the deserts of Chihuahua to Culiacán in the present state of Sinaloa."[40] The Colorado River runs from Colorado through Utah and northern Arizona before forming the border between Nevada and California and emptying into the Gulf of California. The Gila River is a tributary of the Colorado that runs from New Mexico through southern Arizona. The account of this movement of indigenous American peoples between regions, later circumscribed by the borders of two different settler-colonial nations, allows Downing to foreground an indigenous history and geography. In this history and geography, there are no settler-colonial borders between indigenous peoples in the United States and Mexico. Effacing these borders is a step toward building a political and cultural program of anticolonial resistance for American Indians based on what Downing observes in an always revolutionary indigenous Mexico.

In addition to their first contact with Spanish rather than English colonizers, Cherokees have, in contrast to the Mexicas, accounts that they migrated from or through the land that is now Mexico.[41] In his *History of the Cherokee Indians and Their Legends and Folk Lore* (1921), Cherokee historian Emmet Starr explains: "The Cherokees most probably preceded by several hundred years the Muskogees in their exodus from Mexico and swung in a wider circle, crossing the Mississippi River many miles north of the mouth of the Missouri River as indicated by the mounds. [. . .] The Muskogees were probably driven out of Mexico by the Aztecs, Toltecs or some other of the northwestern tribal invasions of the ninth or preceding centuries. This is evidenced by the customs and devices that were long retained by the Creeks."[42] Though Starr leaves room for doubt, he treats this account confidently as empirical history rather than legend or folklore. Contemporary Cherokee writer Robert Conley is less confident but still relates the story as significant to Cherokee history. He summarizes a story by Levi Gritts, who Conley identifies as a Nighthawk Keetowah Cherokee of Oklahoma, about Cherokee origins in South America and an eventual migration through Mexico. The tone of Conley's commentary on the story is remarkably similar to Downing's on the story of Aztlán: "It seems reasonable to say that the Cherokees likely came from South America and migrated north through Central America and Mexico, eventually stopping for a time in the northeast along with the other Iroquoian-speaking tribes there."[43] Conley then makes his own investment in this particular story transparent: "At best, origins are obscure. We tend to believe what we want

to believe."[44] For Conley, specifically, this history of nearly constant Cherokee migration helps him to recontextualize the forced migrations of the
colonial and settler-colonial eras not as aberrations in Cherokee history
but as variations on distinct Cherokee experiences.

Historians, anthropologists, and archaeologists describe in detail the
bonds and migrations documented in these indigenous histories. In her
discussion of the Southeastern Ceremonial Complex, art historian Susan
C. Power reviews the scholarship on and summarizes these bonds: "In
addition to maize, some of the clearest cultural links between North
America and Mesoamerica are flat-topped accretional mounds, the organization of major centers, tobacco, weaponry, metalwork, the Ball Game,
cyclical renewal, and the extinguishing of fires."[45] Power then catalogs the
similarities in the form and content of indigenous art in both regions with
a focus on feathered serpents and winged beings. She concludes: "Archaeology and oral traditions show that the worldview and belief systems of
Mesoamerica and the eastern United States were quite close over a period of many centuries, perhaps millennia."[46] Riley also explores "the idea
of meaningful Mesoamerican influence in the Southwest" in *Becoming
Aztlán: Mesoamerican Influence in the Greater Southwest, AD 1200–1500*
(2005). The focus of his work is the three-hundred-year era of the title in
which "a wave of new religious, ceremonial, and political ideas, as well as
new artistic styles and new technology, swept up from Mexico."[47] He traces evidence of these Mesoamerican influences in ceremonial platforms
and ball courts, as well as town organization and construction tech-
niques. Power's and Riley's scholarship maps an indigenous world from
Mesoamerica through the U.S. Southeast and Southwest populated by a
network of groups with economic, political, and cultural ties.

These histories likely shaped Cherokee views of Spanish Mexico as a
safe haven from British and U.S. colonial violence. The story of the "Lost
Cherokees," as recorded by James Mooney, tells of a group of Cherokees
that protested land cessions by leaving the Southeast for northern New
Spain in 1721. Other Cherokees found them later living in a precolonial
Cherokee world.[48] Historian Dianna Everett cites a report of Cherokees
visiting one of New Spain's northern provinces, Texas, in 1807 and establishing a settlement there in 1813.[49] The Cherokees that followed were
attempting to move beyond the reach of the United States: "Over the winter of 1819–1820, the first Cherokees known to have settled permanently in
Texas crossed the Red River into presumed Spanish territory. The leader

of this group was probably Duwali."[50] Duwali, or Chief Bowls, remained in Spanish and then Mexican Texas. Richard Fields, who Everett argues was a "red" chief, led a delegation to Mexico City beginning in December 1822. Fields hoped to establish an alliance with Mexico, but he returned to Texas in June 1823 without an agreement.[51] The Cherokees eventually signed a treaty with Texas in 1836, establishing a reservation with their "associate bands," including the Choctaws. Texas did not immediately consider ratification of the treaty and then nullified it on December 16, 1837.[52] Following the Texas revolution, a Republic of Texas militia attacked Duwali's band, killed him, and drove the rest of the band to Indian Territory. While the Texas Cherokees negotiated with Mexico and the Republic of Texas, John Ross in the Cherokee Nation in Georgia also attempted to make arrangements with Mexico to reserve land for the Cherokees.[53] The famous inventor of the Cherokee syllabary, Sequoyah, also made a journey to Mexico at the end of his life in an attempt to find Cherokee relations living there.[54] Daniel F. Littlefield Jr. (Cherokee) describes a Cherokee delegation sent to Mexico in the early 1840s by the Old Settlers, under John Brown, and another larger delegation of Old Settler and Treaty Party Cherokees in 1845.[55]

Several generations after Sequoyah and Brown, Mexico maintained its presence in the Cherokee political imaginary. When Cherokee citizens faced the allotment of their nation's land in the late nineteenth century, some of them looked to Mexico as a possible sanctuary. From 1895 to 1908, Indian Territory and Oklahoma newspapers reported on various plans by Cherokees and groups from other tribal nations to emigrate to Mexico.[56] Conley describes one of the most prominent plans: "Bird Harris proposed that the Cherokee Nation go ahead and sell all of its land to the United States, use the money to purchase land in Mexico or South America, and then remove the entire Cherokee Nation once more, this time completely beyond the long and greedy reach of the United States."[57] Conley connects Harris's proposal to the movement led by Redbird Smith, a Keetowah Cherokee. The Keetowahs were "traditional Cherokees [. . .] devoted to the preservation of Cherokee culture and politically opposed to mixed-bloods in the tribal government."[58] They were also abolitionists who later resisted allotment. Conley relates that when some Keetowahs decided to enroll on the lists used for allotments, Smith formed the Nighthawk Keetowah Society and continued to resist. In 1910, Redbird Smith, by then the chief of the Nighthawk Keetowahs, "went to Mexico with a document dating from 1820 hoping to prove a claim to land under that government."[59] The journey, an attempt to realize what Littlefield calls "the utopian dream of the Cherokee fullbloods," was unsuccessful.[60] Yet the journey made clear again that for some Cherokees, Mexico was a place associated not only with precolonial histories but also with resistance to colonialism. Riggs's own frequent visits to Mexico in the 1930s, and perhaps his long relationship with the Mexican dramatist Enrique Gasque-Molina (Ramon Naya), confirmed for him this view of Mexico.

The connections that Downing and McNickle make among indigenous U.S. and indigenous Mexican peoples are a product of their personal, political, and historical interests in the indigenous people of contemporary Mexico. The most common Choctaw explanation of their origins describes their emergence from the earth out of a mound called *Nanih Waiya* in what is now the state of Mississippi.[61] However, Downing spends the first half of his eleven-page *Cultural Traits of the Choctaws* (1973) tracing the cultural influence of indigenous Mexico on the Choctaws. The Choctaws, like the Cherokees, had first contact with Hernándo de Soto and the Spanish.[62] Groups of Choctaws began arriving in Texas as early as 1814, while it was still a northern province of Spanish colonial Mexico. They continued to arrive after Mexican independence.[63] A little further north, Downing's paternal grandmother reached Indian Territory in 1832, during the removal of the Choctaws from Mississippi.[64] Her family settled in the Choctaw Nation, which, before Texas independence, shared its southern border for two years, from 1834 to 1836, with Mexico. A century later, Downing experienced Mexico primarily as a visitor with political and intellectual interests. He was a tour guide in Mexico during the summers in the late 1920s and early 1930s, and his personal library of more than 1,500 volumes, which he donated to Southeastern Oklahoma State University, contains many volumes on Mexico as well as Latin America.

McNickle was involved with John Collier's administration at the Bureau of Indian Affairs (BIA), and he shared Collier's interest in Mexico's federal Indian policy as a model for the United States. Like Collier, he attended the first Inter-American Congress on Indian Life in Mexico in 1940. His journey to Mexico occurred in a busy season of conferences in the United States and Canada, during which activists and organizers held the discussions that led to the formation of the National Congress of American Indians in 1944. This influential intertribal organization, therefore, appears to have at least one root in Mexico. McNickle's family history also includes a flight from persecution across another settler-colonial national border between Canada and the United States. McNickle's maternal grandfather, Isidore Parenteau, participated in Louis Riel's resistance movement in 1885. He fled with his family to Montana after Canada executed Riel.[65] While several generations of Cherokees unsuccessfully negotiated for or otherwise sought sanctuary in Mexico, McNickle's family successfully found refuge among other indigenous peoples across another southern settler-colonial border.

A generation after Redbirth Smith traveled to Mexico in search of sanctuary for the Nighthawk Keetowahs, Downing, Riggs, and McNickle took the same journey. During and following those visits, they wrote about the indigenous Mexican past and contemporary indigenous Mexican life. They tended to emphasize the anticolonial histories of the Mexicas, Mayans, and Yaquis, rather than the Tlaxcaltecas, for example, who aligned with Cortés.[66] They rejected the anxiety of nonindigenous American authors from the United States and other nations about Mexico's perceived propensity for violence and narrate it as a desirable force of indigenous revolution. They saw in the indigenous worlds of Mexico the political, historical, and cultural materials that allowed them to contemplate a politically and culturally robust future for Native peoples and communities in the United States.

Literary Revolutions

The murder of two Mexican college students by deputy sheriffs in Ardmore, Oklahoma, on June 8, 1931, dramatically altered the life of Choctaw author Todd Downing, one of the most prolific and neglected American Indian novelists of the twentieth century and the focus of chapter 1. Downing immediately suspended the summer tours that he guided in Mexico and started a writing career that included ten novels. In a novel such as *The Cat Screams* (1934), Downing appropriates and refigures indigenismo—the official celebration of Mexico's indigenous history and culture—to reveal evidence of the modern indigenous people obscured by indigenismo discourse. These indigenous people persevere in a world in which two postcolonial settler governments, the United States and Mexico, are in conflict with each other, while maintaining the colonial practices of the European empires from which they secured their independence. In his novels, Downing makes three extraordinary discoveries in the context of mid-twentieth-century American Indian literary history. He detects a persistent though enervated European colonial presence in Mexico and a more potent neocolonial invasion of Mexico by U.S. tourists, academics, smugglers, drug addicts, and criminal venture capitalists. Even more surprising in an era widely perceived by scholars as politically impotent, Downing identifies a contested yet enduring indigenous Mexican resistance to this neocolonial invasion and the oppressive Mexican state. Finally, Downing finds in this resistance a model for Choctaw self-determination that he puts into practice in a bilingual (Choctaw and English) education program that he helped to create in the early 1970s. His detective novels provide, within the American Indian novel tradition as it existed in the middle decades of the twentieth century, a consistently hopeful though not fully developed narrative of contemporary indigeneity.

Lynn Riggs, the celebrated Cherokee playwright of *Green Grow the Lilacs*, on which Richard Rodgers and Oscar Hammerstein based *Oklahoma!*, is, in addition to Downing, part of a productive and well-known group of Indian Territory–born writers who were publishing during the middle decades of the twentieth century. He set his plays *A World Elsewhere* (1947) and *The Year of Pilár* (1947) in the 1930s, when President Lázaro Cárdenas began a reform program called *agrarian cardenismo* that involved redistributing land from the hacendados to indigenous communities. In *A World Elsewhere*, General Gonzalo Fernandez Aguirre, a former hacendado, starts a counterrevolution and takes U.S. tourists hostage as indigenous service workers organize against him behind the scenes. In *The Year of Pilár*, an expatriate Yucatecan family returns to its home prior to the redistribution of its land, discovers its blood kinship with local Mayans, then must flee an armed indigenous revolution. Riggs dramatizes the possibility of and justifies indigenous revolution, but he is more reluctant than Downing to celebrate it. The menacing violence in these plays suggests some anxiety about social upheaval. However, when placed within the context of his entire career and read through the perspective of early twentieth-century Cherokee history in Indian Territory and Oklahoma, *World* and *Pilár* demonstrate that Riggs saw Mexico, like Downing, as a place where indigenous people could more forcefully assert themselves.

During a particularly difficult era for the Choctaw Nation in Oklahoma, from statehood in 1907 until 1970, Downing also wrote *The Mexican Earth* (1940), a history of Mexico as an indigenous nation that interprets optimistically Cárdenas's reforms and identifies, nearly half a century before anthropologist Guillermo Bonfil Batalla, a México profundo at the center of Mexican national life. In chapter 3, I consider this work within the context of the diplomatic moments in nonfiction published in this period by Rogers, Standing Bear, and Mathews, and discuss the political implications of Downing's effort to map an indigenous-to-indigenous diplomatic relationship between tribal nations in the United States and indigenous communities in Mexico. Downing developed the views of indigenous Mexico presented in *The Mexican Earth* during the formative moments of the transnational and hemispheric political perspectives adopted by indigenous people in the next generation. He highlights the specific histories that define indigenous Mexican communities, but, similarly to Acoma Pueblo author Simon Ortiz, for example, he also encourages indigenous solidarity against colonial dominance by emphasizing diplomacy among all indigenous peoples who share the experience of originating and continuously residing in the Americas.[67] The diplomatic obligations of indigenous nations and communities with roots in a shared homeland, he indicates, provide the foundation for socially transformative international relations and a more promising indigenous American future.

Confederated Salish and Kootenai author D'Arcy McNickle's *Runner in the Sun*, the focus of chapter 4, foregrounds the kinship of indigenous U.S. and Mexican peoples and connects the maintenance of this relationship to the health of indigenous nations and communities. As the federal government was terminating its trust relationship with tribal nations and encouraging American Indians to move to urban centers in the early 1950s, McNickle crafted a narrative of migration that establishes the cultural and historical kinship of a cliff-dwelling community in the southwestern United States and Culhuacan in central Mexico. The novel is a handbook for rebuilding tribal nations during an era of attacks against them as well as a reimagined Inter-American Congress on Indian Life. In *Runner in the Sun*, the cliff dwellers face drought and political factionalizing, and they send a runner to their central Mexican homeland to find solutions to these crises. The runner returns with the knowledge to lead a new community on the plains below the cliffs. McNickle correlates the recognition of intertribal kinship to the peaceful establishment of new communities, imagines a model for international diplomacy that preserves the integrity of indigenous communities, and alludes to the potential of an indigenous American coalition to challenge the hemisphere's settler-colonial governments.

The move in chapter 5 from the early 1950s to the early 1990s produces a different lacuna in American Indian literary history than the more familiar one that runs from the 1920s to the 1960s, when N. Scott Momaday's 1968 novel *House Made of Dawn* inaugurated the Native American literary renaissance. By producing this gap, I suggest only that there are many literary histories still to recover and assess and that the field-wide production of a dominant literary history focused on the renaissance figures tends to impede this work.[68] In 1991, Leslie Marmon Silko and Gerald Vizenor published *Almanac of the Dead* and *The Heirs of Columbus*, respectively, in anticipation of the Columbian quincentennial. Indigenous Mexico figures prominently in both novels. Like Downing, Riggs, and McNickle, Silko and Vizenor see a Mexico that promises indigenous political strength, historical continuity, and cultural cohesion. Indeed, Sean Teuton's characterization of Red Power literature of the early renaissance era accurately describes the work on indigenous Mexico by Downing, Riggs, and McNickle: "During the era of Red Power, Native writers imagined a new narrative for Indian Country, and they did so neither by longing for an impossibly timeless past nor by disconnecting Indians' stories from the political realities of their lives. Instead, writers of the era struggled to better interpret a colonized world and then offered this new knowledge to empower the people."[69] These literary historical and political bonds among the earlier generation of writers, and two of the most celebrated American Indian renaissance authors, help to rehabilitate the reputation of this neglected era of American Indian literature.

Tribal Nations and Trans-Indianism in Greater Indian Territory

The Red Land to the South, in theory and practice, shifts constantly among distinct and overlapping territories and jurisdictions. It implements the tribal-nation specificity of Craig Womack and Daniel Justice in the chapters on Todd Downing and Lynn Riggs and in the readings of John Oskison and Will Rogers. Downing was born a citizen of the Choctaw Nation and Riggs, Oskison, and Rogers of the Cherokee Nation, and they witnessed the dissolution of their national governments. Their tribal-nation political and cultural identities remained important to them, however, and continued to inform their literary production. I will embed my readings of Downing and Riggs, Oskison, and Rogers, therefore, in Choctaw and Cherokee contexts, respectively, including those tribal nation–specific contexts shaped by familial and local histories. I also rely on the tribal nation–specific work of anthropologists such as Valerie Lambert and Circe Sturm and historians such as Andrew Denson and Robert Conley. In the chapter on McNickle, I will focus primarily on his work within the broader pan- and intertribal American Indian literary contexts that Jace Weaver documents in such detail in his work and to which many other scholars gesture from a more specific tribal-nation base.

This study also shares with the work of scholars who identify as American Indian literary nationalists a concern for the politics of literature and literary criticism, particularly as those politics potentially influence contemporary efforts by tribal nations to practice self-government. Throughout *The Red Land to the South*, I follow the guidance of critics such as Justice, Weaver, and Womack, as well as Robert Warrior, who situate Native writing in those political contexts that are most urgent for Native peoples. In an assessment of the institutional history of the interpretation of American Indian writing, Crow Creek Sioux scholar Elizabeth Cook-Lynn observes that "the literatures themselves are rarely conceptualized as foundations for native political insight and action, and the result is that the study of their own literatures by tribal people becomes irrelevant to their lives."[70] Downing's, Riggs's, and McNickle's works are not only foundations for Native political insight and action; they are explicitly political in their narration of a revolutionary, anticolonial indigenous Mexico and an American Indian struggle—in McNickle's novel a successful one—to maintain cohesive communities and nations. The works by Downing and Riggs in particular dramatize what Cook-Lynn calls a major feature of Native nationalism—retribution.

The pan- and intertribal contexts of American Indian political activity and U.S. and Mexican federal Indian and immigration policies, as documented by historians such as Francisco Balderrama and Raymond Rodríguez, Thomas Cowger, Daniel M. Cobb, Ben Fallaw, Donald Fixico, Alan Knight, Stephen E. Lewis, Rick López, and Mary Kay Vaughan, will also inform my readings. The making of Indian and immigration policy in the United States and Mexico diverges and converges throughout the four central decades of this study. In 1924, the U.S. Congress passed the Indian Citizenship or Snyder Act. In that same year, it passed the National Origins Act and created the U.S. Border Patrol in response to illegal immigration and the smuggling of alcohol. Downing, Riggs, McNickle, and the other authors in this study were writing within this context and the context of a U.S. national history shaped by the Indian Reorganization Act of 1934 and the Oklahoma Indian Welfare Act of 1936, the massive deportation and repatriation of Mexican nationals and Mexican Americans, and a Mexican national history of postrevolutionary nationalism that included indigenismo as well as land reform under President Lázaro Cárdenas.[71] McNickle published his novel *Runner in the Sun* a decade into his work with the National Congress of American Indians (NCAI) and during the era of termination and relocation in the United States in the 1950s. His work with the NCAI coincides in part with the federally sponsored guest worker or *bracero* program with Mexico, which ran from 1942 to 1964.

The Red Land to the South focuses primarily on the movement of American Indian minds and bodies across the U.S.-Mexican border, but it does so within the context of these other, often indigenous, removals and migrations. It is, therefore, a borderlands study, at least geographically. These authors see through that which is "vague and undetermined" in the Anzaldúan borderlands, or see through the "shifting mosaic of human spaces" in the fugitive landscapes of historian Samuel Truett's borderlands, to a coherent indigenous world.[72] This act of seeing is both historical recovery and political strategy, and it involves the derecognition of colonial and settler-colonial worlds and the borderlands that they produce. Their historical and political vision transforms Américo Paredes's Greater Mexico, "all the areas inhabited by people of Mexican culture— not only within the present limits of the Republic of Mexico but in the United States as well—in a cultural rather than a political sense," into both a Greater Indigenous Mexico and a Greater Indian Territory.[73]

By mapping an indigenous American world that existed prior to the colonial era and that continues to span settler-colonial national borders, these authors produce an indigenous American transnational or transborder imaginary. This study thus participates in what Rachel Adams describes as the "'transnational turn' in American literary and cultural studies."[74] Adams explains: "Many scholars have come to see the nation, which had long been the implicit organizing principle of much work in the field, as constrained by rigid borders and teleological narratives about the origin and destiny of the American people. Whereas once the 'America' of American studies could be assumed to lie within the geographical borders of the United States, this is no longer the case." Instead, many American studies scholars have become "attentive to the significance of geography and place while seeking to avoid the limitations of an exclusively nation-based paradigm." "At its best," she concludes, "[transnationalism] does not seek to ignore borders or to bypass the nation altogether, but to situate these terms within a broader global fabric."[75] Adams uses the term "indigenous transnationalism" in her discussion of Silko and Thomas King "to describe these authors' representation of the divisive, centrifugal forces of modernity that have dispersed North American Indians, but also of the drive to form coalitions across the boundaries of tribal nations and nation-states. In their work, such coalitions are not simply a reaction to the fractious power of the nation-state, but rather the resumption of alliances and networks of filiation that were severed by the conquest and its aftermath."[76] This definition of indigenous transnationalism also accurately describes the work of the authors central to this study and therefore makes legible a literary and political link between the mid-twentieth century and the post–civil rights era. However, *The Red Land to the South* emphasizes tribal nations and other forms of indigenous community as major historical and political factors in the discussion. It makes an effort to consider the implications for American Indian literary history and politics of reading the "national" in "transnational" as referring to the tribal nation rather than the settler-colonial nation-states of the United States and Mexico and, in the case of Adams's study, Canada.

The Red Land to the South also has an affiliation with *Mapping the Americas*, in which Shari Huhndorf considers the ways that "indigenous transnationalisms in particular extend existing American studies critiques of national identity and imperialism as they radically challenge the histories, geographies, and contemporary social relations that constitute America itself."[77] Downing, Riggs, McNickle, and other writers in this study rigorously challenge these histories, geographies, and social relations in the generation preceding the renaissance. My interest is what these challenges suggest about the constitution of Native nations in the mid-twentieth century and in the indigenous futures these authors imagine. Therefore, while the transnationalism under my purview also "refers to alliances among tribes and the social structures and practices that transcend their boundaries, as well as processes on a global scale such as colonialism and capitalism," I strive to maintain a focus on indigenous-to-indigenous relations.[78] These relations are transnational in the context of tribal nation to tribal nation, tribal nation to indigenous community, tribal nation to settler-colonial nation, or settler-colonial to settler-colonial nation. They are what Paul Lai and Lindsey Claire Smith call "alternative contacts," and they form the social component of an indigenous transnation, the aforementioned Greater Indigenous Mexico or Greater Indian Territory.[79]

These relations are, as anthropologist Lynn Stephen explains, always more than transnational. Stephen uses "transborder" to describe the experience of indigenous Mexican immigrants to the United States beginning in the 1940s:

> The borders they cross are ethnic, class, cultural, colonial, and state borders within Mexico as well as at the U.S.–Mexico border and in different regions of the United States. Regional systems of racial and ethnic hierarchies within the United States are different from those in Mexico and can also vary within the United States. Thus the ways that "Mexicans" and "Indians" have been codified in California and Oregon can differ from how they have been historically built into racial and ethnic hierarchies in New York or Florida. While crossing national borders is one kind of crossing undertaken by the subjects of this book, there are many others as well.[80]

At times, indigenous Mexican immigrants also cross tribal-national borders or class and cultural borders between themselves and American Indians. The authors at the center of *The Red Land to the South* draw our attention to the indigenous American-specific histories of these border crossings and their potential contribution to political, cultural, and tribal-national revitalization efforts.

Downing culturally and McNickle and Vizenor narratively reconstitute these transnational and transborder experiences as tribal nation or tribal community–specific, and these contacts are at the moment they occur intertribal and trans-Indian but not pan-Indian. Robert Warrior explains a crucial difference between pan-Indianism and intertribalism in *The People and the Word* (2005). He uses as his example the Native prisoners at Fort Marion in the 1870s under the supervision of Richard Henry Pratt. Warrior views the interaction of the seventy-one prisoners—Cheyennes, Arapahoes, Kiowas, Comanches, and one Caddo—as an example of "the intertribal sociality that later helped produce American Indian powwow culture."[81] He elaborates, "People from different tribes at Fort Marion shared songs and their situation provided a forum for developing the ethic of respect for particularity and sameness that remains an ideal of intertribal gatherings and organizations. Intertribalism, importantly, stands in marked contrast to Pan-Indianism, which seeks to blend and homogenize Native cultures."[82] While Warrior indicates that intertribalism and pan-Indianism are incompatible, intertribalism and trans-Indianism, or the indigenous specific rejection of the borders of settler-colonial nations, work together to reject those nations as, for example, geographically, historically, or politically determinant of indigenous life.

The Red Land to the South contributes to the scholarship that documents Mexico's place in Chicana/o, U.S., and British cultural imaginaries and prepares the groundwork for various comparative studies. Historical, political, and cultural contexts shape the key distinctions among the views of Mexico held by American Indian writers, such as Riggs and Downing, and U.S. and British writers. D. H. Lawrence portrays indigenous Mexicans in his novel *The Plumed Serpent* (1926) as alien and repulsive; thus, their revolution is ominous. To Hart Crane and Graham Greene, indigenous Mexicans were unfathomable or a source of Mexican national evil and brutality.[83] Riggs and Downing, however, recognize a historical and cultural kinship with indigenous Mexicans. As denationalized citizens of the Cherokee and Choctaw nations, respectively, indigenous Mexican revolution held for them a promise of retribution or tribal-national revitalization. The politics of their representations of indigenous Mexico are coherent with the same representations in civil rights and post–civil rights era Chicana/o literature. The literary productions by Downing, Riggs, McNickle, Vizenor, and Silko are, in Ana Patricia Rodríguez's words, "fictions of solidarity."[84] These fictions privilege American Indian rather than indigenous Mexican subject positions, and writing them involved a process of appropriation. Yet these fictions of solidarity differ in historically and politically significant ways from Lawrence's fiction of an alien south or Kerouac's fiction of a "magic *south*" in *On the Road* (1957).[85] A comparative study of American Indian and Chicana/o fictions of indigenous Mexico would illuminate both literary histories and suggest other possibilities for political solidarity.

Instead, within the context of contemporary American Indian literary critical practice, *The Red Land to the South* assesses the pattern of narration and representation about indigenous Mexico only in the work of these American Indian writers. It offers several answers to the question posed by Womack in *Red on Red*: "How do Indians view Indians?"[86] Downing, Riggs, and McNickle view indigenous Mexicans as revolutionaries, while

Oskison and Rogers, for example, see a Mexican nation but appear not to see indigenous Mexicans at all. In the additional context of their depictions of historical and contemporary Cherokees, Choctaws, Osages, Salish, and American Indians more generally, these authors and the others under consideration in this study show a robust and prolific era of American Indian writing in which the real and imagined revolutions in Mexico speak with particular clarity to the next two generations of American Indian writers and intellectuals.

Renaissance Reconsidered

The surprising politics of the mid-twentieth-century writing by Downing, Riggs, and McNickle about Mexico, particularly in contrast to both their own work set in American Indian nations or the United States and the work of many other American Indian writers of the period, establishes an international route from these authors to the American Indian civil rights movement and literary renaissance of the next generation. A full accounting of the accomplishments of the writers of this interwar and early contemporary era forces a reconsideration of that renaissance as a movement that both emerged from a period of quiescence and dramatically redirected the course of American Indian literary history. In the decades between the progressive era and the first wave of the renaissance from 1968 to 1992, only McNickle has a secure place in the conversation, as a writer who serves as a bridge, though a very narrow one, between the two periods. *The Red Land to the South* begins to fill this lacuna in American Indian literary history by examining some of the astonishing amount of writing, much of it extraordinarily popular, by American Indians in this era.[87]

One of the characteristics of this period, and perhaps one of the reasons for its marginal presence in American Indian literary studies, is the dominance of nonfiction, particularly history and biography.[88] There was not as much fiction, drama, or poetry by American Indian authors in the mid-twentieth century, but the authors who were publishing were popular and prolific. Mathews followed *Wah'kon-tah*, "a phenomenal success and [. . .] a featured selection of the Book-of-the-Month Club," with his novel *Sundown* (1934).[89] Oskison wrote numerous short stories and three novels. McNickle published two novels during his lifetime, while Downing published ten. Riggs wrote short stories, poems, at least eighteen one-act and full-length plays, and at least seven others that were produced but not published. Phyllis Braunlich notes that critics discussed two of his plays, *Green Grow the Lilacs* (1931) and *Russet Mantle* (1936), as contenders for Pulitzer Prizes.[90] In addition to the posthumous publication of McNickle's novel *Wind from an Enemy Sky* (1978), Timothy B. Powell and Melinda Smith Mullikin have recovered Oskison's *The Singing Bird*, while Weaver has recovered Riggs's play *Out of Dust* (2003).

Ruth Muskrat Bronson, Ella Deloria, Downing, Sunshine Rider/Princess Atalie Unkalunt, Riggs, Rogers, and Luther Standing Bear represent an impressive group of American Indians with national reputations in writing, performance, and/or politics. Indeed, Rogers was one of the most popular writers and celebrities in the world in the 1920s and 1930s.[91] He and the others also share the era with Nicholas Black Elk. His specific contributions to *Black Elk Speaks* (1932) only became clear more than fifty years after initial publication of the book, but the spiritual worldview associated with him has been influential both within and outside Native American communities since that time.[92] Vine Deloria Jr. calls *Black Elk Speaks* "perhaps the only religious classic of this [the twentieth] century," and Arnold Krupat calls it "perhaps the single best-known Indian autobiography of all."[93] The public presence of American Indians in this period—in newspapers, on the radio, in film, on stage, in conversation with presidents—is comparable to the preceding and succeeding periods.[94]

The Red Land to the South introduces to a contemporary audience some of the American Indian writers of this neglected interwar and early contemporary era. They are a diverse and prolific group with a broad range of political affiliations. However, the anticolonial spirit of some of their work, as they articulate it within an indigenous Mexican landscape, speaks across the generations to contemporary critics interested in the political projects to which American Indian literatures might contribute within tribal-nation contexts and on behalf of tribal-nation sovereignty. This study attends to the "refiguring of the period to take into account the multiplicity of voices" and thus joins a project that Warrior contends in *Tribal Secrets* "has become an obvious necessity in American Indian critical studies."[95] It attempts to move the authors' writing during this period from the margins to a more prominent place in the field. It argues, too, that these middle decades of the twentieth century constitute a major era of American Indian literary production on par with the eras that frame it. We cannot understand the accomplishments of either the preceding reform era or the succeeding American Indian literary renaissance without a comprehensive view of the writers and writer-activists at work between 1920 and 1960. In particular, the continuities of intellectual and political purpose will appear surprising when viewed against conventional American Indian literary history.

CHAPTER 1

Dreadful Armies

Indigenistas and Other Criminals in
Todd Downing's Detective Novels

Todd Downing, one of the most prolific and most neglected American Indian writers of the twentieth century, began his career as an author of detective fiction after working as a tour guide in Mexico during the summer months of the late 1920s and early 1930s. Like the other American Indian authors under consideration in this study, Downing traveled in a postrevolutionary Mexico that was in the process of incorporating indigeneity into a unified national identity. In eight of the ten novels that he published between 1933 and 1945, Downing appropriates and refigures this indigenismo—the official celebration of Mexico's indigenous history and culture—to reveal evidence of the modern indigenous people obscured by indigenismo discourse. These indigenous people persevere in a world in which two postcolonial settler governments, the United States and Mexico, are in conflict with each other while also imposing upon indigenous populations within their borders the colonial practices of the European empires from which they secured their own independence and sovereignty.[1]

Downing makes three extraordinary discoveries in his novels in the context of twentieth-century American Indian literary and activist histories. He detects a persistent though enervated European colonial presence and a much more potent neocolonial invasion of Mexico by U.S. tourists, academics, journalists, smugglers, drug addicts, kidnappers, and criminal venture capitalists. He also identifies a contested yet successful indigenous Mexican resistance to this invasion as well as to the oppressive policies of the Mexican state. Finally, in a novel such as *The Cat Screams*, his depiction of a determined attempt to maintain indigenous autonomy anticipates the anticolonial discourses of the American Indian civil rights movement of the late 1960s and early 1970s and the literary renaissance that attended it.

Downing began to publish these narratives that both condemn the criminal abuse of indigenous people, material culture, and bodily remains and depict individual efforts at indigenous self-determination in the same year that President Franklin Roosevelt nominated John Collier as commissioner of the Bureau of Indian Affairs. As commissioner, Collier facilitated the U.S. Congress's passage of the Indian Reorganization Act in 1934 and started to encourage the U.S. federal government to use Mexico's Indian policy as a guide for reform.[2] Downing's understanding of indigenous self-determination is, however, more tribally specific and less paternalistic than Collier's brand of reform. When put into practice in the early 1970s, Downing's version of self-determination found expression in his work with a grassroots Choctaw bilingual education program for which he authored some of the classroom materials. By devoting himself to this program, Downing contributed intellectually to a Choctaw national context in which a coalition of Choctaw citizens mobilized against both the Choctaw Termination Act of 1959 and their own fellow citizens and politicians that supported it.[3]

Atoka, Norman, Ardmore: The Local Roots of Downing's Mexican Mysteries

George Todd Downing was born in 1902 in Atoka in the Choctaw Nation, Indian Territory, now Oklahoma, to Maude (Miller) Downing and Samuel Downing.[4] Samuel Downing was the son of George Downing, a farmer from Fannin County in north Texas via Indiana and Kentucky. George left his first wife and thirteen children to move to Boggy Depot, Indian Territory, in 1866, where he married Mary Armstrong, whose parents came to Indian Territory in 1832 during the removal of the Choctaws from Mississippi. George and Mary had four children, including Todd's father, Samuel.[5] In "A Choctaw's Autobiography," published in 1926 in a Tulsa periodical called *The American Indian*, Todd Downing observes,

> My father has always been a power among the Choctaws. During the Spanish-American war he was a member of Theodore Roosevelt's Rough Riders, serving the incomparable "Teddy" as interpreter with the Choctaw and Chickasaw members of this organization. He was a member of the statehood delegation to Washington that secured statehood for Oklahoma. At present he

is a member of the Choctaw Tribal Council and is taking a leading part in the efforts to wrest from the United States government
the fulfillment of promises which have never been fulfilled and to
prevent further encroachment upon the rights of the Indians.[6]

Downing published this autobiography almost twenty years after the final
stages of allotment culminated in Oklahoma statehood and in the middle
of an era characterized by what Choctaw anthropologist Valerie Lambert
calls "the very high level of attenuation of Choctaw tribal relations and
structures."[7] Downing presents his father as a political activist working
as a member of an official Choctaw government body to maintain those
Choctaw tribal relations and structures and to defend all American Indians from a settler colonial government.

Downing took the legacy of his father's political activities quite seriously. "A Choctaw's Autobiography" includes the outline of a political
platform that Downing develops in greater detail in his novels and then in
The Mexican Earth. Downing begins the autobiography by providing what
he calls a "brief summary of the history of the tribe of American Indians
in which I am proud to claim membership—the Choctaws."[8] After asserting himself as a Choctaw, Downing emphasizes that he does not intend to
encourage a focus on tribal nation differences. Instead, at least for the sake
of presenting a united front to the invasive United States, he argues that
American Indians should assert themselves as a single ethnic bloc:

> Their fatal fault and weakness in the past has been this inability
> to cement an effective union on racial, instead of tribal grounds,
> a consistent weakness which rendered unavailing their efforts to
> resist the encroachments of the white man. This still remains the
> hardest single obstacle in the path of those Indians who are not
> [*sic*] attempting to hold the United States government—a govern-
> ment dedicated to liberty and the proposition that all men are
> created equal—to the promises made to their fathers. It seems to
> the writer that it is indeed high time we Indians thought more of
> ourselves as Indians and less as representatives of a single tribe.[9]

In his *Cultural Traits of the Choctaws*, published in 1973 just before his
death, Downing repeats this concern: "Let's not, in our talk about the
Choctaws and our concentration on the Choctaws, get to thinking that

the Choctaws are so entirely different from other people. [. . .] Keep in mind that we are stressing the differences, but more important than those differences is the fact that the Choctaws simply belong to the human race."[10] The differences, for Downing, are "geographical and historical," not racial.[11] Elizabeth Cook-Lynn and Simon Ortiz, who were born during Downing's most prolific years and became influential renaissance-era writers, engage in this same negotiation between respect for tribal-nation specificity and desire for indigenous solidarity.[12]

Though Downing rejects tribal specificity in his autobiography as a political position, at least when the United States is the antagonist, he practices it during his life, especially on a local level. He calls his autobiography a Choctaw's rather than an American Indian's life story and publishes it in a magazine edited by Lee F. Harkins, the Choctaw writer, printer, editor, publisher, and rare book collector.[13] He continues, too, to identify himself to a broad audience as Choctaw throughout his life, and he helps to develop a Choctaw bilingual education program within the Choctaw Nation, rather than participate in an organization such as the National Congress of American Indians. In his life and work, Downing reconciles the different political strategies that tribal national, U.S., and, as in the novels and *The Mexican Earth*, transnational contexts demand. Each strategy, whether it appears as Choctaw specific or as a nascent continental ethnic indigenous nationalism, has a contribution to make to the health of indigenous communities.[14]

Downing wrote "A Choctaw's Autobiography" while he was a twenty-four-year-old MA student at the University of Oklahoma in Norman. After graduating from high school in Atoka, he entered the university in 1920, earned his BA in 1924, and continued as a graduate student with his work in indigenous and colonial Latin American literature and history. By the time he completed a master's thesis on Florencio Sanchez, a Uruguayan dramatist, Downing was an accomplished intellectual who spoke five languages (Choctaw, English, French, Italian, and Spanish). After completing his graduate degree, he remained as a faculty member in the Department of Modern Languages at the University of Oklahoma, where he taught Spanish. He was also a reviewer of books in French, Italian, and Spanish for *Books Abroad*, the forerunner of *World Literature Today*, for which he also served as advertising and then business manager from 1928 to 1934; a voracious reader of American, English, Mexican, and Latin American history and literature; and an equally avid reader of mystery novels by Agatha

Christie, Sir Arthur Conan Doyle, Dashiell Hammett, Dorothy Sayers, Ellery Queen, and Wilkie Collins, whose collected works are part of the library of more than 1,500 volumes that Downing donated to Southeastern Oklahoma State University. During the summers, he worked as a tour guide in Mexico.

Organized crime and murder in Mexico became Downing's specialties, but he began to write his first detective novel following a local act of violence that posed a serious threat to the already strained diplomatic ties between the United States and Mexico: the murder of two young Mexican college students by deputy sheriffs in Ardmore, Oklahoma, about seventy miles from Atoka, on June 8, 1931.[15] Emilio Cortes Rubio and Salvatore Cortes Rubio, both relatives of Mexico's president, and Manuel Gomez were traveling together from colleges in Atchison, Kansas, and Rolla, Missouri, to Mexico City when they stopped in Ardmore. The conflicting testimonies of the survivor, Salvatore Cortes Rubio; the law enforcement officers; and the eyewitnesses frustrate attempts to reconstruct the sequence of events that culminated in the murders. The men with badges, however, had the legal and cultural sanction to tell the most authoritative, if perhaps not the most plausible, narrative. After stopping to question the men, Deputy Sheriff William E. Guess, who was no stranger to shooting men while on the job, and Deputy Sheriff Cecil Crosby claimed "that the shooting occurred after the two youths had drawn guns, although they did not fire; that Crosby disarmed one youth; that the other emerged from the car with a gun protruding from a blanket thrown about his shoulders; that thereupon Guess fired, killing the student; that then the first youth, who had been disarmed, produced a small pistol, and Guess fired on him."[16] Representatives at the highest levels of the Oklahoma, U.S., and Mexican governments corresponded in a diplomatic language of earnest regret as opaque as the specific circumstances of the fatal confrontation that early summer morning. A jury acquitted Crosby and Guess, and the United States sent $30,000 as reparations to the victims' families in Mexico.[17]

Following the murders in Ardmore, Downing wrote his first novel, *Murder on Tour* (1933). In a letter to his sister, Ruth Shields Downing, he announces the exciting news that G. P. Putnam's Sons purchased the book and offered him a contract for two books a year: "There's no need for me to tell you," he writes, "how I am floating around in the clouds." He also anticipates with some eagerness the possibility of a career change from university professor to professional author: "I am going to hang on as long as possible, of course, but if the book sells well, I can be independent of the State of Oklahoma if I want to be. It's a great feeling. [...] I am about on the point of giving up the tour racket and doing some writing down in Mexico."[18] After the publication of *Murder on Tour*, Downing resigned from the University of Oklahoma and moved to New York, rather than Mexico, to become a professional writer.

While he lived in New York and then Philadelphia in the 1930s and 1940s and worked for several advertising agencies, including the famous firm N. W. Ayer and Son, Inc., Downing achieved as an American Indian fiction writer a level of success matched only at the end of the twentieth century by writers such as Louise Erdrich (Turtle Mountain Ojibwe) and Sherman Alexie (Spokane and Coeur d'Alene).[19] Downing had the powerful New York publisher Doubleday Doran promoting him as a Choctaw author to a broad, international audience that appears to have relished his novels.[20] Doubleday Doran published eight of his ten mysteries for its Crime Club and advertised his novels in the *New York Times*. The same newspaper reviewed at least eight of those novels and made announcements about Downing's career.[21] Four of those novels were reprinted at least once in the United States, and at least nineteen editions or translations of Downing's novels were published in European countries.[22]

Three novels were also reproduced in other popular or mass culture formats. Downing's second novel, *The Cat Screams* (1934), was published in England by Methuen, translated into Italian, reprinted in the United States by the Popular Library, and adapted by Basil Beyea into a Broadway play, also called *The Cat Screams*, in 1942.[23] The *New York Times* reported on the play during every step from preproduction to its opening on June 16, 1942, at the Martin Beck Theatre and its closing on June 20, 1942, after seven shows.[24] Downing's third novel, *Vultures in the Sky*, was printed in 1935 in four successive issues of *Short Stories Twice a Month*, a pulp magazine published by Doubleday Doran, then printed in its entirety on December 15, 1935, in newspapers such as the *Detroit Free Press* and the *Philadelphia Inquirer* as the featured Sunday novel of the week. It was then reprinted in England by Methuen (1936), in 2 *Detective Mystery Novels Magazine* in the spring of 1950, and in translation in Finnish, Spanish, and Italian. The Italian translation was reprinted as late as 1977. Downing's fifth novel, *The Case of the Unconquered Sisters*, was reprinted in *Detective Novel Magazine* in August of 1943. Three of Downing's other novels were reprinted, and *The Lazy Lawrence Murders* earned mention in the "Murder

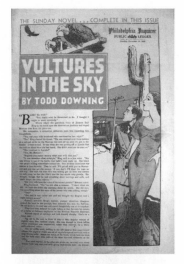

Figure 1.1 Todd Downing's novels were distributed nationally and internationally in many different formats. His third novel, Vultures in the Sky *(1935), was published in book form but also in the* Philadelphia Inquirer *as the illustrated "Sunday Novel" on December 15, 1935. The* Inquirer *published the Sunday novels from 1934 to 1949.* Murder on Tour *(1933) is his first novel. The image shows the first and only edition in the original dust jacket.* Kuoleman Linnut *(1942) is the Finnish translation of* Vultures in the Sky. *Downing's fifth novel,* The Case of the Unconquered Sisters, *was published as a book in 1936 and again in* Detective Novel Magazine *in August of 1943. The reprints indicate that the popularity of his novels extended through the early 1940s. From the author's collection. Photos by Johannah Hochhalter.*

in May" section of *Time* magazine on June 9, 1941. The reviewer called the novel "pretty good."[25]

Yet even following the reprinting of Downing's *The Mexican Earth* in 1996 by the University of Oklahoma Press, we have not turned to his mystery novels in order to assess his place in twentieth-century American Indian literary history. The lack of attention scholars have given Downing is at least curious in light of the critical scrutiny of popular culture productions about indigenous people by nonindigenous artists. The oversight is particularly astonishing if we consider that by placing Downing's work into a Choctaw literary history, an American Indian literature of Oklahoma tradition, and a twentieth-century American Indian literary history where it properly belongs, the number of novels by American Indian authors under consideration prior to the publication of N. Scott Momaday's *House Made of Dawn* in 1968 nearly doubles.

Downing's focus on indigenous people in Mexico rather than in the United States explains in part his almost complete absence from scholarship on twentieth-century American Indian writing. Yet that absence is still a mystery that would test even the extraordinary skills of ratiocination of Downing's detective, Hugh Rennert. Downing has escaped our notice, including my own, even though his popularity and production can be compared favorably to a contemporary such as Lynn Riggs. Downing's popularity in the 1930s and 1940s led Marion E. Gridley, a prolific author of popular histories about and biographies of American Indians, to devote entries to him in the 1936 and 1947 editions of *Indians of Today*. Works such as Mary Marable and Elaine Boylen's *Handbook of Oklahoma Writers* (1939) and fellow Choctaw Muriel Wright's *A Guide to the Indian Tribes of Oklahoma* (1951) also celebrate Downing's literary accomplishments.[26] A. S. Burack included an essay by Downing, along with contributions by such luminaries in the field of detective fiction as Dorothy L. Sayers and S. S. Van Dine, in the edited collection *Writing Detective and Mystery Fiction* (1945). After his death in 1974, Downing continued to secure mention in local publications such as *Tales of Atoka County Heritage* (1983) and in reference works such as Bill Pronzini and Marcia Muller's *1001 Midnights: The Aficionado's Guide to Mystery and Detective Fiction* (1986). Pronzini and Muller devote an entry to Downing and *Vultures in the Sky*, though they also praise *The Cat Screams*, *The Case of the Unconquered Sisters*, and *The Last Trumpet*.[27]

That Downing wrote in a popular genre likely has some correlation to the critical inattention. Arnold Krupat argues that on the "odd but powerfully operative scale" of the American literature canon in the late 1980s, two decades into the Native American renaissance, popular literature placed fifth and Native American literature "a distant sixth" at the bottom of the hierarchy.[28] With the welcome exception of recent work such as Phil Deloria's *Indians in Unexpected Places* (2006) and Amy Ware's articles on Will Rogers, American Indians also have been more readily identified as objects rather than producers of popular culture in this era. Even more contemporary American Indian authors of detective novels, such as D. L. Birchfield (Choctaw), Sara Sue Hoklotubbe (Cherokee), Carol LaFavor (Anishinabe), Thomas King (Cherokee), Ron Querry (Choctaw), and William Sanders (Cherokee) have not received much critical consideration.

Another potentially illuminating explanation for this neglect can be reached by taking a cue from Downing's novels and conceptualizing literary critics as detectives searching for a particular kind of textual indigeneity. Louis Owens's *Other Destinies* (1992) is an example of first-generation renaissance scholarship that covers novels in this period. Owens points to identity as the primary focus of American Indian writers: "In spite of the fact that Indian authors write from very diverse tribal and cultural backgrounds, there is to a remarkable degree a shared consciousness and identifiable worldview reflected in novels by American Indian authors, a consciousness and worldview defined primarily by a quest for identity."[29] Downing's indigenous Mexican characters are not, however, on a quest for identity. Charles Larson's *American Indian Fiction* (1978) and Kenneth Lincoln's *Native American Renaissance* (1983) also cover, in part, the middle of the twentieth century. Larson and Lincoln, respectively, identify explicit resistance to assimilation and distinctly Native oral traditions as characteristics of Native literature most worthy of scholarly consideration. Their critical assumptions preclude the detection of Downing, whose main characters are predominantly, though not exclusively, nonindigenous; who does not privilege indigenous beliefs and cultural practices; and who, with the exception of *The Cat Screams*, rarely draws from oral storytelling traditions and Native epistemologies to frame his narratives, as many of the next generation of renaissance writers born during the 1930s and 1940s do.

Even in a more recent era characterized by the recovery of many American Indian authors and the emergence of American Indian literary nationalism, which foregrounds tribal national histories rather than issues of identity and cultural authenticity, Todd Downing remains almost completely overlooked. Until LaVonne Ruoff's *American Indian Literatures: An Introduction, Bibliographic Review and Selected Biography* (1990), scholars of American Indian literatures did not recognize Downing's contributions to American Indian literature. Downing does not appear in bibliographies such as Arlene Hirschfelder's *American Indian Authors* (1970) and Tom Colonnese and Louis Owens's *American Indian Novelists* (1985) or in the aforementioned influential monographs by Owens, Larson, and Lincoln.[30] In the only scholarly article about Downing, Wolfgang Hochbruck discourages further intellectual inquiry by concluding that Downing does not explore issues important to indigenous people and defining Downing's work as existing outside what he calls "the core" of indigenous literature. This core, argues Hochbruck, consists of "works that are consciously written about or use Native issues and materials and that are intended for both Native and non-Native audiences on a larger scale."[31] Hochbruck's derecognition of Downing as a writer of American Indian literature is symptomatic of broader forces at work in the field; Indiana Miami scholar Malea Powell identifies "the utter ease with which counter-stories are unseen and, ultimately, unheard by even the most well-intentioned scholar."[32] Indeed, by Hochbruck's own definition, a Downing novel such as *The Cat Screams* occupies a space at the core of American Indian literature.

Downing's novels show an author interested in much more than mining incidents of lethal force by the local police for plot material. The *New York Times* covered the murder of the Mexican college students and the subsequent trial and then reported almost a decade later: "Todd Downing got his start as a writer because an Oklahoma deputy sheriff shot down two Mexican boys as they were returning from school in Kansas in the Spring of 1931. At that time Mr. Downing was teaching Spanish at the University of Oklahoma and was conducting tourist parties to Mexico during his Summer vacations. Because of the shooting, it was feared that Oklahomans would not be welcome in Mexico at that particular time, and so Mr. Downing was at loose ends."[33] Gridley is only a little more revealing: "In 1931, the murder of two Mexican youths disrupted the plans for one of [Downing's] tours, for warnings were issued by the Mexican government of the dangers to Americans vacationing there. The details of the murder were an inspiration for plot material, and encouraged to write by a university professor, he launched his fictional career and produced 'Murder on Tour.'"[34] The indictment of a culture of U.S. violence in these novels includes an unwavering indignation at the treatment of Mexican citizens, especially the indigenous population, and an incisive critique of the sustained, criminal abuse of Mexico by a U.S. neocolonizing force that augments and, Downing suggests, rivals the already present settler colonialism at work in Mexico for sheer brutality and contempt for indigenous life.[35] By also engaging Mexican national discourses about indigeneity, specifically indigenismo, Downing sustains in his novels a two-pronged, transnational reproach to settler-colonial aggression.

Postrevolutionary Indigenismo and Mestizaje: The Mexican Context of Downing's Mysteries

The family politics that Downing inherited from his father shaped his appropriation of these Mexican national discourses as well as indigenous Mexican history and culture and Mexican federal Indian policy. Following the end of the Mexican revolution in 1920, indigenismo made indigeneity a much more significant feature of national identity in Mexico than in the United States. Though according to most commentators the contribution of indigenous people to indigenismo was negligible, indigenismo as a Mexican national discourse provided Downing with a public space in which he could imagine indigenous Mexican people as modern political and cultural actors.[36] Historians Mary Kay Vaughan and Stephen E. Lewis describe the origins of indigenismo: "In 1921, on the heels of the twentieth century's first social revolution, the Mexican government launched a nationalist movement celebrating the culture of Mexico's mestizo and indigenous peoples and recasting national history as a popular struggle against invasion, subjugation, and want."[37] Even during the era of the Society of American Indians from 1911 to 1924, American Indians had a much more uncertain place in national U.S. discourses. At that time, explains Phil Deloria, "according to most American narratives, Indian people, corralled on isolated and impoverished reservations, missed out on modernity—indeed, almost dropped out of history itself. In such narratives, Native Americans would reemerge as largely insignificant political and cultural actors in the reform efforts of the 1920s and 1930s."[38] While American

Indians in the United States continued in the early twentieth century to experience the rejection of their place in both history and modernity, "the revolutionary version of history" in Mexico, assert Vaughan and Lewis, "placed greater emphasis on Mexico's indigenous foundations and contemporary cultures."[39] In his study of two celebrations of independent Mexico's centennial in 1921, Rick López provides a more dramatic reading of this context: "According to the emerging nationalist rhetoric first articulated by Manuel Gamio in 1916, to be truly Mexican, one had to be part indigenous or at least to embrace the idea that indigenousness was vital to the national consciousness. Rejection of Mexico's contemporary indigenous peoples and cultures, de rigueur before the revolution, was now criticized as a mark of unpatriotic xenophilia."[40] In the United States, as Shari Huhndorf demonstrates in her analysis of the racial politics of the 1893 World's Columbian Exposition in Chicago and the 1909 Alaska-Yukon-Pacific Exposition in Seattle, the national ideal was white racial purity. Huhndorf assesses Chicago's White City and Seattle's Cascade Court as the spatial and material expressions of the whiteness that indigenous racial difference threatened to attenuate.[41] Postrevolutionary Mexico offered, therefore, an attractive alternative present for American Indian authors like Downing. Neither history nor modernity in Mexico had been settled, as it had according to dominant narratives in the United States, so decisively in favor of non-Native people.

Yet indigenismo in Mexico had U.S. roots. López argues of the centennial celebrations that "both reveal the extent to which the turn toward an 'ethnicized' or 'Indianized' definition of Mexico's national culture did not flow inevitably out of Mexico's historical experience, as is generally assumed, but instead resulted from a distinct movement led by cosmopolitan nationalists inside and outside the government [. . .] in a profoundly transnational context."[42] Two cosmopolitan nationalists, Adolfo Best Maugard and Manuel Gamio, were principal organizers of these celebrations: Best of the Noche Mexicana in Chapultepec Park and Gamio of the Exhibition of Popular Arts. Best and Gamio were influenced by the time they spent in the United States with Franz Boas, the anthropologist who launched a critique of evolutionary anthropology in the 1880s and 1890s while arguing that "race, language, and culture were not now and probably never had been closely correlated."[43] The anthropologist and historian George Stocking Jr. argues that Boas influenced two "of the most fundamental orientations of modern American cultural anthropology: on the one hand, the rejection of the traditional nineteenth-century linkage of race and culture in a single hierarchical evolutionary sequence; on the other, the elaboration of the concept of culture as a relativistic, pluralistic, holistic, integrated, and historically conditioned framework for the study of the determination of human behavior."[44] In addition to his long affiliation with Columbia University and his influence on such American Indian intellectual-activists as Arthur C. Parker (Seneca), Archie Phinney (Nez Perce), and Ella Deloria (Yankton Dakota), Boas served in 1910 as the first director of the Escuela Internacional de Antropologia in Mexico.[45] Boas's former student Gamio was "the founder of postrevolutionary indigenismo" and one of the leading indigenistas—a non-Native promoter of indigenismo.[46]

This shift in the United States to Boasian anthropology in the early twentieth century helped to undermine dominant theories of race but also kept politics secondary if not irrelevant.[47] As Hazel Hertzberg reminds us, Boas "remained aloof from all Pan-Indian movements" and maintained an "indifference to Indian causes" throughout his career.[48] In Mexico, as intellectuals and federal officials during the 1920s increasingly used indigeneity—indigenous history and material culture—as the thread that bound Mexican citizens to each other, settler-colonial policies of violent containment remained in place: the Mexican air force dropped bombs on the Yaquis in 1926.[49] Indigenismo was not incompatible with racism, historian Alan Knight explains, as it functioned in Mexico and was even closely linked, he argues, to Mexican Sinophobia in the 1930s.[50]

These centennial celebrations, federal policies, and the national discourse of indigenismo were symptoms of the mestizo dominance of Mexico. Twentieth-century Mexican mestizaje, the mixture of Spanish and indigenous that produces mestiza/os, is closely related to indigenismo.[51] The celebration of mestizaje in Mexico, however, did not involve according indigeneity an equal role on the national stage with mestiza/o, European, or other nonindigenous identities. Instead, "advocating mestizaje served," asserts Rafael Pérez-Torres, "to effectively erase the presence of a contemporary indigenous identity in Mexico, relegating the Indian to the mists of a tragic and oblivious past."[52] In her study of race and modernity in Latin America from 1910 to 1940, Tace Hedrick observes, "Part of what undergirded the political use to which mestizaje was put was the sometimes explicit, sometimes implicit idea that through race and cultural mixing the Indians, *qua* Indians, would eventually die out, and there would be left a modern nation of mixed Indo-Hispanic mestizos who, as José Vasconcelos suggested, since they could not return to the ways of their (Indian) ancestors, would have no choice but to make of themselves a bridge into the future."[53] Guillermo Bonfil Batalla describes mestizaje in Mexico as "de-Indianization" or "ethnocide."[54] While mestiza/os have indigenous ancestry, in many cases enough to enroll in an American Indian tribal nation with the most stringent blood quantum requirements, their self-identification as mestiza/o indicates a social, cultural, and political rejection of this ancestry.

Thus nonindigenous Mexican people, even if mestizo-identified, were the primary actors in the creation of a postrevolutionary national identity. Put another way by Knight, "The Indians themselves were the objects, not the authors, of indigenismo."[55] The indigenistas argued among themselves about how to incorporate indigeneity into a unified Mexican national identity. For example, Best and the prominent intellectual and bureaucrat Vasconcelos thought that Native material culture required interpretation and improvement by nonindigenous artists, while Gamio and Gerald Murillo, the painter, writer, and centennial celebration organizer known as Dr. Atl, wanted to maintain the "authenticity" of indigenous arts. According to López, Dr. Atl saw "indigenous artisans as primitive producers isolated from modern commercialization."[56] In this context characterized by postrevolutionary nationalism and indigenismo, López explains, "the masses can contribute only passively to the nation, through their instincts and intuition, not through their self-determined cultural or political genius."[57] In López's assessment of the Mexican context, there is an echo of Deloria's observation that Native people in the United States were "largely insignificant political and cultural actors" in the 1920s and 1930s.

Downing was most interested, however, in contemporary indigenous Mexicans, such as the Yaquis in Sonora, as actors. Popular and official histories asserted that the Yaquis, who are separated from Yaquis in Arizona by the Mexican-U.S. border, had never been conquered. Though some Yaquis had experienced removal to Yucatán in 1908, a year after Oklahoma statehood, they were still resisting militarily in the 1920s. This history of military resistance led to the creation of an anomaly in indigenous Mexican life. There were no reservations in Mexico, but in the late 1930s President Cárdenas "recognized the authority of Yaqui governors and set aside 450,000 hectares as Mexico's only tribal land grant."[58] Cárdenas had also started his land reform program that involved the redistribution of

the land owned by the large haciendas to indigenous communities. Ben-
eficiaries of the Cárdenas land-reform program included the Kickapoos,
who began arriving in Mexico in the late 1830s, following a long migration
from the U.S. upper Midwest.[59]

Indigenous people were not silent in this era, either. In 1939, Lewis
explains, after indigenous leaders requested "separate-but-equal Indian
schools," the Autonomous Department for Indian Affairs responded by
issuing a statement "that Indians had the right to preserve their language
and customs and called for bilingual schools taught by indigenous teachers
and tailored to local customs and needs."[60] Jan Rus also describes assertive
Maya politics and cultural revitalization in Chiapas in the late 1930s and
early 1940s. He observes that, to distinguish this era from the revolution of
the 1910s, "the years from 1936 to the beginning of the 1940s are sometimes
referred to in Chiapas as 'la revolución de los indios.'"[61] Thus indigenismo, particularly in its most radical formulations in the 1930s, created a
public space for indigenous Mexicans to make some political demands.[62]
That public space was also available for appropriation by American Indian
writers who witnessed the brief reform era in the United States that began
with the passage of the Indian Reorganization Act in 1934.

White Villains and Red Herrings: Indigenous
Mexico in Downing's Novels

From within the context of a politicized Choctaw history, Downing
claims in his novels this public space created by indigenous Mexican history and culture and official Mexican indigenismo. A detective novel such
as *The Cat Screams* becomes in Downing's hands an investigation both
of the disregard for Mexican lives represented by the deputy sheriffs of
Ardmore and of the strategies that indigenous Mexicans develop to resist
or evade similar acts of state-sponsored violence and settler-colonial
oppression. Many of Downing's characters view indigenous Mexican people as superstitious and latently violent, even as frequently on the threshold
of armed revolution, but Downing consistently exposes this figuration of
indigenous people as a colonial red herring, as an alibi for non-Native
people that draws the attention of readers away from the crimes that non-
Natives are committing. Downing only once in his ten novels delivers to
readers an indigenous criminal, a young man in the novella "The Shadowless Hour" (1945) named Jesus who kills both his mother's drug dealer,

a former university professor of Mesoamerican studies, and a zealous missionary who discovers evidence of his guilt. Instead, indigenous and nonindigenous Mexicans are frequently victims of crimes committed by visitors, immigrants, and expatriates from various European countries and north of the border; crime is the primary export to—rather than a product of—Mexico in Downing's novels.

In an era in the United States of menacing cinematic Indians, indigenous Mexican peons obstructing modernization, and anti-Mexican hysteria fed by the Great Depression, the novels are an extraordinary public challenge to the dominant U.S. views of indigenous Americans and indigenous and nonindigenous Mexican nationals, as well as to the contemporary (and still prevailing) narrative about the flow of violent crime from the south, especially Mexico, toward the United States.[63] As two postcolonial settler nations vie for power—economically, politically, narratively—and the neocolonial agents of the United States descend on Mexico, Downing finds indigenous people in a vulnerable position but with resources available that help them to escape the fray. Indigenismo made indigenous Mexico part of a daily conversation in which indigenous Mexicans had a limited role. By identifying in a novel such as *The Cat Screams* the strategies that contemporary indigenous Mexicans use to maintain their communities as the battle rages around and against them, Downing appropriates indigenismo and forces Native voices, beliefs, and bodies into that conversation. He then takes this reconstituted Mexican national discourse, incorporates it into his understanding of the place of the Choctaw Nation in the United States, and near the end of his life begins to practice his own version of Choctaw self-determination.

Criminality in *The Cat Screams* has the same European and U.S. origins as it does in his first and third novels, *Murder on Tour* (1933) and *Vultures in the Sky* (1935). In *Murder*, a U.S. couple smuggle indigenous Mexican artifacts into the United States and commit murders to hide their illicit business. This theft of indigenous Mexican cultural productions by U.S. criminals is an apt metaphor for indigenismo, the intellectual and bureaucratic theft of Mexican indigeneity by a predominantly nonindigenous and mestizo Mexican elite. In *Vultures*, a kidnapper flees south Texas on a train to Mexico in disguise as a businessman interested in purchasing mining leases from indigenous people. He hopes to escape prosecution in south Texas by participating in the state-sanctioned criminal activity of dispossessing Native people. The kidnapper murders several passengers and an indigenous porter to avoid detection, and he finds unexpected cover when a French citizen and dangerous Catholic militant also traveling to Mexico City consumes the attention of the authorities. A Yaqui platoon of Mexican soldiers eventually captures the Cristero. To any members of a U.S. audience predisposed to seeing either dangerous Mexican immigrants undermining the U.S. economy or childlike Mexican peons, the image of Yaqui soldiers marching with a Catholic militant as their prisoner would likely have been disconcerting. The image is a surprising reversal of the dominant representations of indigenous Mexicans in the United States and Mexico, as well as an assertion that indigenous Mexicans have an active role to play in a modernizing Mexico.

Downing disguises a story of indigenous resistance and revolutionary promise within a conventional story of detection in *The Cat Screams*. In the novel, the suicides of several women haunt the U.S. colony in Taxco in the southwestern Mexican state of Guerrero.[64] The deaths can be traced to the narcotics trafficking of Madame Céleste Fournier, the daughter of French immigrants, including a father who was an administrator in

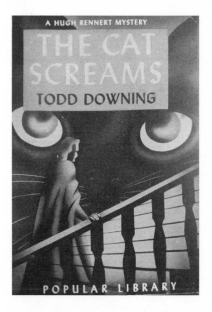

Figure 1.2. The Cat Screams (1934) was reprinted by the Popular Library in 1945. The biography on the back cover identifies Downing as Choctaw and Mexico as "an Indian country." From the author's collection. Photos by Johannah Hochhalter.

Maximilian's court during the French occupation of Mexico from 1862 to 1867.[65] Fournier's home is an alien colonial space: "Madame Fournier during her occupancy installed modern plumbing and called the house a pension, so that the discriminating tourist might distinguish it from the many native *casas de huéspedes* in the town."[66] Downing then confirms that we should read Fournier, one of the few non-U.S. villains in his canon, as the sign of an unassimilated European presence in Mexico, for "on Bastille Day she always hung out the Tricolor and invited her guests to drink champagne with her."[67] Her current guests comprise a rogue's gallery of U.S. citizens that includes Donald Shaul, a predatory tabloid journalist from New York; Dr. R. L. Parkyn, an archaeologist from Chicago looking for potentially lucrative jade deposits; and Gwendolyn Noon, a New York stage actress and drug addict. These visitors are the privileged guests of a caste system that structures a colonized indigenous Mexico dominated by Europeans and their descendants. While the guests at the pension are all nonindigenous visitors from the United States, the members of the staff are all indigenous Mexicans: Esteban, the *mozo*, or servant; Micaela Guerrero, the cook, who shares a name with the Mexican state in which she lives and works; and Maria, the *criada*, or waitress.

Yet Fournier is an infirm sign of French colonial aggression and European or nonindigenous dominance, and the recognition of her vulnerability is crucial to Downing's identification of possible sites of indigenous resistance. Benito Juárez, the liberal reformer and president of Mexico, led the successful fight against the occupying French army and had Maximilian executed. Downing's allusion to this era of Mexican history draws our attention to Juárez as the indigenous face of Mexican resistance to foreign invasion. At the same time, neither Juárez's Zapotec identity nor his dedication to reform should imply a political alliance with indigenous people. The liberal government that defeated Santa Anna in 1855 and in which Juárez served as secretary of justice forced indigenous communities to sell their communally held land, the ejidos. Juárez's relationship with the United States also does not translate easily into Downing's critique of the criminal, neocolonial U.S. presence in 1930s Mexico. Juárez lived in exile in New Orleans prior to the defeat of Santa Anna. In addition, during the French occupation, the United States recognized Juárez's government, not Maximilian's, and helped to arm Juárez.[68] Juárez was an indigenous revolutionary, or a revolutionary who was indigenous, but he was not a revolutionary fighting for indigenous Mexicans.

The nonindigenous residents of Fournier's fragile world fear indigenous Mexicans, but they do not take seriously the possibility of an assault on them by indigenous revolutionaries. *The Cat Screams* begins with a translation from the Spanish of an article from the Mexico City *Mundial*. The introductory headings to the newspaper article, which has a dateline of June 18, 193- from Taxco, announce "FOREIGNERS IN PANIC" and link the aforementioned suicides of U.S. citizens to a "*Revival of Primitive Practices*." The author of the article foments anti-indigenous hysteria that could be read as a refraction of the anti-Mexican hysteria in the United States in the 1930s: "Queer rumors were current about the plaza. That native witch doctors still ply their trade among the ignorant persons of Taxco is a well-established fact, and one of these, a woman famous in her trade, is being sought by the police. These *curanderas*, the ignorant ones believe, can injure or drive insane any person, provided they possess an article of his clothing."[69] As in *Murder on Tour* and *Vultures in the Sky*, Downing uses indigenous Mexican beliefs and practices in *The Cat Screams* to imbue the atmosphere with fear and suspicion and to suggest a possible source of the crimes.[70] Readers soon learn that Micaela Guerrero, the cook at Fournier's pension, is the "woman famous in her trade," but the close proximity of these "primitive practices" to the colonial center never manifests as a dramatic display of anticolonial or domestic revolution. Instead, again as in *Murder on Tour* and *Vultures in the Sky*, the threat of indigenous violence with origins in those revived "primitive practices" is a red herring, and the gravest threat to Fournier is her own involvement in the criminal underworld sustained by visiting U.S. nationals with disposable incomes, a contempt for Mexican law, and a disregard for their own and others' lives.

Indigeneity, however, does threaten Fournier's world, though much less sensationally and more strategically than the newspaper article suggests. The novel's title alludes to the practice of nagualism by many indigenous groups in Mesoamerica. Antonio de Herrera and Bernardino de Sahagún refer to nagualism in their sixteenth-century *historias*, while Daniel G. Brinton's *Nagualism: A Study in Native American Folk-lore and History* (1894) is the first attempt to produce a comprehensive study.[71] The *nanahualtin* (singular *naualli* with alternate spellings such as *nagual, nahual, naual,* and *nawal*) are either animal guardians or "masters of mystic knowledge, dealers in the black arts, wizards or sorcerers" who have the power to transform into animals.[72] Though consistently and often brutally suppressed by the Catholic Church, the practice was still common when

Brinton wrote his study. A generation after Brinton, Downing's indigenous Mexican characters continue to practice nagualism.

Indigenous revolution is a real possibility in *The Cat Screams*, though the simulation of hysteria in the discourse of sensationalistic journalism about a revival of primitive magic helps to keep nagualism, the potential driving force of the revolution, hidden in plain sight. The newspaper article foments anxiety while disparaging the source of it and discouraging critical investigation. Downing introduces nagualism as part of the narrative thread about Esteban, the mozo who begins the novel bedridden and hidden from the view of readers and the other characters. Fournier describes Esteban's mysterious illness to Hugh Rennert, a customs agent for the Department of the Treasury and the primary detective in nine of Downing's ten novels. In her description of the illness, Fournier mentions that the screaming of the titular Siamese cat, Mura, frightens Esteban. She tells Rennert that after the cat screamed, "He said something in a low voice, something that I could not understand. Then he turned his face to the wall."[73] When the local government places the pension under quarantine in response to Esteban's undiagnosed illness, the novel begins to function as a pseudocaptivity narrative with Esteban and his mysterious illness as the figurative captors of the visitors from the United States. Throughout the novel, Esteban's illness then shadows the central mystery: the deaths that start at the pension soon after Rennert's arrival.

The solution to the mystery of what Esteban says to himself requires knowledge of indigenous languages that only Professor Parkyn has. Parkyn plays a recurring character type in Downing's novels: an academic with some appreciation for indigenous history and culture but with a concomitant belief in his superiority. He is not overtly villainous, but he is a U.S. indigenista, a U.S. practitioner of indigenismo: he values indigenous history and material culture rather than indigenous people. Parkyn consults Aztec manuscripts for clues that will lead him to the jade deposits he seeks, but he views indigenous religious beliefs and practices as superstition. Downing's cast of academics from the United States studying and at times exploiting indigenous Mexico includes Dr. Xavier Radisson, a linguist of indigenous languages and the murderer in Downing's sixth novel, *The Last Trumpet: Murder in a Mexican Bull Ring* (1937).[74] Radisson's Mexican counterpart is the drug dealer and former university professor of Mesoamerican studies Don Evaristo Montellano in "The Shadowless Hour." The representations of Radisson, the linguist-cum-murderer, and

Montellano, the professor-cum-drug dealer, make legible the violence of intellectual indigenismo.

As he fights his illness, Esteban refuses to speak in Spanish and, therefore, constantly reminds readers of the indigenous presence at the spatial center of the pension. Strategic linguistic separatism and bilingualism are the primary tools of cultural preservation and anticolonial resistance in the novel: the indigenous characters speak colonial languages, Spanish, English, and French, but only one nonindigenous character speaks Nahuatl. Fournier finally identifies the word—*nagual*—that she failed to hear earlier but that Esteban repeats frequently in his conversations with Micaela. Fournier shares the information with Rennert, who plans to take the word to Parkyn for translation and explanation. Downing delays for many chapters the meeting between Rennert and Parkyn, but in those chapters he consistently emphasizes both the significance of nagualism to the main mystery and the connection between nagualism and the screaming cat. Rennert attempts, for example, to secure the guests' fingerprints by writing nagual on a sheet of paper and then asking each guest about the word with the expectation that they will hold the paper while they ponder his question. Downing stages two mysteries simultaneously in this scene: as Rennert tries to solve the overt mystery of who is killing the guests, Downing considers the covert mystery of how indigenous people can survive and thrive in the twentieth century. They can thrive, Downing proposes, by exploiting the settler-colonial state's inability to contain and control indigenous knowledge. As the only character that can translate the word *nagual* or understand the implications of Esteban's use of it, Parkyn is also the only character that the settler-colonial state could use to infiltrate and observe the indigenous world. He is, however, only interested in jade.

To extend the life of the mystery, Downing obstructs Rennert's attempts to discuss nagualism with Parkyn until two-thirds of the way through the novel. At that point, Parkyn gives Rennert a lecture that reads like a condensed version of Brinton's study and provides an authoritative guide for reading the indigenous knowledge—and the indigenous resistance to linguistic and religious domination—that structures the novel:

> It really goes back to pre-Conquest Mexico, where the belief in the practice of the black arts was prevalent, as indeed it is today. More so, perhaps, than we realize. [. . .] In the time of the Aztecs the Naualli was a high priest who possessed magical powers, including those

of levitation and the assumption of animal form at will. He acted
as the general guardian of the city against sorcerers and gave warning of approaching famine or pestilence. After the Conquest by the
Spaniards, the belief in such powers by certain individuals became
very widespread and resulted in the formation of a regular cult, the
members of which were called Nagual. They were believed to have
animal familiars, whose shape they could assume, and to hold regular
"witches' sabbaths." Under torture, many of the natives confessed to
such practices and the Spaniards had great difficulty in stamping out
the cult, which had for its avowed object the elimination of Christianity in Mexico.[75]

Like an orthodox indigenista, Parkyn dismisses these indigenous beliefs as
superstition and indigenous people as primitive. Yet the three members of
the indigenous staff seize upon the possibility that a malevolent nagual has
attacked Esteban after the doctor who practices Western medicine fails to
diagnose his illness accurately. Despite Parkyn and Rennert's doubts about
nagualism, the failure of Western medicine, the failure of the doctor to
detect the cause of Esteban's illness, creates a fissure in the empirical and
rational foundation of the detective novel genre and opens a space for the
application of indigenous religious knowledge to the mystery.[76]

Through that fissure emerges the covert mystery that Downing is
investigating: the status of internally colonized indigenous people in the
twentieth century and the strategies available to them to maintain or
revitalize their communities. Esteban's ravaged body represents the state
of this dominated indigenous world; to identify the disease, however, is
to begin the process of finding a cure. Left with the mystery of why Esteban is dying, Micaela, a healer or *curandera*, applies her religious-medical
knowledge to the case and makes a diagnosis of witchcraft. Downing's
representation of colonialism as witchcraft anticipates one of the most celebrated novels of the first generation of the American Indian renaissance.
In Leslie Marmon Silko's *Ceremony* (1977), a contest between witches
leads to the creation of brutal and terrifying European colonizers.

Micaela's diagnosis also introduces other mysteries: has a nagual transformed into Mura to attack Esteban, and what are the motives for the
attack? The violence directed against Esteban initially appears to have
indigenous origins: the Native witch doctors to which the journalist
refers in the prologue to *The Cat Screams* are nanahualtin, practitioners

of nagualism, and therefore are the most obvious suspects. Yet the pos-sibility of indigenous-against-indigenous violence is another red herring. As S. S. Van Dine (Willard Huntington Wright) insists in his influential essay "Twenty Rules for Writing Detective Stories," the criminal in a mod-ern detective novel must play a major role in the story.[77] Downing cites Van Dine in his own essay about writing detective novels, "Murder Is a Rather Serious Business," and suggests to beginning authors that "there is a premium for originality in tales of crime [. . .] but this originality must lie within certain prescribed bounds, and until the writer is familiar with these he is venturing among pitfalls if he gets off the beaten path."[78] Charles Rzepka elaborates on this unique characteristic of detective fiction: "This concept of fairness is alien to nearly every other form of literary realism, where we rarely assume the author to be ethically delinquent when he or she withholds certain facts, feeds us misinformation, or is mistaken him- or herself."[79] Downing strategically leaves the nanahualtin at the margins of the narrative, off the beaten path; they are not the practitioners of the mystic arts that have attacked Esteban and threaten to destroy Fournier's carefully arranged domestic colonial space.

Downing provides for readers many suspects that might be the witch attacking Esteban and the indigenous world that he embodies. The most obvious suspects include the drug-dealing Fournier, who murders to cover her tracks; the neglectful doctor who misdiagnoses Esteban; or even Parkyn, the condescending, opportunistic archaeologist whose interest in Mexico extends to ancient jade but not to the health or reli-gious practices of contemporary indigenous Mexican people. However, Downing most explicitly connects Gwendolyn Noon to the cat, the nagual's familiar in the context of Micaela's diagnosis of Esteban's illness. Noon fulfills the role of the nagual in part as the agent that sets disaster in motion: she decides not to marry Stephen Riddle, the son of an Okla-homa oil man, and instead comes to Taxco to get a quick divorce from her secret first husband. Her flight to Taxco draws several of the other characters there, too: Shaul to write about her in his gossip column; Riddle to convince her to marry him; and George Crenshaw, a private investigator from Dallas, to gather information about her for Riddle's father. Shaul and Riddle are two of the murder victims; the other charac-ters discover them dead in their rooms.

Noon also shares physical characteristics with her familiar. Downing describes Noon as explicitly white—her fingers, dress, face—offset only with the red of her fingernails. When Rennert approaches Noon with the intention of confronting her about a chloroform attack on Fournier, he watches her carefully: "As if conscious of his scrutiny she quickly let her hand fall to her side and her fingers clenched themselves with a febrile movement. Their crimson nails seemed to be digging into the white skin. *Curiously*, he thought, *like the painted claws of a cat*."[80] When he finally confronts her, Noon's eyes begin to twitch like a cat, and "incredibly, her white face seemed to have grown whiter."[81] The screaming cat is a nagual, the avatar of malevolent magic—the tabloid journalism and celebrity obsession that worships whiteness; the morphine addiction that leads to suicide and murder—that originates with and is most clearly exemplified by Noon.

While Noon is the primary locus of nagualism, the avarice that motivates Parkyn's attempted pillaging of indigenous Mexican wealth also feeds the malevolent magic that is attacking Esteban. Downing owned two copies of Wilkie Collins's *The Moonstone* (1868), a detective novel that is, according to John Reed, an indictment of the crimes of British imperialism.[82] Rzepka provides additional, specific, and compelling textual support to Reed's reading of *The Moonstone*, which opens at the battle of Seringapatam in what is now southern India in 1799: The Brahmins sent to retrieve the stolen moonstone are, like Downing's latently dangerous Indians, only red herrings as suspects; they do not fulfill the stereotype of the "blood-thirsty Asiatic maniac," much as Downing's indigenous Mexicans do not fulfill the same "blood-thirsty savage" stereotype so familiar in the Americas.[83] English characters, not the Brahmins, are the drug addicts in *The Moonstone*, just as the American visitors to Taxco rather than indigenous Mexicans are addicted to morphine in *The Cat Screams*. Collins accommodates the culturally specific Hindu caste system and belief in reincarnation, just as Downing accommodates nagualism. Lastly, Godfrey Ablewhite, "the real thief of the Moonstone," contains in his name that whiteness that so thoroughly defines Gwendolyn Noon.[84] *The Cat Screams* shares other characteristics with *The Moonstone*, such as Shaul's journal entries that he writes after smoking marijuana and that correspond to the journal entries made by Ezra Jennings while he is under the influence of opium. The Siamese cat Mura, Noon's nagual familiar, however, is the most important clue to the connection between these two novels and to Downing's interest in using the detective novel genre to investigate stereotypical depictions of the colonized population of Mexico, the crimes committed against them by the settler-colonial Mexican government and neocolonial U.S. presence, and the possible ways for indigenous people to resist that presence or escape it entirely. In Thai, Siamese cats are called "wichien maat," or "moon diamond."[85]

Fournier's illicit drug trade and the rampant drug addiction fed by her dealing reinforce nagualism as a key both to the novel's mysteries and to Downing's search for evidence of indigenous Mexican resistance. Brinton's study includes an overview of the intoxicants used by practitioners for visions or other spiritual insights: *peyotl*, or peyote; the seeds of the *ololiuhqui*, or *coaxihuitl*; and the bark of the *baal-che* that makes a drink called by the Mayas *yax ha*, first water, and by the Spanish *pitarilla*. While the use of intoxicants can produce spiritual insight, the abuse of the spiritual power gained from these insights makes nanahualtin dangerous. The drug use by bourgeois Anglo American and French Mexican women is, too, an abuse of privilege that makes them dangerous to themselves as well as to others: Fournier murders Shaul and Riddle to prevent them from exposing her other criminal activities; Noon chloroforms Fournier and leaves her to suffocate to death while she searches desperately for Fournier's morphine stash, and then she pulls a gun on Rennert; and drug addicts continue to commit suicide when the quarantine on Fournier's pension obstructs access to their supply. Most dramatically, a young indigenous man of the Mexican class of working poor lies dying throughout the novel while members of the American privileged class destroy themselves because they are tormented by love affairs gone sour, insomnia, and existential anguish.

A scene in which Downing parodies what Phil Deloria calls "playing Indian" in his study of the same name confirms the connection that Downing encourages readers to draw between Noon and the neocolonial U.S. presence in Mexico figured as a dangerous supernatural power. After Noon chloroforms Fournier and fails to find any drugs in her room, she disguises herself behind a jade mask of the Aztec god Xipe as she returns to her room. Parkyn identifies Xipe as "the god of sacrifice by flaying," which, in turn, explains the fright of the waitress, Maria, when she witnesses Noon holding the mask in front of her face.[86] Noon's travesty of indigenous religious belief and practice is a compelling representation of a long history of colonial criminality that in *The Cat Screams* culminates in the absurdity of a drug addict disguising her identity behind a tiny mask.

The mask carries another meaning equally germane to the mystery of Esteban's illness and revelatory of the anticolonial resistance at the heart of the mystery. Parkyn explains that "those who were suffering from diseases of the skin were believed to be under the protection of Xipe."[87] Prior to Noon's appropriation of Xipe in order to hide her criminal activities, Micaela takes the mask in an effort to draw on Xipe's power to protect Esteban. Micaela's theft of the mask potentially implicates her in the murders. As he summarizes the case, however, Rennert exonerates her:

> The cook had nothing to do with these deaths. She took the arsenic
> from the kitchen and attempted to poison the cat, yes, thinking to
> protect Esteban. [. . .] She may even, conceivably, have believed
> herself that the cat was a human being in animal shape, threatening
> him. She did certainly take the jade mask of Xipe from Madame
> Fournier's room, in the belief that it would afford some protection
> for one afflicted with a disease of the skin. She escaped at the first
> opportunity, knowing that she would be under surveillance and
> not wanting to run the risk of another encounter with the police.
> Further than this, however, she has no connection with this case.[88]

Micaela Guerrero, whose last name translates as "warrior" and who takes her first name from the archangel who leads heaven's armies, evades the authorities like one of her curandera ancestors, Maria Candelaria, described by Brinton as a famous nagual who led an indigenous revolution in Chiapas in 1713 and escaped after the revolution failed.[89] This indigenous woman is not a suspect in the murders at the pension, though the police consider her responsible for several deaths linked to her medical practice as a curandera. Downing suggests that indigenous people and their cultural beliefs and practices are always under suspicion and surveillance, always in question, but in the case of *The Cat Screams*, a powerful indigenous woman whose name invokes sacred warfare maintains those beliefs and practices while Western medicine surveys the repercussions of its failures: Esteban's death and the other deaths made possible by the misdiagnosis that trapped Fournier's guests in a quarantine.

Downing does not foreground indigenous epistemologies, as his literary descendants of the American Indian renaissance so frequently do, but nagualism becomes for him a means of conveying an anticolonial critique of the U.S. presence in Mexico and identifying indigenous languages and spiritual traditions as a resource for resisting that presence. Downing asks readers to recognize nagualism's crucial presence in his literary practice and in indigenous Mexican communities; nagualism as Downing presents it in the novel has unequivocal literary, ideological, and political value. Nagualism is a sign of untranslatable indigenous difference and a separatist indigenous cultural and political position. When Esteban first whispers the word *nagual* to Micaela, Downing reveals a separate indigenous religious world still inaccessible to colonial, neocolonial, and settler-colonial authorities. Fournier overhears but does not and cannot understand. This indigenous difference is inflected by modernity: Downing presents Micaela, Maria, and Esteban as members of a servant class that uses indigenous American spiritual traditions to navigate a transnational tourist industry. The adaptation of nagualism to this world is unsuccessful in the case of Esteban, who dies of acute appendicitis. Yet as the nonindigenous world feeds on itself with drug abuse, suicide, and murder, and the infirm colonial agent, Madame Fournier, kills herself with arsenic to avoid arrest, the indigenous archangel warrior, Micaela Guerrero, escapes, survives, and lives to continue her fight.

Micaela is an unfamiliar figure in the discourse of indigenismo; she is not a variant of what Hedrick describes as "the figure of the Indian mother as the archaic source of national as well as continental renewal."[90] Instead, she is an indigenous actor adapted to the modern world while interpreting it through an indigenous religious worldview. She engages, too, in what Bonfil Batalla calls "linguistic resistance." "The preservation of one's own tongue," he argues, "has a fundamental importance in maintaining the deeper codes that express one's way of seeing and understanding the world."[91] He observes as well in Mexico the "importance of women as transmitters of their own languages."[92] Micaela resists incorporation into a European or mestizo-dominated nation, and if she represents continental renewal, it belongs to indigenous, not settler-colonial, North America.

The Cat Screams and the American Indian Novel Tradition

The unusual though not anomalous focus by Downing on Mexico has apparently made it difficult to recognize his work as part of an American Indian literary tradition. Yet a novel such as *The Cat Screams*, with its consideration of the religious practices of the indigenous population of a neighboring settler-colonial nation, enriches our discussions of American Indian literary history—particularly the prerenaissance novel tradition. Some prerenaissance novelists eschew any references to distinct American

Indian religious practices. Others, such as Ella Deloria in *Waterlily* (1988) and McNickle in *Runner in the Sun* (1954), depict vibrant American Indian spiritual traditions in the past. Deloria set her novel, which she wrote in the 1940s, in the mid-nineteenth century, while McNickle set *Runner* in the early fifteenth century.[93] Other novelists depict the desire and struggle to maintain these traditions. American Indian religious practices in novels by American Indian authors thus have a rich history, too often understood as intransigently vexed, prior to the renaissance.

Of the novels published prior to the mid-twentieth century, John Rollin Ridge (Cherokee) does not include Cherokee religion in *The Life and Adventures of Joaquín Murieta, the Celebrated California Bandit* (1854), and S. Alice Callahan (Creek) rejects distinctly Creek religious traditions in favor of Anglo Christianity in *Wynema: A Child of the Forest* (1891). In the three Indian Territory and Oklahoma novels published during his lifetime, *Wild Harvest* (1925), *Black Jack Davy* (1926), and *Brothers Three* (1935), Oskison also does not represent the distinctly Cherokee religious practices of previous generations. The absence of these religious practices, however, is not a threat to the nation. Cherokee political autonomy, rather than static cultural or religious tradition, sustains the nation in his novels. He makes an explicit argument for the historical significance of this political self-determination, for example, in both *Wild Harvest* and *Black Jack Davy*.[94]

There is a longing for the religious practices of previous generations, however, in Oskison's posthumously published novel *The Singing Bird* (2007), written circa 1935–45, as well as McNickle's *Wind from an Enemy Sky* (1978), started in the late 1930s and early 1940s.[95] *The Singing Bird* tells the stories of Cherokee removals between 1818 and 1865 from the perspective of the narrator Paul Wear, a white missionary. This narrative structure elicits strikingly divergent assessments of the novel. Jace Weaver argues that the novel can "plausibly be read as an assimilationist work (much like Callahan's *Wynema*)"; the novel is "ultimately about white missionaries as much as it is about Cherokees."[96] Daniel Justice asserts in contrast that by embedding the novel in Cherokee social and political contexts, Oskison makes the novel "far more a story about Cherokee sovereignty and survival than about Christianity or Eurowestern 'civilization.'"[97] The narrator's position on the Cherokee future, however, is explicit. While Paul wonders if "perhaps we are the heathens," he adds, "Yet Dan was right when he said that, like it or not, the Indians must learn our language and adjust themselves to what we called Christian civilization. English-teaching schools must be opened to them, and shops and mills provided. The white man's knowledge of farming must be theirs."[98] Though their perspectives become a little more accommodating of Cherokee worldviews, Paul and his uncle, Dan Wear, repeat this sentiment throughout the novel.

Yet at least one prominent Cherokee contests the view that the Wears have of the Cherokee future. As these missionaries work among the Cherokees in Arkansas Territory and then Indian Territory, they hear one Cherokee leader, Ta-ka-e-tuh, comment on "the old beliefs that were passing."[99] But Sequoyah, the inventor of the Cherokee syllabary, and others of his generation still practice some of the "old ways," and he wants "the old beliefs and the old stories of our people" to be printed in the syllabary.[100] Dan Wear, who agrees to use the press for this purpose, eventually also learns "[to] accept him on his own terms"—that is, as a Cherokee unconverted to Christianity.[101] Near the end of the novel, Sequoyah plans a journey to Texas and Mexico in an effort to persuade Cherokees who had fled there to return with him to Indian Territory. Dan, who accompanies Sequoyah on the journey, speculates that he also hopes to recover these old beliefs in the form of Cherokee sacred symbols—ancient and powerful religious items stolen by the Delawares.[102]

Mexico, for Oskison's Sequoyah, is a possible source of indigenous cultural revitalization, as it is for Downing. "It is believable," Dan writes of Sequoyah to Paul back in Indian Territory, "that he hopes to restore the faith of the Cherokees in their old god."[103] In the final stage of his journey, Sequoyah even goes to the homeland of the Yaquis, the indigenous Mexican nation celebrated as unconquerable by Downing and many other writers. Those who remain in Indian Territory, however, do not hear from Sequoyah or Dan again. The history of the Cherokees that Sequoyah planned to write with the help of the sacred symbols will not be written, at least by him. Paul wonders, "Who among the Cherokees [. . .] could do what Dan suspected Sequoyah was doing, write the history of his people, express their philosophy, put meaning into their old beliefs?"[104] Some hope remains, as a fellow missionary suggests her son or some other scholar might succeed in this endeavor.

We learn, finally, that Sequoyah apparently shared his desire for recovery of the old beliefs with many Cherokees. Paul notices the lingering anxiety in the nation even during a relatively peaceful time prior to the Civil War: "It seemed to me that amongst the people there was a frantic yearning for something to symbolize the sustaining strength of their old beliefs. Could it be, I wondered, the things which Sequoyah had hoped to recover in Mexico, and in the quest of which I believed that he and Dan had lost their lives?"[105] Neither Oskison nor his narrator Paul provides any evidence that Paul's belief is inaccurate; Sequoyah and Dan do not return. There is not a direct correlation between Sequoyah's unsuccessful search and the political and cultural status of the Cherokee Nation, though the novel ends with the nation divided again, this time by the Civil War.

The desire to recover the religious materials of previous generations—"the old Indian power"—also remains unfulfilled in McNickle's *Wind*. In *Wind*, a dam has flooded an important holy site of the fictional Little Elk people. "The white man," the tribal leader Bull says to his grandson, Antoine, "makes us forget our holy places."[106] The Little Elks also seek the return of the powerful Feather Boy medicine bundle.[107] Bull explains to Antoine that Feather Boy is a manifestation of Thunderbird, a child of the sun. After a long flight to the south, to a land that must be Mexico or Mesoamerica more generally, Feather Boy returns to the Little Elks with "the most powerful present of all," tobacco. He then left the Little Elks with the medicine bundle: "All the good things of life are inside. [. . .] Never let it get away from your people. So long as you have this holy bundle, your people will be strong and brave and life will be good to them. My own body is in this forever."[108] Henry Jim, Bull's estranged older brother, gave this powerful religious object to the local missionary, Reverend Stephen Welles, thirty years ago. Welles then sent it to the Americana Institute, a museum owned by Adam Pell, who also runs the company that constructed the dam. Just as Sequoyah had faith in the power of the missing Cherokee sacred items in *The Singing Bird*, Henry Jim believes as he approaches death that the recovery of the bundle will unify the Little Elk people and prepare them for a more certain future. His kinspeople agree with him and wait, optimistically, for its return.

McNickle then directs our attention, as Downing does in his novels set in Mexico, to an indigenous world to the south. Pell finally finds the bundle destroyed by neglect. Only a little buckskin eaten by mice and a few pebbles and feathers remain. He decides to give the Little Elks instead an artifact called the Virgin of the Andes, a nine-inch-high sculpture in gold of a nude adolescent girl. The artifact had been smuggled out of Peru, where indigenismo was, as in Mexico, a significant cultural and social force. Pell describes an indigenous-based social revolution there: "What I found in Cuno [. . .] was an extraordinary human community. After almost four

centuries of conquest, which is to say of murder, pillage, rape, sacrilege—
all those outrageous defilements of the conquered man—these people
were discovering what it meant to be human. [. . .] I suppose if one traced
the historical process at work, it wasn't all so sudden, but one had the
impressions of an overnight revolution."[109] Pell's attempt to appease the
Little Elks by giving them an item stolen from another indigenous community is unsuccessful. When they learn at the end of the novel that the
Feather Boy medicine bundle has been destroyed, Bull shoots and kills
Adam Pell and Toby Rafferty, the superintendent of the Little Elk Agency.

The loss of specific spiritual practices appears final in *Singing* and *Wind*,
though the unsuccessful effort at religious revitalization does not doom
the Cherokee Nation in *Singing*. The Cherokee Nation thrives in the generation after Sequoyah, and the evidence indicates that they will meet
the conflict of the Civil War with the same resilience. The loss is more
devastating in *Wind*. In the final two chapters of McNickle's novel, Two
Sleeps, the tribe's adopted holy man, and other members of his generation
make elegiac statements that suggest the loss of the Feather Boy bundle
is a disaster from which the Little Elks will not recover. As Bull predicts
early in the novel, the Little Elks still have a future leader in Antoine, and
Antoine will be powerful, according to Two Sleeps.[110] When Bull lifts a
rifle to shoot Pell, Antoine feels proud of him. Though the head of the
tribal police then kills Bull, Antoine's surge of pride in Bull and Little Elk
history rather than grief is the lesson that he takes from his grandfather's
death. Yet the novel then ends "*and the world fell apart.*"[111] If there is hope
for the Little Elk people in *Wind*, it is tenuous.[112]

Indigenous spiritual beliefs and practices in other novels such as *Cogewea* (1927) by Christine Quintasket/Mourning Dove (Okanogan and
Colville), *Sundown* (1934) by John Joseph Mathews (Osage), and *The Surrounded* (1936) by McNickle continue to sustain the older generations in
the contemporary world. In each novel, however, there are young people
participating in the ceremonies as well. In *Cogewea*, contradictory statements by Cogewea and intrusive authorial voices make the contemporary
state of indigenous religious beliefs and practices difficult to assess.[113] Further complicating Mourning Dove's representation of Okanogan religion
through Cogewea's grandmother, Stemteema, is Cogewea's statement,
unsupported by other evidence in the novel, that Stemteema and her
other granddaughters are Catholic.[114] Cogewea's grandmother is part of the
older generation that Mourning Dove characterizes as incompatible with

modernity: "Ever suspicious of the whites and guardedly zealous in the secrecy of their ancient lore, seldom do the older tribesmen disclose ancestral erudition, and when they do, their mysteries are not comprehended. The young people, as a rule, are interested in their tribal legends only to the extent of 'cramming' some ardent writer with palpable absurdities."[115] Stemteema is, Cogewea explains, "lingering pathetically in the sunset of a closing era."[116] Of the ceremonies still practiced, Cogewea observes, "These ceremonies, held sacred by the more primitive tribesmen, are now, shame to say, commercialized and performed for a pittance contributed by white spectators who regard all in the light of frivolity."[117] Yet in chapter 8, "The Indian Dancers," members of all generations, including Cogewea, participate. She defends oral Okanogan history to Alfred Densmore, an easterner hired as a ranch hand who hopes to marry her, and then, during an argument with him, announces: "The true American courses my veins and *never* will I cast aside my ancestral traditions!"[118] Cogewea wavers in this commitment several times, but the novel ends with an endorsement of the Okanogan religious worldview of her grandmother.[119]

The indigenous religious context is similar in *Sundown* and *The Surrounded*, in which the older generations continue to practice Osage and Salish religious practices, respectively, and pass them to the younger generations, though to neither of the protagonists—Challenge or Chal Windzer in *Sundown* and Archilde Leon in *The Surrounded*. Warrior observes, "*Sundown* chronicles the self-destructive descent of the mixed-blood protagonist into alchoholism, debilitating self-hate, and spiritual despair."[120] He then shifts the critical focus from Chal Windzer's nearly naturalistic, individual decline to the political context, to "the undermining of Osage sovereignty and the repression of Osage traditional life of the period" and argues that the novel "is a nuanced description of what Mathews saw as the weaknesses of two internal political and social strategies in the midst of an oppressive situation."[121] Within this oppressive situation, Osage religious practices—what the religious leader Road Man calls the "old road of our People" (the "old beliefs" of *Singing* and "the old Indian power" of *Wind*)—are fully functional: as in *Cogewea*, there are summer dances in *Sundown*, for example, and peyote ceremonies attended by members of the younger generation such as Chal's friend Sun-on-His-Wings.[122]

Similarly to Chal Windzer, Archilde Leon experiences a decline in *The Surrounded* following his return from boarding school. Yet as in *Sundown*, a Salish religious world continues to function around Archilde in

the form of secret meetings of elders such as Old Modeste and Archilde's
mother, Catharine, who renounces Catholicism at the end of her life and
returns to the Salish religious practices of previous generations. She also
helps prepare Archilde's nephews, Mike and Narcisse, for the midsum-
mer dances. When in the final scene of the novel the Indian Agent Horace
Parker arrests Archilde following the murder of Sherrif Dave Quigley by
Archilde's girlfriend Elise La Rose, he says angrily, "You people never learn
that you can't run away."[123] John Purdy proposes that the end of *The Surrounded* "is not as bleak as one would assume": "The Salish *have* run away.
As Modeste tells us earlier, the future resides in his grandchildren. Like all
the Salish characters in the novel, they too have renounced the teachings
of the priests and returned to earlier traditions and ceremonial practices.
[. . .] *The Surrounded* demonstrates a reaffirmation of traditional ways to
gain and employ—through verbal arts and ceremony—the knowledge
necessary to act and react. McNickle asserts the efficacy of old ways in
modern times."[124] Purdy asserts more emphatically that the novel offers "a
view of dynamic, enduring Native cultures."[125] Even in Oskison's *Black Jack
Davy*, Ned Warrior ponders the invasion of the Cherokee Nation by Anglo
criminals that has almost led to his dispossession and death. He then wonders about the traditionals in the hills: "Ned understood better than ever
before why old Running Rabbit and his fellow full-bloods of the hill country met in secret councils and planned to drive out the aliens and close the
borders to them. If they only could!"[126] In contrast to Ned Warrior in *Black
Jack Davy* but similarly to Mike and Narcisse in *The Surrounded*, Micaela
Guerrero literally runs for the hills—or the mountains—of Guerrero.

The Cat Screams is thus one of a small but still significant number of
novels by American Indian authors before the renaissance begins in the
1960s in which indigenous spiritual practices are a possible foundation
of twentieth-century life and a potential motivating force of anticolonial
resistance.[127] The inquiry into the status of indigenous religious traditions in these novels, and in particular Downing's depiction of nagualism,
anticipates the work of writers and activists such as Vine Deloria Jr. during
the American Indian civil rights era, as well as late twentieth- and early
twenty-first-century cultural and literary nationalists such as Cook-Lynn,
Justice, Ortiz, Warrior, Weaver, and especially Womack and Taiaiake
Alfred (Kahnawake Mohawk). All these authors to varying degrees advocate anticolonial scholarship, community activism, and self-determination
that rigorously foreground indigenous religious and intellectual traditions,

history, politics, and culture.[128] A generation before Deloria Jr. and two generations before literary nationalism became an influential intellectual mode of inquiry in American Indian literary studies, Downing published a novel that earnestly considered indigenous resistance that rejects assimilation and advocates separatism.

The indigenous religious traditions in these novels provide refuge from the myriad forces of racial terrorism, while in *The Cat Screams*, Downing depicts as functional the kind of contemporary, revolutionary indigenous religious power so desirable but more difficult to secure in the other novels of the period. *The Cat Screams* is, at least in this regard, an anomaly in the prerenaissance novel tradition. Though this religious power surfaces only intermittently in Downing's other novels, he introduces and sustains in those novels, with the exception of his eighth and ninth, an explicit condemnation of colonial and neocolonial practices in Mexico. For American Indian writers, the 1930s immediately preceded what Chadwick Allen characterizes as "an important prepatory period of indirect opposition to dominant discourses that attempted to direct an indigenous minority 'self-determination' on nonindigenous terms." Of the authors deploying these "relatively quiet" narrative strategies, Allen asserts that "they questioned the assimilationist orthodoxy of the day and prepared the way for the more explosive tactics of the indigenous minority renaissance of the late 1960s and 1970s."[129] Similarly to the narrative strategies used by the authors under Allen's consideration, the challenge to colonial dominance in Downing's mystery novels can be understood as quiet and indirect or covert.

Yet between his ninth and tenth novels, he published *The Mexican Earth*, a well-reviewed history that celebrates Mexico as an unconquered collection of indigenous groups, posits explicit connections between those groups and American Indian nations in the United States, and makes frequent and far more direct assertions of indigenous Mexican cultural, political, and social strength in the present: "The great conquest of the Revolution was a return to Indian values. [...] There is no wall around Mexico, of course, but whatever form its national life ultimately assumes it is going to have its roots in Mexican soil, like corn and the maguey. The issue was decided during the days of Cortés and the viceroys, when the Spaniards failed to annihilate either the Indian or his culture. Now Mexico is an Indian country, where the white man is rapidly being bred out."[130] By writing the history of Mexico as a statement of the continuous centrality of indigenous people to the life of that nation, Downing produces an early articulation of Native-centric writing that most clearly anticipates the work of renaissance-era nonfiction writers such as late McNickle and early Deloria Jr.[131] Downing leaves the mystery of Micaela Guerrero unresolved in *The Cat Screams*. We do not know where she is going or what she is planning to do when she arrives. However, the history of indigenous Mexico that Downing tells in *The Mexican Earth* suggests that he envisioned many others like her evading settler-colonial authorities, speaking indigenous languages, practicing indigenous religions, and contributing, therefore, to a Mexican-wide, centuries-old resistance to colonial, settler-colonial, and neocolonial dominance.

Downing Detected

While Rennert gathers the clues and solves the homicides committed at Madame Fournier's, evidence in the real world rarely produces such a coherent understanding of a crime. The investigation of the Ardmore murders on June 8, 1931, yielded conflicting testimony about what happened between the moment that Deputy Sheriffs Guess and Crosby emerged from their car and the fatal shooting of Rubio and Gomez. The newspaper articles conveyed the details of an enduring mystery to the reading public: the deputy sheriffs claimed to have identified themselves as officers of the law and even to have displayed their badges, while the survivor, Salvatore Rubio, asserted that they did not. The young men were reported to have mistaken the deputy sheriffs for bandits, while Deputy Sheriff Guess, according to an Associated Press story on the front page of the *New York Times*, "believed he had encountered desperadoes."[132] An eyewitness gave testimony that Deputy Sheriff Crosby pointed to Emilio Cortes Rubio and said, "I got that boy," while Crosby called the accusation a "falsehood."[133] The trial did not reconcile any of these discrepancies or solve the mystery, but the basic outline of events remains clear: the deputy sheriffs killed two men and were arrested, charged, tried, and acquitted. Will Rogers reported briefly on the murders in his Daily Telegram for the *New York Times* on June 12, 1931, and Mexican Americans immortalized the victims in the corrido "La Tragedia de Oklahoma." Downing chose to respond in a genre that guaranteed his detective always reconstructs the specific details of the mystery and the U.S. citizens that perpetrate crimes against Mexican nationals—indigenous and nonindigenous—always face punishment.[134]

Though Rubio and Gomez were not indigenous, their murder by state authorities in Oklahoma also led Downing to investigate in his detective novels the place of indigenous people in a world in which the international relationship of two postcolonial settler nations evokes the long history of conflict between the U.S. settler government and its citizens and the indigenous domestic dependent nations within its borders: armed authorities in the United States kill Mexican citizens under suspicious circumstances; the U.S. government removes by mass deportation Mexican and Mexican American citizens from their homes; U.S. citizens occupy Mexican land as tourists and consumers; the U.S. government and its corporations, as eager for the completion of the Pan-American highway in the 1930s as they were for the transcontinental railroad in the 1860s, exploit Mexican resources. In the process of writing these detective novels, most explicitly *The Cat Screams*, Downing finds compelling evidence of indigenous resistance to domination and the maintenance of indigenous languages and ways of life.

During this politically, socially, and economically difficult era for the Choctaw Nation, Downing followed what Lambert identifies as one of four typical patterns of Choctaw urban migration: following birth in the Choctaw Nation, this type of migrant goes to an urban area or a series of urban areas before returning permanently to the nation.[135] While Downing lived abroad from the Choctaw homeland, he looked to Mexico for examples of indigenous strategies to resist settler governments as well as to maintain and revitalize tribal nation traditions. He was still thinking of the murders in Ardmore when he wrote *Murder on the Tropic* (1935), in which a young man named Esteban Flores returns to his family's old hacienda in Mexico from the college that he attends in Kansas. In the same novel, an indigenous mother, Maria Montemayor, covertly uses the hacienda's water supply to sustain the flowers in the plaza under which her son has been buried. "The flowers," Montemayor says to Hugh Rennert, "were here before men."[136] As he contemplates Montemayor's devotion to the flowers and her son, Rennert thoughtfully observes: "[Maria] stood, the embodiment of the Mexico that stands self-sufficient by the side of the road while conquering armies pass by, to be replaced in days or years or centuries (it doesn't matter) by other armies under other banners. *Along the paved highway to the east* [...] *will come another, more dreadful army with billboards and refreshment stands and blatant automobile horns, but Maria and her kind will stand when they have passed by.*"[137] *The Mexican Earth* is a celebration of this self-sufficient and explicitly indigenous Mexico. As a teacher and writer outside his homeland, Downing also practiced this patient self-sufficiency, which Momaday characterizes in *House Made of Dawn* as the "long outwaiting" of the residents of the Jemez Pueblo.[138]

His detection of this indigenous world in Mexico and his development of a Choctaw transnational optic influenced his increasingly active role in the life of the Choctaw Nation. Downing returned permanently to his homeland in 1951 after teaching one year as an assistant professor of Spanish at Washington College in Chestertown, Maryland.[139] He cared for his parents, lived with his fellow Choctaw citizens more than a decade under the threat of the termination of their tribal nation, and helped to create a Choctaw language revitalization program.[140] In the early 1970s, Downing published his last two works: *Chahta Anompa: An Introduction to the Choctaw Language* (1971) and *Cultural Traits of the Choctaws* (1973). Both works were assigned as part of the Choctaw Bilingual Education Program (CBEP), to which Downing devoted the last years of his life. This program was in part the product of his ability to see through the many strata of internal and U.S. neocolonial oppression in Mexico and to detect a thriving indigenous world there. The goals of the program were "(1) to help each child to develop a positive self-concept—to be proud of himself and his heritage, and to have a positive attitude toward the language or languages familiar to him; (2) to help each child to progress rapidly toward mastering standard English as well as the other tool subjects; and (3) to encourage teachers to learn to recognize individual differences, particularly those rooted in language and culture, and to make these differences contribute to the total learning process."[141] Students in the program learned that part of their heritage and culture was Mesoamerican—for Downing spends the first half of the eleven pages of *Cultural Traits* outlining the influence of indigenous Mexico on the Choctaws. They learned from Downing that the Choctaws lived in the northern region of a Greater Indigenous Mexico—a cultural, geographical, and political zone that existed prior to and continues to exist after the invention of settler-colonial borders.

Downing's participation in the CBEP as an administrative assistant and "writer, translator and professor" coincided with a moment of activism that galvanized the Choctaws.[142] The program began in July 1970. One month later, on August 24, the federal government responded to the resistance of culturally and politically invigorated Choctaws by repealing the Choctaw termination act one day before it would have ended the federal trust relationship between the United States and the Choctaw Nation.[143] Lambert marks this moment as the key origin point in the Choctaw Nation's resurgence. Within the context of Downing's writing, the moment also demonstrated that, similar to their indigenous Mexican relatives, the Choctaws could successfully challenge their own dreadful antagonists.

CHAPTER 2

¡Indian Territory!

Lynn Riggs's Indigenous Geographies

I N THE MID- TO LATE 1930s, as Todd Downing was establishing himself in New York as a professional author of detective fiction, Cherokee dramatist Rollie Lynn Riggs was enjoying a celebrated career, earning mention as a contender for Pulitzer Prizes, working on screenplays in Hollywood, and writing two plays set in Mexico, *A World Elsewhere* (ca. 1934–37) and its companion play *The Year of Pilár* (ca. 1935–38).[1] *A World Elsewhere* is a satire of a failed counterrevolution by hacendados longing to recover the haciendas that the government of President Lázaro Cárdenas returned to indigenous people in the 1930s. Riggs stages in *The Year of Pilár* the contemporary indigenous Mexican revolution that exists as a covert but real threat in Downing's *The Cat Screams*. This revolution confirms that the possibility of armed anticolonial resistance and dramatic social change for indigenous peoples in Mexico was quite real for Riggs. While Downing's challenges to colonial dominance in his novels are quiet or indirect, to recall Chadwick Allen's general assessment of American Indian writing in the mid-twentieth century, Riggs's representations of indigenous Mexican revolution are loud and unequivocal. *World* and *Pilár*, therefore, have an indigenous transnational connection to the more explicitly anticolonial literature of the renaissance era.

The anticolonial politics of the Mexico plays are not an anomaly in Riggs's canon but, rather, the most assertive statement of his interest in dramatizing the legacy of the familial, tribal-national, regional, and even global ruptures produced by British and U.S. as well as Spanish and Mexican colonialisms. Early in his career, Riggs set plays such as *Big Lake* (1927) and *Green Grow the Lilacs* (1931) in an Indian Territory landscape marked specifically as Cherokee. There is a confounding Cherokee absence in these plays, though the federal authorities in both *Big Lake* and *Green Grow the Lilacs* and the "furriners" or "United Statesers" in the latter represent a dangerous settler-colonial U.S. presence.[2] Riggs started *The Cherokee Night* in 1928 in France as he was completing *Green Grow the Lilacs*, but he did not finish it until 1931. While *The Cherokee Night* features Cherokee characters, the play's pervasive sense of doom vexes many contemporary scholars. Riggs indicates that this doom, however, is an explicit product of a devastating colonial and settler-colonial history that includes removal, the land run, and Oklahoma statehood. The Santa Fe play *Russet Mantle*, which Riggs completed in 1935, features only Salvadore, an almost completely silent resident of the San Ildefonso Pueblo. Riggs makes clear that, similar to the despair of early twentieth-century Cherokees, this silence is the product of the enduring colonialist perspective of the region's European-descended residents.

Riggs was producing drafts of *World* and *Pilár*—the plays that complete the dramatic move from the deracinated "citizens without a state" in *The Cherokee Night* to indigenous Mexican revolutionaries reclaiming their land and defending it against counterrevolutionaries—before he finished *Russet Mantle*.[3] Samuel French published *Cherokee* and *Russet* together in 1936, and in September of that year, Riggs was making plans to go to Mexico to continue writing *World*. He completed a draft of the play while in Mexico in the summer of 1937 and then flew to Mexico City to finish it at the end of the same year. By September 1938, Riggs had completed *Pilár*, too. *World* premiered at the San Diego Community Theater on April 8, 1940, during the particularly auspicious few months for American Indian writers and Mexico. Though Phyllis Braunlich does not list a production of *Pilár*, the play was performed at the Amato Opera in New York in January 1952.[4]

The revolution available to the Mayans and other indigenous Mexicans in *World* and *Pilár* was, however, apparently unavailable to the Cherokees of Indian Territory. Following the Mexico plays, Riggs turns his attention again to a Cherokee family, the Sawters, who, like several characters in his first published play, live on the shores of Big Lake in the Cherokee Nation in Indian Territory. While the Sawters fight among themselves rather than against a readily identifiable colonial antagonist, *The Cream in the Well*, which Riggs completed in 1940, includes Riggs's most politically empowered Cherokee character. Sean Teuton demonstrates that the process of coming to political consciousness through a critical engagement with Native experiences is a defining characteristic of protagonists in influential novels of the early renaissance era. This process does not occur in a single

Riggs play, but it does happen for his Native characters from *Big Lake* to *Cream*.[5] *Cream* was published in *4 Plays* (1947) with *World*, *Pilár*, and *Dark Encounter*, an exploration of the devastating global legacy of colonial violence that Riggs completed in 1944.[6]

From *Big Lake* through *Dark Encounter*, Riggs imagines the dramatic geographies of the many Indian territories of the United States and Mexico. Riggs rarely leaves these territories in his work. Though some of his plays might not appear to be about Indians, they are almost always explicitly about Indian territories. These geographies as imagined by Riggs are so similar historically, emotionally, sexually, and spiritually, for example, that they appear interchangeable: the Cherokee Nation is Indian Territory; Indian Territory is indigenous Mexico; and indigenous Mexico is, in Riggs's dramatic imaginary, Indian Territory and the Cherokee Nation. Like Downing and McNickle, Riggs produces a Greater Indian Territory or Greater Indigenous Mexico, though only a consideration of his entire corpus makes this intertribal as well as indigenous and settler-colonial transnational space legible. This more comprehensive view of his career also helps to establish Riggs as a major contributor to a major era in twentieth-century American Indian literature.

Coming Down to Tahlequah: The Stateless Citizens of *The Cherokee Night*

Discussions of Riggs usually begin with *Green Grow the Lilacs* or *The Cherokee Night*, his most well-known plays and, in the case of the latter, the one most explicitly about the Cherokees as a polity. This section examines the reception of *The Cherokee Night*, which is also the play of greatest interest to American Indian literature scholars, to establish the literary critical and historical contexts for the subsequent consideration of the other plays about Indian Territory and Mexico. Each critic's assessment of *The Cherokee Night* constitutes a determination of the dramatist's place in American Indian literary history. A reading of the play as nihilistic or racist tends, in either the more culturally oriented critical context of the first twenty-five years of the renaissance or the more politically and historically oriented critical context of the next generation, to challenge the value of Riggs's plays in this literary history. A more hopeful reading in either critical context tends to position Riggs more securely within it. However, neither *The Cherokee Night* nor our readings of it need to weigh so heavily or exclusively in our assessment of Riggs, as Riggs dramatizes the legacies of colonialism in other plays. When he imagines a cognate Indian Territory in Mexico, the future of the colonial world, rather than the future of indigenous people, is grim.

The recovery of Riggs by scholars such as Weaver, Womack, and Justice begins with and sustains a focus on *Green Grow the Lilacs* and *The Cherokee Night* while opening new lines of political and literary historical inquiry. For all three scholars, the recovery process involves situating Riggs's plays within tribally specific Cherokee and broader American Indian histories and experiences.[7] They read *The Cherokee Night* as a statement on a doomed Cherokee world and support this evaluation with close readings of the play and two additional pieces of evidence: Riggs's description of the play in a letter dated March 10, 1929, to fellow dramatist and friend Barrett H. Clark and Riggs's life as a closeted gay man. The letter reads, "The play will concern itself with that night, that darkness (with whatever flashes of light allowably splinter through) which has come to the Cherokees and their descendants. An absorbed race has its curiously irreconcilable inheritance. It seems to me the best grade of absorbed Indian might be an intellectual Hamlet, buffeted, harassed, victimized, split, baffled—with somewhere in him great fire and some granite."[8] Riggs ends his review of the play's seven scenes in the letter with a vague comment: "But this is the cloud out of which something will come."[9] While Weaver, Womack, and Justice agree that the play deserves a secure place in American Indian literary history, they disagree on the social and political value of the play for contemporary Cherokees.

Weaver's reading is the most optimistic of the three. He shares Womack's and Justice's view of *The Cherokee Night* as a play that plots the doom of the Cherokees, but he situates it within a long history of communitist writings by American Indian authors. Weaver defines communitism in *That the People Might Live* (1997): "It is formed by a combination of the words 'community' and 'activism.' Literature is communitist to the extent that it has a proactive commitment to Native community, including what I term the 'wider community' of Creation itself. In communities that have too often been fractured and rendered dysfunctional by the effects of more than 500 years of colonialism, to promote communitist values means to participate in the healing of the grief and sense of exile felt by Native communities and the pained individuals in them."[10] As a communitist play, *The Cherokee Night* represents doom in order to encourage resistance to the forces pushing Cherokees toward it; the play is critical commentary of and not capitulation to these forces. Weaver's reading of the play focuses on its protest against the destructive legacies of assimilation and the demonstration of memory as a resource that could bind together the members of the community. For the characters in the play, Weaver concludes, "Only before statehood, before the loss of political, territorial sovereignty, was there any hope for wholeness. Now the hope rests in memory, in not forgetting one's Indianness and in moving ahead along an uncertain path."[11] Though it is uncertain, at least there is a path into the future for the Cherokees of the play. As Riggs writes about the play in his letter to Clark, "something" will be there when the clouds clear. Weaver ends his consideration of Riggs in 1936, when *Russet Mantle* and *The Cherokee Night* were published, but prior to the writing and publication of the two Mexico plays as well as *The Cream in the Well* and *Dark Encounter*. These later plays show Riggs attempting to make that path to the Cherokee future more clear both by exploring other colonial histories and by dramatizing the historically specific trauma of a Cherokee family.

For Womack, the torment of living as a gay man in a violently homophobic world also finds expression in the pervasive sense of doom in *The Cherokee Night*. His reading of *The Year of Pilár* and *The Cream in the Well* in *Art as Performance, Story as Criticism* (2009) also focuses primarily on the "gay subject matter" in these plays.[12] Riggs's Indian and gay identities are, Womack asserts, "the two most relevant aspects of his life and work," and his plays are the expressions of "a closeted gay man dealing with an incredibly oppressive societal realm that sanctions what a gay man can say, sanctions what an Indian can say."[13] Crucial to Womack's reading of Riggs's plays is his argument that they depict the contours of "an Oklahomo's interior landscape rather than Oklahoma physical geography."[14] Riggs banishes Indians, Womack suggests, from this interior landscape; he fails to account for Indians in Oklahoma and for the history of their displacement by non-Native settlers. Womack's critical approach raises the possibility, however, that Riggs keeps Indianness as well as queerness in the closet. The "incredibly oppressive societal realm" had a racial component that motivated writers and artists such as Anatole Broyard, George Herriman, or, according to Henry Louis Gates and Rudolph Byrd, Jean Toomer to pass as white in this era, just as a gay man might pass as heterosexual.[15] Thus, while Riggs as an adult did not keep secret either his gay or Cherokee identity from his friends, the absence of Cherokees in the plays that Riggs wrote prior to *The Cherokee Night* could indicate a reluctance to come out of the closet as an American Indian author. Unlike fellow Cherokee Will Rogers, Riggs appears not to have made a consistent effort to identify himself as Cherokee to a broad public.

Following this analysis of Riggs's erasure of Indians from his imagined Oklahoma landscapes, Womack offers a sobering assessment of *The Cherokee Night*. Riggs gives "some attention [. . .] to the loss of Indian lands after the Dawes Act" in the play, but it endorses "racial purity" and dramatizes "the doom of Cherokees."[16] In comparison to Weaver's reading, Womack's is far less hopeful: "The question is, can a cohesive tribal communal worldview be brought forward into contemporary circumstances? The play, on the surface, seems to say no."[17] Yet the play is still worthy of celebration: "As an Indian work, *The Cherokee Night* is a good play. As a queer Indian work, *The Cherokee Night* is a fabulous play; haunting, poetic, layered in meanings."[18] Like Weaver, Womack balances critique with an affirmation of the value of the play for the view it provides of Cherokee—and gay Cherokee—life in the first part of the twentieth century.

In *Our Fire Survives the Storm*, Daniel Justice situates Riggs's dramas within a Cherokee literary history shaped by Cherokee authors seeking to walk either the Beloved Path of peace and balance or the Chickamauga Path of fierce defiance. He argues that Riggs wrote plays that were part of a "rhetorical battle for nationhood" in the Cherokee Nation as well as responses to the centuries of conflict over land between the Cherokee Nation and the United States.[19] More specifically, Riggs dramatizes the legacy of the massive land loss and dissolution of tribal governments following allotment and Oklahoma statehood, as well as the continuing federal policy of coercive assimilation. Though Justice identifies a "geographic connectedness [. . .] a consciousness and conscience rooted in the land of their birth" in the writing by Oskison, Rogers, Riggs, and Emmet Starr, he concurs with Weaver and Womack that for Riggs this connection does not produce a vision of a healthy, sovereign Cherokee future.[20] After he cites the aforementioned letter by Riggs about "absorbed Indians," Justice situates *The Cherokee Night* within the specific critical context of his study: "The play seems to be Riggs's attempt to travel the Beloved Path of accommodating change while maintaining a coherent sense of Cherokee centrality, but it fails in that mission, ultimately giving way to despair and the doomed fading of Cherokees as deracinated shadows of a once great nation."[21] Justice completes an analysis of the argument between the Cherokee sisters Sarah and Viney with the following observation about the play: "The Beloved Path here leads nowhere; a state of balance is impossible, for both defiance and submission bring about the destruction of the self. Whether Indian, White, Black, or somewhere in between, all is struggle and pain. There is no safe state of being for Riggs's Cherokees— the 'vanishing Indian' is invoked again, this time by an Indian."[22] Of these three influential readings of Riggs's plays, Justice's is the most devastating. The play, for Justice, is an elegy; night has come to the Cherokees, and there is no promise of dawn.

The nearly exclusive focus on *The Cherokee Night* by other scholars emphasizes that the discussion of this play continues to determine Riggs's place in contemporary American Indian and American literary critical debates. This scholarship includes an emphatic statement on the play's failures, particularly its perpetuation of dominant racial and racist logic, by theater scholar, playwright, and director Julie Little Thunder (Creek); an equally emphatic statement on the play's accomplishments "as a carefully crafted assertion of Native performance elements and communal values in deliberate opposition to mainstream American dramatic conventions and individualistic ideology of the 1920s and 1930s" by Jaye Darby; and a discussion by Qwo-Li Driskill of a Cherokee-based hermeneutic that could be used to recuperate the play as a drama of Cherokee resistance.[23] Darby makes the most earnest effort to date not only to recover the play but, like Driskill, to recuperate its potential to speak of survival and resistance rather than doom to contemporary Native audiences.

These assessments of *The Cherokee Night* within the contexts of allotment and Oklahoma statehood, Riggs's gay identity, and modern U.S. drama demonstrate that the play offers a still compelling picture of turn-of-the-century and early twentieth-century Cherokee life in Oklahoma. Even the most problematic part of the play—what Womack argues is its endorsement of racial purity and what Little Thunder identifies as Riggs's representation of mixed bloods as racial degenerates—has its origins in a Cherokee-specific history of what anthropologist Circe Sturm calls blood politics. "In the Cherokee community," Sturm explains, "race mixing has become directly associated with cultural loss. Many Cherokees express the belief that as blood connections are stretched thin over the generations, so too are cultural connections, and the degree to which individuals still have a Cherokee culture can be measured by their degree of Cherokee blood."[24] More forcefully, Sturm asserts that "race and culture are conflated in Cherokee social classification."[25] *The Cherokee Night* is an exploration of and challenge to these blood politics just as it is a challenge, in Darby's reading, to modern U.S. drama. In the final scene, the full-blood John Gray-Wolf tells the mixed-blood outlaw Edgar Spench that his criminal ways have their origins in a lack of Indian blood. Yet as he loses blood from injuries he has sustained escaping the posse, Spench says, "White blood, Indian—it don't matter."[26] When the marshal, Tinsley, shoots Spench, the blood is neither white nor Indian but "cold."[27] Then Gray-Wolf, disregarding his own implicitly superior claim to Cherokeeness, claims Spench as belonging to the Cherokees and not to the authorities who have violated the sanctuary of Gray-Wolf's home by killing the outlaw.

Riggs's comment to Clark about "absorbed Indians" and the debilitating anxiety produced in the play by Cherokee blood politics suggest that Riggs is dramatizing a primarily cultural and racial decline. Yet Riggs's deracialization of blood and Gray-Wolf's assertion that Spench belongs to us, to Cherokees, establish a political dimension to the anomie at the heart of Riggs's Cherokee world. Though Riggs calls his Cherokees "absorbed Indians," he also identifies them as "citizens without a state."[28] When Gar Breeden, Edgar Spench's son, finds himself captured by members of a religious cult, he explains to them his unwelcome presence: "No place for me anywhere! Come down to Tahlequah yesterday to see if—to see—I thought this bein' the head of—Listen, I'm half Cherokee. I thought they could help me out here, I thought they—Old men sittin' in the square! No Tribe to go to, no Council to help me out of the kind of trouble I'm in. Nuthin' to count on—!"[29] Gar's predicament is explicitly political: he does not need an infusion of Cherokee blood or culture but a political organization, a tribe, a council. He needs both the claim of kinship and Cherokee jurisdiction that John Gray-Wolf extended to his father. The cultural and racial anxiety in the play almost overwhelms the political, but the political context that is present—the sabotage of the Cherokee Nation—links *The Cherokee Night* to the much more overtly political and anticolonial Mexican plays.

The Cherokee Night will likely remain one of two plays by Riggs that most consistently receive the attention of literary scholars, and part of my project is to provide—like Weaver, Womack, and Justice—another context in which to examine it. As Weaver in his most recent article on Riggs, "A Lantern to See By," and crime historian Albert Borowitz document in persuasive detail, the lawlessness and violence in Indian Territory and personal family disasters shaped Riggs's entire body of work. This violence and disaster even provide the narrative structure, Borowitz reveals, of an unfinished novel, "The Affair at Easter," on which Riggs was working immediately prior to his death.[30] I am emulating Borowitz's and Weaver's attention to Riggs's full career to demonstrate that Riggs had an attendant desire to find a political path—for everyone but particularly for poor and indigenous people—out of the chaos. The search for this path takes him eventually to Mexico, where he sets *A World Elsewhere* and *The Year of Pilár*. These plays are much more optimistic than *The Cherokee Night* about the future of contemporary indigenous communities. Though the Mexico plays are not explicitly about Cherokees, the consistency of Riggs's interest in the legacies of violent colonial histories, including in his Indian Territory plays, encourages us to examine the direct correlations among these histories and to consider how those correlations illuminate the Cherokee past, present, and future.

The Dramatic Geography of Riggs's Indian Territories

The Cherokee Night dramatizes several of those legacies, including the constant disruption of the Cherokee Nation's healthy relationship to the land. A "fissure like a trench" that "is gashed into the cliff" on Claremore Mound, according to the stage directions for scene 1, provides a visual image of the damage to this relationship.[31] *The Cherokee Night* shares with Riggs's Indian Territory plays—*Big Lake, Roadside* (1930), *Green Grow the Lilacs*, and *The Cream in the Well*—this careful attention to the specific physical geography of the Cherokee Nation.[32] Indeed, the setting that Riggs identifies as Indian Territory is almost always geographically coterminous with the Cherokee Nation. Riggs also archives the human geography of the Cherokee Nation in the Indian Territory plays. In all these plays, characters travel to and from Cherokee towns, and they constantly express anxiety about the various uses to which they are putting the land. In addition, many of his plays are about what Edward Said calls the central feature of imperialism: the fight over land.[33] These plays feature violent crimes, especially homicides, as well as intrusions and invasions and histories of resistance and dispossession. Thus whether or not Riggs identifies his characters as Cherokee or American Indian, the plays confirm familiar Cherokee or American Indian histories in the Cherokee Nation, Indian Territory, and later, Oklahoma.

This preoccupation with a people's orientation to a specific landscape and their use of that land is a familiar feature of American Indian literature and literary criticism, especially in the renaissance era. As Sean Teuton observes in *Red Land, Red Power*, a study of three foundational early renaissance novels by Momaday, James Welch, and Silko, "a central social construction in Native thought [is] that Indigenous people, by definition, grow from the land, and that everything else—identity, history, culture—stems from that primary relationship with homelands."[34] Of the three concepts that comprise Chadwick Allen's blood/land/memory complex employed by many indigenous writers to define identities and reclaim

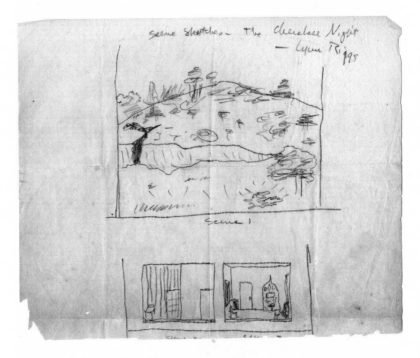

Figure 2.1. The fissure that cuts like a wound into Claremore Mound is prominent in this drawing, titled "Scene Sketches—The Cherokee Night—Lynn Riggs." Riggs orients the entire play to this feature of the Cherokee Nation landscape that stands as a reminder of the battle with the Osages following removal of the Cherokees from the Southeast and of the social, racial, and political divisions within the nation. From the Lynn Riggs Papers, 1971.004. Department of Special Collections and University Archives, McFarlin Library, University of Tulsa, Oklahoma.

histories, land is the most stable in Riggs's plays.[35] In his tribal nation–specific study of Creek literature, Craig Womack asserts, "What identifies a Creek work, in my mind, in addition to its authorship by a Creek person, is the depiction of a geographically specific Creek landscape and the language and stories that are born out of that landscape."[36] Similarly to the dialect letters of his Creek Nation neighbor to the immediate south and east, the Indian Territory–born Alexander Posey, Riggs's plays depict a geographically specific landscape—Cherokee rather than Creek—and the language and stories born there. His plays, even when they do not overtly feature Cherokee characters, are Cherokee specific, and the stages on which the actors perform his plays are Indian Territories.

We must account for these specific geographical spaces and historical moments when assessing Riggs's contributions to American Indian and American literary history. Riggs reminds his audience of the history of and his experience in the Cherokee Nation, for example, throughout *The Cherokee Night*: the aforementioned Claremore Mound is visible in the foreground or background of every scene. Like the town of Claremore, Claremore Mound is named, Cherokee historian Rachel Caroline Eaton explains, for the Osage leader Chief Clermont who was killed by Old Settler Cherokees in 1818. His name, Osage author John Joseph Mathews suggests, "is very likely the result of the Frenchman's attempt to pronounce the name Grah Moh (Arrow Going Home)."[37] In her short piece on the battle, Eaton describes the "border warfare" between the Osages and Cherokees and the attack on Chief Clermont's village by a "war-party" of Cherokees as well as some Choctaws, Shawnees, and eleven white men. Chief Clermont and many other Osages died in what Eaton calls "one of the bloodiest Indian massacres of modern history."[38] Cherokee author and public school teacher Mabel Washbourne Anderson narrates a more nationalistic story. When the Old Settlers arrived, she notes, "they were surprised and disappointed to find themselves among the wild and warlike Osages. These wild Indians did not like the intrusion of a superior and more civilized race, and immediately began hostilities."[39] After the Osages violated a peace treaty, the beleaguered and "greatly outnumbered" Cherokees were victorious in a "dreadful and final battle" that led to the Osages "inglorious flight."[40] The family cemetery on the farm north of Claremore owned by Riggs's mother, Rosie Buster, was near the site of this historical touchstone for the Cherokees. "As a child," Phyllis Braunlich reveals, "Lynn played in this meadow near Claremore Mound, where narrow stones mark the dozen or so graves of his Indian ancestors, sheltered by a grove of oak trees."[41] Riggs orients all the action in the play to this site of intertribal violence within the boundaries of the Cherokee Nation, and he adopts a similar strategy in his Indian Territory plays to ground them in a definitive Cherokee place.

The geographic space to which the terms "Indian country" and later "Indian Territory" refer was always changing shape and size, and throughout its history this constantly redefined space fell under many different indigenous (Great Plains, migratory, immigrant, refugee, and removed or exiled), colonial (Spanish, French, British), and settler-colonial U.S. (organized territory and state) jurisdictions. The region as a destination for indigenous peoples removed from the eastern United States began to take legal shape in the early nineteenth century. Independent scholar Jeffrey Burton summarizes the historical context:

> "Indian Territory" was a geographical expression which evolved from a policy. Its formal origins are found in an act of Congress of March 2, 1819. [. . .] At first the sole legal identity of this area of more than 62,000 square miles was contained in the words "the Indian country," but it was commonly, and legitimately, written and spoken of as "the Indian territory." Thence it was but a short step to the general adoption of the style "the Indian Territory." This was the form that appeared in many congressional bills from the 1860s onward, though it was not until well into the 1890s that the term "the Indian country" was replaced by the newer phrase in prosecutions undertaken by the United States court. Even then it was no more than a regularized solecism: *the Indian Territory was United States territory, but it was never a Territory of the United States.*[42]

The Indian Territory that Riggs remembers, imagines, celebrates, and elegizes encompasses the area in what is now eastern Oklahoma that remained after forced land cessions following the Civil War and the subsequent creation of Oklahoma Territory in 1890.

This area was dominated by the Five Tribes (Cherokee, Chickasaw, Choctaw, Creek, Seminole). The Cherokee Nation occupies much of the northeastern part of Indian Territory and the state of Oklahoma. Their neighbor to the immediate south is Downing's Choctaw Nation, and Mathews's Osage Nation is to the immediate west. The Cherokees also owned the Cherokee Strip and Cherokee Outlet, land to the west of the nation guaranteed by the Treaty of New Echota of 1836. Following the Civil War, the Cherokee Nation was forced to cede the Cherokee Strip and to accept the settlement of other tribal nations, including the Osage, in the eastern part of the Cherokee Outlet.[43] As historian Andrew Denson explains, the Cherokee Nation leased the remainder of the Outlet to non-Native ranchers through the Cherokee Strip Livestock Association.[44] Clement Vann Rogers, the father of Cherokee writer and celebrity Will Rogers, opposed this policy.[45] As Clement Rogers feared, what remained of the Outlet was ceded to the United States in 1893.

The subsequent land run was the largest in U.S. history. Mathews tells the history of the Cherokee Outlet in part 2 of his biography of E. W. Marland, *Life and Death of an Oilman* (1951). Though Mathews notes the hostilities between the Cherokees and the Osages, he does not mention the battle of Claremore Mound that figures so prominently in *The Cherokee Night*. He describes in careful detail, however, the land run:

> When at last the carbines were fired, signaling the opening of the Outlet, the race started over the charred grass. Sweat made little lines through the black dust on the strained faces. Little whirlwinds raced playfully with, or athwart, the runners. Wagons were tipped over and their contents spilled on the black plains. Sweating race horses, their nostrils distended, their barrels moving like bellows, their heads high with nervous excitement, whinnied to each other across the acrid plain or trotted off with dragging reins while their owners pounded their stakes or disputed a claim.[46]

Mathews adds that the Osages no longer threatened their enemies after the land run. This land cession immediately preceded the allotment of tribal-nation land bases and, eventually, Oklahoma statehood.

With *The Cherokee Night*, the Indian Territory play *Green Grow the Lilacs* occupies an important place in the recovery of Riggs, in part as a consequence of its use by Rodgers and Hammerstein as the source material for *Oklahoma!* Weaver reads a Native presence in *Green Grow the Lilacs*: "Set just outside Claremore, the play takes place, as the playscript states explicitly, in Indian Territory—not Oklahoma. Claremore, Riggs's birthplace, is in the heart of the Cherokee Nation. I am suggesting that it is not devoid of Indian characters at all but is, in some sense, a play *about* them."[47] Of the play's singing-cowboy protagonist, Weaver makes the additional and surprising observation that "it is entirely possible that Curly McClain is actually an Indian."[48] Weaver provides a catalog of specific textual examples from the play to support his assertion.[49]

Weaver's attentive reading of the Native presence in *Green Grow the Lilacs* is critical to my own assessment of Riggs as an author much more deeply invested in historical and contemporary indigenous American lives than previously acknowledged. His efforts encourage a further search of *Green Grow the Lilacs* for possible markers of Native presence. For example, early in the play, Curly responds to Aunt Eller's request for a song: "Must think I'm a medicine man a-singin' and passin' the hat around, the way you talk!"[50] The remark appears casual, but there are additional references to Curly's status as a healing force in the community. He has knowledge of the medicinal uses of local flora, as he later references the Indian turnip, which can be used to treat a variety of ailments. After his future wife Laurey tells him she is going to a party hosted by Old Man Peck with Curly's sinister and possibly homicidal rival, Jeeter Fry, Curly sings the title song and is "miraculously healed."[51] During a conversation with Jeeter in the old smokehouse in which Jeeter resides, Curly advises him: "Why don't you do sump'n healthy onct in a while."[52] Finally, while Weaver suggests that the applause of the partyers following Old Man Peck's singing of "Custer's Last Charge" indicates a celebration of Custer's bravery, it is possible to read their praise of the song as a celebration of Custer's defeat and the slow march of his men toward the "doom" conventionally reserved for Indians in some European American storytelling traditions.[53]

The depiction of a specific Cherokee Nation geography under siege, however, establishes most clearly *Green Grow the Lilacs'* correspondence to *The Cherokee Night* and the Mexico plays. The date of the play is 1900, seven years after the loss of the Cherokee Outlet and the subsequent land run and seven years prior to Oklahoma statehood. It was also two years after the passage of the Curtis Act, which, in order to break the Cherokee resistance to the 1887 Dawes or General Allotment Act, "abolished tribal laws, confirmed the extension of federal jurisdiction, and declared the residents of the Indian Territory to be under American authority."[54] Negotiations with the Dawes Commission, the authority responsible for making an allotment agreement with the Cherokee Nation, continued into 1902. Riggs maps *Green Grow the Lilacs* across this contested territory, which includes references to Dog Crick (Dog Creek) and the Verdigree River (Verdigris River) as well as to Catoosie (Catoosa), Sweetwater, Justus, Claremore, Vinita, Bushyhead, Pryor, and Sequoyah. Curly even hires the surrey with a fringe on top later made famous in *Oklahoma!* in Clare-more, where he is later incarcerated.

Aunt Eller's hostility to "furriners" and the federal authorities from which Curly escapes in the last scene, therefore, is comprehensible primarily when situated within the specific Cherokee historical context. After Curly's escape, he observes to Laurey, "Don't know whut's got into Indian Territory nohow! They puttin' everbody in jail—women and all!"[55] When the men deputized as federal marshals appear to return Curly to jail, Aunt Eller protests, "Why, the way you're sidin' with the federal marshal, you'd think us people out here lived in the United States! Why, we're territory folks—we ort to hang together. I don't mean *hang*—I mean *stick*. Whut's the United States? It's jist a furrin country to me. And *you* supportin' it! Jist dirty ole furriners, ever last one of you!"[56] Several people in the crowd then insist that they are Indians born in Indian Territory. This anonymous, disembodied announcement of "Indian blood" is additional evidence that Riggs disguises his Indian characters or that he imagines them on stage passing as white. Curly's comment about the emerging police state in Indian Territory and Aunt Eller's ominous reference to hanging, the method of capital punishment used with considerable frequency by Judge Isaac Parker until 1896, also evoke the historical battles over jurisdiction in the tribal nations of Indian Territory. Parker's last death sentence was for Cherokee Bill, the famous outlaw hanged March 17, 1896.

The specific setting of *Big Lake*, the first of his published Indian Territory plays, also falls within the boundaries of the Cherokee Nation immediately prior to its dissolution by Oklahoma statehood and, similarly to Claremore Mound in *The Cherokee Night*, evokes a land dispute between Cherokees and Osages that was settled in this case in favor of neither tribal nation. The play is set on the shores of Big Lake in the Cooweescoowee district of the Cherokee Nation, now Rogers County, Oklahoma, and is, therefore, a drama about life in the Cherokee Nation. The program of the play's first production on April 8, 1927, at the American Laboratory Theater in New York prepares the audience for the setting: "The action takes place in Indian Territory, now Oklahoma, in the year 1906."[57] The stage directions situate scene 1 more specifically in "the woods adjoining the Big Lake, near Verdigree Switch, Indian Territory, 1906." Borowitz provides a brief history of the Big Lake district: "Big Lake, located about 13 miles southwest of Riggs's hometown, Claremore, is a natural body of water over which Cherokees and Osages quarreled. The Department of

the Interior resolved the dispute by declaring the area Government property, and in the second decade of the twentieth century put the Big Lake
district up for sale; it was privately developed as a gated community."[58]
Riggs also situates the action in *Big Lake*, as in the other Indian Territory
plays, within a constellation of Cherokee Nation towns: Claremont (Claremore), Verdigree (Verdigris), Foyil, Sageeyah, Pryor Crick (Pryor Creek
or Pryor), and Grand River. Riggs embeds the play's plot in this Cherokee Nation–specific landscape, in the histories of violence that shaped it,
and in the disruption of Cherokee national life imminent in the play but
already experienced by Riggs and the other citizens of the nation.

Violence is a defining feature of Riggs's Indian Territory and Oklahoma plays, as Weaver observes in "A Lantern to See By," and a violent
crime has been committed before *Big Lake* begins. A bootlegger, "Butch"
Adams, kills a man, Jim Dory, who has informed federal officers of
Butch's criminal activity. Butch kills Dory while the informant is on his
way to the Binghams—a family that lived in the disputed Big Lake area.[59]
Borowitz establishes the context of the crime: "Prohibition of intoxicants was required in the Indian Territory and Osage Nation for a period
of 21 years by the Enabling Act authorizing Oklahoma statehood and was
extended to the entire State in response to lobbying by dry groups."[60]
When Butch returns to his cabin on Big Lake, a young couple, Lloyd and
Betty, who have arrived early to a school picnic, appear and ask to borrow a boat. Butch's companion, Elly, played in *Big Lake*'s first run by the
renowned actress and acting teacher Stella Adler, complains that authorities intended prohibition to protect Indians. However, she says, "I ain't
saw two Indians since I come to Indian Territory."[61] She then considers
framing Lloyd for the attempted murder. Though Elly changes her mind,
Butch adopts her idea and tells the sheriff about his imaginary homicidal brother who killed Jim Dory. Elly confirms Butch's story when the
sheriff asks her about it; then Butch tells the sheriff that his armed
brother is on the lake with a pretty young woman who is, he suggests,
in danger. Later, the sheriff believes Lloyd is Butch's brother and fatally
shoots him. Betty then drowns herself. Elly ends the play with a fatalistic
statement on the frequency and inevitability of violence around the lake.

While the stage bears the weight of the Cherokee Nation history that
shapes this dramatic geography, Riggs does not identify any of the characters as Cherokees, Osages, or Indians. In the stage directions for scene
1, Riggs introduces Lloyd and Betty and marks Lloyd as racially other

than white: "Lloyd and Betty come from the left, softly over the matted earth. They are very young. Lloyd is tall, dark; he has black hair; his face is sensitive; [. . .] Betty's hair is yellow. She has let it down. It frames her white, delicate face."[62] Though dark skin and black hair do not necessarily indicate a Cherokee or an American Indian, just as white skin and yellow hair do not necessarily indicate an Anglo American, Riggs is making visible a physical distinction between the characters that a 1930s audience would likely read as racial and, with a reminder that the setting is in Indian Territory, as Indian and white. In his discussion of the direct correlation between the degree of blood quantum and a character's connection to Cherokee culture in *The Cherokee Night*, Justice observes, "as blood quantum (thus ethnicity) is, to Riggs, evidence of stronger cultural connection to both other people and to the land itself, *visible* difference thus implies the ultimate melding of self, community, and land."[63] After citing a comment by Womack about Riggs's attraction to dark-skinned men, Justice continues, "I would assert that Riggs's erotic attraction is deeply embedded in a desire to connect to something that he believes rests in dark skin—namely, a *legitimized* cultural connection."[64] If Justice's analysis is applicable across Riggs's canon, then we can read Lloyd as a Cherokee or an Indian with at least some cultural connection to his tribal nation. In this historicized and politicized reading, *Big Lake* dramatizes an organized Anglo criminal enterprise that leads to the murder of a young Cherokee man by U.S. authorities acting, as in *Green Grow the Lilacs*, within the boundaries of the Cherokee Nation.

The play is thus an allegory for the threat of imminent Oklahoma statehood and the attendant dissolution of the Cherokee Nation's government in the following year, 1907. The relationship of the characters to the landscape elucidates this allegory. Riggs connects both Lloyd and Butch explicitly to the land. Butch has living arrangements similar to Jeeter Fry's in *Green Grow the Lilacs*: he lives in a cabin partially underground. In the cabin, "it is dark and gloomy; no direct sunlight has ever reached this secret place."[65] Butch does not work the land or work on it; he is a bootlegger and has possibly murdered other people than Jim Dory. In contrast, in scene 1, Lloyd pays homage to Big Lake with a brief speech that is *"like a prayer."*[66] He is in awe of the lake's beauty and knows the area around Big Lake well. After he tries to give Betty a flower for her hair, a gesture that connects him more explicitly to the land, Betty expresses a fear of the woods. Lloyd is initially unable to resist this fear, though he dismisses it quickly then insists that they ask the owners of the cabin, Butch and Elly, to borrow their boat rather than simply take it. Later, Lloyd and Betty escape Betty's fear of the woods by going onto the lake, which Lloyd associates with the sun and freedom: "I wish I could be a lake. I wish I could be that big, that deep! [. . .] It moves when the wind moves. It holds the sun. It's a cup with gold in it."[67] Betty adds that Big Lake holds the dawn; Lloyd says it holds the sunset, the starlight, and the moon. Like Ned Warrior in John Milton Oskison's 1926 novel *Black Jack Davy*, Lloyd embodies the land, the Cherokee Nation, and Cherokee law and order. His murder at the end of the play at the hands of invasive colonial agents posing as law and order is an evocative rendering of the material consequences of Oklahoma statehood for the Cherokee Nation.

Riggs continues to embed his plays within a specific history and landscape of the Cherokee Nation in *Roadside*, though, once again, he does not identify his characters as Cherokees or Indians. The program for the first performance of *Roadside* in New York at the Longacre Theatre on September 26, 1930, identifies the setting of act 1: "By the side of a road through the woods in Indian Territory. Sunset of a June day in 1905."[68] Act 2, scene 1, and act 3 occur on the same roadside, while act 2, scene 2 occurs in Verdigree Switch, the town of Verdigris. It is, like Big Lake, in the Cooweescoowee district of the Cherokee Nation. The characters in *Roadside* also visit or work in the towns of Claremore, Vinita, and the nation's capital, Tahlequah. The date of June 1905 is, again, as in *Big Lake* and *Green Grow the Lilacs*, an inauspicious one for Cherokees and the other Native nations of Indian Territory.

As he does most famously in *Green Grow the Lilacs*, Riggs dramatizes in *Roadside* the conflicts that characters have over the proper relationship of people to the land. Like his Mexican plays, *Pilár* and *World*, *Roadside* and *Green Grow the Lilacs* can be read as companion pieces. *Roadside* tells the story of a Western folk hero named Texas and his encounter with Buzzey Hale, Hale's ex-wife Hannie Rader, and Hale's former father-in-law, Pap Rader. Hannie entrapped him in an infidelity in order to escape their marriage and what is to her their banal life on a farm. Buzzey defends this way of life. He calls farming "livin' outa the ground" and asks Pap, "I'd like to know whut's better?"[69] Pap spends his life, in contrast, wandering throughout the West and stealing rather than raising food. Hannie was raised in this environment as a child, and she has left Buzzey in order to return to it. Pap has an unequivocal response to Buzzey's question: "This *here's* better. An' I'm tellin' you Hannie'd *orter* divorced you like she did. You ain't no kind of a man, and yore life ain't no kind of a life fer Hannie to be havin'. She's a strappin' girl that wants to roam, like me, and see life 'stid of a milk churn."[70] Hannie adds with some equivocation, "Men is s' crazy. Some wants to set on a farm till they dry up and blow away—like Buzzey here. Or some wants to go streakin' across the country, hell-bent for high water—like Paw. If they was jist a half-way crazy man who like to streak, and liked to set—*both*."[71] There is not "a half-way crazy man" in the world of the play, however, and Texas, who complains about the new laws and new fences in Indian Territory, is this narrative's wandering hero. In the contest between farming and roaming in *Roadside*, roaming clearly triumphs at the end of the play, when Pap, Hannie, Texas, and Buzzey's hired hands, Black Ike and Red Ike, head down the road with a defeated Buzzey and two law enforcement officers watching.

Riggs provides in *Green Grow the Lilacs* a different resolution to this tension between two ways of relating to the landscape. In *Green Grow the Lilacs*, Riggs places the cowboy Curly McClain in conflict with the hired hand and farmer Jeeter Fry. Curly says, "In this country, they's two things you c'n do if you're a man. Live out of doors is one. Live in a hole is the other."[72] The cowboy, to Curly, lives the life out of doors, while the farmer, though working the land, returns at the end of his day to the hole in which he lives. Later in the play, Curly bemoans the end of the cowboy era as the ranches break up and the cattle business slows dramatically, and then by the end of the play says, "I got to learn to be a farmer, I see that! [. . .] Country a'changin', got to change with it!"[73] Though Curly concedes that ranching and the cowboy life will surrender to farming as the primary relationship people have to the land in the new state of Oklahoma, there is a tremendous sense of loss in the change.

As in *Green Grow the Lilacs*, Riggs refers to American Indians within the Cherokee Nation landscape only at the end of *Roadside*. In an effort to win back Hannie's affection, Buzzey offers to help her with her chores: "Air you goin' to pick up sticks?" he asks before adding "Er find wild ingerns?"[74] This absence of characters identified as American Indian makes Texas's statement to the town marshal during the final showdown startling. As the town marshal, the jailer Neb Withers, and Buzzey confront Texas, Hannie, Pap, Black Ike, and Red Ike, Texas observes to the marshal: "You're the only white man in the whole shootin' match."[75] If the marshal is the only white man, then it is possible, indeed likely, that there are American

Indians on the stage. Riggs appears to take delight in implying that his characters are Native without committing to these racial identities.

A racist rhyme by Black Ike and Red Ike includes the only other specific reference to a character's racial identity in the play. The Ikes chant the rhyme, which suggests that Texas is actually African American, both times that Texas prepares to fight with the marshal.[76] The casting of Mexican-born actor Anthony Quinn as Texas in a 1950 production of *Roadside* pleased Riggs enough for him to mention it in a letter to his friend Spud Johnson in June of the same year.[77] It also suggests that Riggs did not want audiences to see Texas as white. Quinn was well known for his "ethnic roles" such as the American Indian Charley Eagle in Phil Karlson's *Black Gold* (1947) and Eufemio Zapata, the brother of Zapotec revolutionary Emiliano Zapata, in the 1952 Elia Kazan film *Viva Zapata!*[78]

The tension in *Green Grow the Lilacs* and *Roadside* between farming and ranching and farming and roaming, respectively, becomes in *Out of Dust* (ca. 1948) the struggle over ranching and town life. Weaver published *Out of Dust* for the first time in 2003 for the University of Oklahoma Press in an edition with *The Cherokee Night* and *Green Grow the Lilacs*. Riggs sets the play in Indian Territory on the Shawnee Cattle Trail in the early 1880s during about forty-eight hours of a cattle drive similar to the one from the Texas panhandle to western Kansas on which Will Rogers rode in 1898.[79] The three sons of Old Man Grant—Teece, Bud, and Jeff—chaff against the rule of their dictatorial father.[80] As they ponder the paucity of other employment options, Bud threatens to leave: "I'll light out for Mexico before I'll work for him again!"[81] Jeff also expresses his desire to leave the cattle trail and settle in Baxter, Kansas, with his fiancée, Rose. The trail sub-boss, King, who has spent some time in the penitentiary, encourages the sons to kill their father. Teece and Bud respond eagerly, but to manipulate Jeff into participating in the plot, King reveals to him that Old Man Grant had an affair with the young, vulnerable Maudie prior to Maudie's marriage to Teece. Jeff does not agree to help with the patricide, but after another confrontation in which his father threatens to control Jeff's future wife as well, Jeff tells his brothers and King to do whatever they want.

Like many of the homicides in Downing's detective novels, the killing of Old Man Grant is staged to look like an accident. While Riggs presents the murder as less brutal than Butch's killing of Jim Dory in *Big Lake* or Art Osburn's killing of his wife in *The Cherokee Night*, it captures the same desperate ruthlessness of Riggs's Indian Territory. After Old Man Grant's death, King introduces the recently arrived Rose to this Indian Territory:

"Where do you think you are, anyway—in a storybook someplace? This is Indian Territory and a man's life is worth nuthin' much from the cradle. And less than that when the breath is stopped. We'll get away from here—and leave the dead to shift for theirselves."[82] Twain's Huck Finn likely would not have survived long here. Jeff learns later that King stabbed their father to death after the staged accident only injures him. The resulting family turmoil ends with Rose shooting and killing King, Jeff going to tell the authorities, and Bud and Teece fleeing. Maudie speculates to the arresting officer, Mr. Osborn, that they are on their way to Mexico, the region that in Riggs's plays is most like Indian Territory: "They lit out from here—like you see. They talked about Mexico." Osborn responds, "They'll never make it. They'll be stopped before nightfall."[83] Out of Dust, written about a decade after the Mexico plays, shows Riggs again thinking of the kinship between these geographies but also about the sanctuary that Mexico often promises in Cherokee history.

As Riggs moves farther temporally and spatially in the settings of his plays from turn-of-the-century Indian Territory and Oklahoma, he maintains his sense of the way that the conflict over land shapes a region and its people while also more explicitly and frequently critiquing the dominance of oppressed communities and finding indigenous people who are not vanishing. While suffering from an illness variously described as "consumption, severe depression, or a nervous breakdown," Riggs followed his lover Witter Bynner to Santa Fe in the fall of 1923 and became a patient at Sunmount Sanatorium.[84] At Sunmount, where Riggs quickly recovered, he met N. Scott Momaday's future mentor, Yvor Winters. Russet Mantle, set in the 1930s in Santa Fe, features a blistering satire of the white, privileged classes and both their patronizing and more malevolently racist views of the local indigenous population from the surrounding pueblos. Like all Indian territories in the United States, New Mexico has a colonial history of which Riggs reminds the readers. It had only recently become a state, too, in 1912. Horace Kincaid, the owner of the ranch on which Riggs sets the play, explains to John Galt, an alienated and idealistic poet who he employs, why he came with his wife Susanna to New Mexico: "Have you ever been to Spain? New Mexico is Spain, my boy—the same hills, the same sun, the same arid and cruel earth."[85] Like Downing's Madame Fournier, who in The Cat Screams marks her pension as French territory with a flag and annual ceremonies, Kincaid superimposes the settler-colonist's homeland, Spain, onto the occupied colonial landscape, the U.S. Southwest. When Horace's sister-in-law Effie arrives, she expresses a desire to see "real live redskins," to see indigenous people that she views as "red and bloodthirsty" and as "savages."[86] She is also surprised to learn that Native people live in towns. Riggs contrasts Effie's imaginary Indians with the stoic and nearly silent local residents represented by the character Salvador from the pueblo of San Ildefonso. This satire of reductive representations of American Indians will appear familiar to readers of contemporary writers such as Sherman Alexie, Thomas King, and Gerald Vizenor. To a 1930s audience, however, the satire would likely have been more surprising. The disorientation that the non-Native characters experience, in addition to their failure to see or hear the local indigenous population, reinforces the representation of these non-Native characters as alien to this landscape.

Riggs treats the alien European visitors to these New World shores tragically rather than comically in *Dark Encounter*. A careful consideration of the specific references to Puritans and Pilgrims landing near Cape Cod shows *Dark Encounter* to be an astute contemplation of the nearly apocalyptic legacies of colonialism and racism. Riggs embeds the D-day setting of the play in a specific colonial landscape at one of the most celebrated sites of English invasion and settlement. As Allied forces invade Normandy across the Atlantic, Teek, a member of the Coast Guard stationed on the East Coast of the United States, surveys the sea and shore for any German presence. Teek eventually murders a U.S. Marine Corps lieutenant, Tom Patch, whose view of killing is reminiscent of Emo's in Silko's *Ceremony*. Patch had been ordered by his friend, Ancil Bingham, an honorably discharged U.S. Army officer seriously wounded in action, to kill a third man, Karl Enright. Enright immigrated as a child to the United States with his family from Germany, recently enlisted in the U.S. Army, and had an affair with Bingham's fiancée. Teek's murder of Patch in the penultimate scene occurs beneath a pier under a restaurant called the Flagship, after a destroyer, like a twentieth-century Mayflower wearing its intent to commit violence much more explicitly, pulls into the harbor.

The key features of this Indian Territory geography also define Riggs's Mexican plays: colonial and settler-colonial histories of violence and dispossession; deeply troubled families; repressed and traumatized sexualities, including an apparent incestuous relationship between half-siblings Gar Breeden and Bee Newcomb in *The Cherokee Night*; brutal murders; and omnipresent debates about the relationship of a people to the land. Cherokees and Mayans share the stage in Riggs's indigenous transnational imaginary.[87] In his plays, however, the possible coalition between American Indians and indigenous Mexicans in this Greater Indian Territory/ Greater Indigenous Mexico remains, in contrast to Downing's and McNickle's explicit delineations, unarticulated. There is also a crucial distinction between the two Indian territories. For Cherokees in the north, the future is very uncertain. For indigenous Mexicans in the south, the trauma and violence drive a revolution that transforms the landscape and promises healing within their families and communities.

The Greater Indian Territories of *The Year of Pilár* and *A World Elsewhere*

In addition to his career-long concern for keeping alive the memory and geography of the Cherokee Nation in Indian Territory, Riggs had a political interest in the indigenous peoples of Mexico. By the early 1930s, like Downing, Riggs was making frequent trips into Mexico from his home in Santa Fe, and he had an extended stay in Mexico City in 1937 as he finished *A World Elsewhere*.[88] His first completed Mexican play satirizes U.S. tourist culture within the context of a failed counterrevolution by hacendados and the military in Mexico City. Riggs follows *A World Elsewhere* with a drama that ends with the eruption of an indigenous revolution. *The Year of Pilár* is a dramatization of an enervated colonial world collapsing as a result of its inability or unwillingness to adapt and cannibalizing itself with its own oppressive religious and patriarchal traditions. The Mayans in *Pilár*, though not as fully developed as the members of the Spanish-descended or criollo Crespo family and as enigmatic as many of his Cherokee characters, unequivocally gain control of their present and future: Riggs stages the actual process of land redistribution in the Yucatán and justifies the wrath of local Mayans who at the end of the play punish the hacendados for centuries of enslavement and torture. When studied together, *World* and *Pilár* offer a devastating critique of colonialism and an unequivocal assertion about the feasibility of decolonization, including retribution against the settler-colonial landowners, the redistribution of land to indigenous people, and the reconstitution of indigenous self-government.

Riggs sets *A World Elsewhere*, the Mexico play that he completed first, in Mexico D.F. The D.F. might not immediately register as an indigenous territory. As Bonfil Batalla argues, however, there is a long, uninterrupted history of indigenous life in the city built on the site of the Aztec capital,

Tenochtitlan. While the segregated indigenous barrios of the early Spanish colonial era have been nearly overwhelmed in the late twentieth
century by urban sprawl, "Mesoamerican cultural forms" are still identifiable in indigenous and ladino neighborhoods.[89] In addition, indigenous
migration from rural areas continuously "Indianizes" the city; the city's
markets, for example, have a "profoundly Indian character."[90] Indeed,
Bonfil Batalla observes, *Mexico City is the place with the largest number of
speakers of indigenous languages in all the Americas.*"[91] From the laborers to
the indigenous women selling gum on busy street corners, the D.F. is full
of indigenous people maintaining ties to their home communities while
they adapt to urban life.[92]

The affluent Bodine family travels from its U.S. home to this occupied
indigenous territory in *A World Elsewhere*. Though the allusion in the
play's title is to Shakespeare's *Coriolanus*, the setting has affinities with the
quasi–New World island of *The Tempest*. Riggs sets *World* on "a section of
the *patio* of a little inn in Mexico, D.F., on a Spring afternoon in the Thir-
ties."[93] The inn's patrons include Mrs. Annie Bodine, the grandmother;
Phil Bodine, the father; Claire Bodine, his wife and the ex-wife of Stewart Nash; Jabby Nash, her ten-year-old son with Stewart; Janie Nash, her
seventeen-year-old daughter with Stewart; and Elizabeth Martin, the gov-
erness. According to Jabby, Clemente, "a young Mexican mozo, quite dark,
quite Indian," has told him that the military plans to overthrow the government.[94] The Bodines and Stewart Nash, who is also traveling in Mexico,
find themselves in the middle of this counterrevolution as the tempo-
rary prisoners of the U.S.-educated former hacendado General Gonzalo
Fernandez Aguirre. *World* gives Riggs a chance to assert the righteousness
of the revolution that he stages in *Pilár* and to meditate on the dominant
U.S. views of this Indian Territory.

Several members of the Bodine family romanticize Mexico and use
their socioeconomic and white racial privilege to appropriate an imaginary,
ideal colonial space for themselves. Riggs dramatizes the familiar practice
of playing Indian in the United States as playing Mexican in *World*, though
materially and culturally playing Mexican in the play is equivalent to playing
indigenous Mexican. Janie Bodine loves Mexico, especially "the marvelous
peons"; she wants to be "dark and passionate."[95] After she returns from a
shopping excursion, she appears in regional costume from Tehuantepec, a
Zapotec area in the state of Oaxaca, and says she wants to dye her hair black.

Claire and Phil Bodine share Janie's love for the country; it is their
world elsewhere, their paradise. Claire wants to stay forever, have a servant

girl named Manuela and "a *mozo* with his head shaped like a cone," and do nothing.[96] Her desire for an indigenous servant marked by the Mayan practice of skull modification indicates that Claire's interest is in building a utopia on an exoticized and exploited working class of indigenous Mexican people. In response to Claire's expressions of colonial longing, Phil exclaims, "We've both found it! The world everybody's looking for."[97] The desire to live as a member of the ruling class in a colonial regime is apparently a familiar one in the Bodines' world. However, there is a privileged class already in place in Mexico. The conflict between the Bodines, representatives of U.S. democracy, and this Mexican privileged class does not culminate in a statement on the superiority of *norteamericano* civilization. Instead, it makes legible a shared, transnational urge to dominate indigenous Mexico.

Stewart Nash's arrival disrupts the Bodines' daydreaming and introduces an alternative vision of this colonial world elsewhere. While Claire sees "Indians brown and beautiful in the fields," Stewart sees "the greed and hypocrisy, the rape and plunder of this land" and starving, exhausted Indians suffering from disease.[98] As in *Russet Mantle*, which takes its title from act 1, scene 1 of *Hamlet*, in *World* Riggs dramatizes a dialectic in which the opposing positions are founded on reductive representations of indigenous people. Indigenous Mexicans are neither happy fieldworkers nor all starving and diseased; the imminent counterrevolution demonstrates that neither view of Mexico—as a paradise or as a living hell—is accurate.

The sound of machine guns soon after Stewart's appearance announces the beginning of the counterrevolution that disrupts the Bodines' New World paradise, even though the counterrevolution's colonial ideology mirrors their own view of Mexico. As Clemente goes to get his gun, Claire inquires, "Is it a revolution?"[99] A witness to the violence responds, "Those bastard *soldados* at the Palace. We saw it, we knew it, and couldn't believe it! Straight across the Zocalo, they turn their machine gun. Like a mowing machine! Rrrrr—like that! Without warning when the order was given."[100] The general then appears at the inn with a "dynamic Fascistic energy" that anticipates the tyrannical tendencies of the titular Pilár in Riggs's next play. The general takes the Bodines and Nash hostage and announces, "The *hacendados* are having their revenge at last. I, too, am having my revenge. My family *haciendas* were stolen from us and subdivided and given away. I am happy to state that I have taken them back. Not only my own but all those so ruthlessly seized by a government which imagines a grimy Indian has a right to land."[101] The general's anti-Indianism is matched by his contempt for the United States: "You beat the little peoples of the earth for the salvation of their souls and the jingle of coins they can put in your pockets. You steal oil, minerals—wherever you find them. You snatch land away from no matter who,—the Indians who were there before you. Half your august territory you stole from Mexico, to begin with. [. . .] When all else fails you terrorize with your dreadnaughts and your raw-boned Marines. You pollute the world with your smug faces, you change it, you send your sickening jingoistic movies everywhere."[102] The general's speech is far more blunt than the condemnation of U.S. policy in a Downing novel or a Will Rogers newspaper column, but it captures the same sense of outrage in both. His speech also implies a distinction between the old colonial war fought by European nations against indigenous American peoples and the new colonial war fought by competing settler-colonial nations against each other.

Riggs exposes this distinction, however, as the general's attempt to obfuscate the contempt for and domination of non-European peoples at the foundation of both colonialisms. While the general appears as a familiar caricature in U.S. culture of the Mexican strongman, he shares a history of domination with the Bodines. The general tells the family that during his stay, he will choose one of the women as his sexual partner for the night. In an attempt to distract and delay him, Mrs. Bodine and Claire appear with the ostensible goal of seducing him. During their conversations, their similar family histories become clear. The Bodines, as Claire observes, are from St. Louis, while the general is from San Luis Potosí. "Our origins are akin," she tells him.[103] Mrs. Bodine emphasizes the kinship between their histories when she observes that in his persistence the general is just like her husband. They then discuss the past:

MRS. BODINE. [. . .] I remember the way everything used to be.
AGUIRRE. *The way it used to be—is the way it shall be.*
MRS. BODINE. If only I could believe that! When I was a young girl
   I lived on a plantation back in Missouri.
AGUIRRE. When I was a young boy I lived on my father's *hacienda*
   in San Luis Potosí. *Now* I shall live there again.
MRS. BODINE. Oh, if only I could go back to—! "The way it used to
   be is the way it shall be." You give me hope. You give me courage.
AGUIRRE. [*Blandly.*] We are on the same side, you see. You and I.[104]

Even if Mrs. Bodine is acting in order to flatter the general, they are indeed on the same privileged side of history: the plantation and the hacienda are both landscapes of domination. The nostalgia here is not imperialist as defined by anthropologist Renato Rosaldo; Mrs. Bodine and the general mourn the passing of their racial and political dominance, not the passing of colonized, indigenous cultures that their racial and political dominance helped to destroy.[105] However, their shared settler-colonial nostalgia for the loss of their ancestors' legal, social, political, and economic domination makes legible the transnational colonial kinship between Mrs. Bodine and the general.

Like Downing's *The Cat Screams, World* is a captivity narrative, though the indigenous actors in this drama free the white captives from a settler-colonial agent that only Mrs. Bodine recognizes as their historical and ideological kin. Clemente shows Jabby a secret passage, built at the Empress Carlotta's request when she visited the inn with Emperor Maximilian, in the kitchen that leads across the street to the American consulate. By embedding the escape route's origins in the same history of the French occupation of Mexico so important to the historical context of Downing's *The Cat Screams*, Riggs recalls the defeat of Maximilian by the Zapotec political and military leader Benito Juárez. The escape of the Bodines signals the defeat of their imaginary socioeconomic and racial occupation of Mexico. After Claire defends her nation's history with an idealistic, jingoistic speech, Jabby appears with soldiers from the consulate. A soldier announces, "The counter-revolution has collapsed. Mexico lives."[106] After Claire announces that there is no world elsewhere, Phil says that they should all go home. When the counterrevolution fails, the foreigners leave Mexico and leave this Indian Territory to the indigenous revolutionaries. They depart from a Mexico that is neither a paradise nor a hell for an exploited working class of indigenous people. Instead, Riggs portrays indigenous people working and fighting to make Mexico their nation. Mexico lives to assert more forcefully its indigeneity.

Yucatán, the setting for *The Year of Pilár*, is more legible as a coherent indigenous territory than the D.F., and it has a long revolutionary history. Historian Nelson A. Reed tells the more recent part of this history in his study of the Caste War between the Yucatecan Mayans and criollos. The Caste War began in 1847, when Yucatecan Mayans revolted against the system of debt peonage under which they had long suffered. Mexican independence in 1821 simply reinforced criollo dominance:

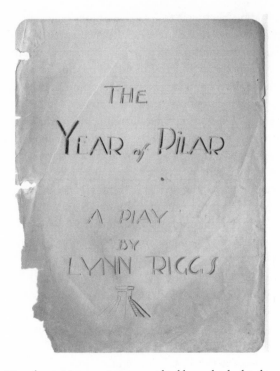

Figure 2.2. Riggs drew a Mesoamerican pyramid in blue and red colored pencil at the bottom of this homemade cover page for The Year of Pilár. *The pyramid represents the Mayan's historical claim to Yucatán and hints at their uprising in the play following the collapse of the haciendas. From the Lynn Riggs Papers, 1971.004. Department of Special Collections and University Archives, McFarlin Library, University of Tulsa, Oklahoma.*

For a large majority of the Mazehual, tied by family or habit to the land, the white man became a more regular presence in the years following independence. He had the power to question the Mazehual at will or make him kneel to kiss his hand; he could demand to be transported for miles in the colche or insist that his baggage be carried on a tumpline. In addition, the Mazehual saw their sacred corn trampled and smashed by unfenced cattle, their very land stolen away. And they had no recourse when their women were sexually exploited.[107]

Specific acts that further aggrieved the Mayans included the criollo appropriation of communally held lands, the ejidos; the elimination of Mayan water rights; the failure of the criollo ruling class to fulfill a promise of land to the Mayans who were armed by and then fought for the Republic of Yucatán (1841–48) against Mexico; and the racially motivated execution by firing squad of three Mayan leaders in Tabi on January 7, 1847.[108]

Until May 1848, the Mayans earned often overwhelming military victory after military victory, though conflict between two Mayan leaders led to the demise of an April 1848 peace plan with very favorable terms, such as debt relief and unobstructed use of the ejidos.[109] Simultaneously, the arrival of the time to plant crops, along with a scarcity of food and ammunition, led many Mayans to return to their home villages. The government of Miguel Barbachano y Tarrazo finally succeeded in first securing aid from Cuba and interested parties in Vera Cruz and New Orleans and then a strategic reunification with Mexico on August 17, 1848. The criollo government reestablished some control and avoided collapse during the next seven years. The arrival of 938 U.S. soldiers in late 1848 contributed to "the reconquest of the peninsula" and briefly opened a southern, trans-Caribbean front in the Indian wars of Mexico's northern neighbor.[110] While Yucatán began to sell Mayans into slavery in Cuba, the religion of the Speaking Cross helped to rally the most determined Mayan revolutionaries. Despite victories in individual battles, they could not completely overwhelm the government's militias. Those militias, however, could not decisively defeat the revolutionaries. When Yucatán conceded in 1855 that it could not win, argues Reed, the Mayans won the war: "Of all the native revolts in America since the Arawaks used their wooden spears against the sailors of Columbus, this one alone had succeeded."[111] Many Mayan communities, with the exception of the followers of the Speaking Cross, signed peace treaties. The trade in Mayan slaves continued.

With a capital at Noh Cah Balam Na Santa Cruz, the followers of the Speaking Cross, the Cruzob, controlled, governed, and defended eastern Yucatán. They had allies on their western frontier, where they occasionally attempted to coerce Mayan towns of Pacíficos to join them. Runaway workers from the haciendas to the north and west often found refuge in the Cruzob region. They functioned as an "independent nation," explains Reed, and "the Santo Cruz Maya were recognized as a de facto nation by the English and a sometimes ally of the British Empire."[112] Military action slowed and internal political conflicts increased in the 1870s and 1880s, and the number of faithful, as well as the overall population of

the region, began to fall. They maintained their independence until they
signed a peace treaty in 1897, the same year that the Cherokee National
Council in Indian Territory was negotiating with the Dawes Commission. Still, a long, slow invasion by the Mexican army culminated in its
arrival in Noh Cah Balam Na Santa Cruz in May 1901. The Cruzob had
abandoned the city.

Many of the Mayans living outside the Cruzob zone continued to work
the haciendas. Reed calls northwest Yucatán in the late nineteenth century
"one vast cleared plantation" with the Mayan population still living in debt
peonage.[113] "By the 1880s," he reports, "20,767 men were listed as indebted
servants; together with their families they numbered over 100,000, or a
third of the population."[114] The Mayans remember the era as the "time of
slavery."[115] In 1910, Meyer and Sherman assert, "It is certain that conditions
on the henequen haciendas of Yucatán were the worst in the republic.
Because many of the peones in Yucatán were deportees from other parts
of Mexico (some were recalcitrant Yaqui Indians from Sonora, and others
were convicted criminals), they were forced to work in chains, and flog-
ging was not uncommon."[116] Thus in the decade of Oklahoma statehood
and the dissolution of Indian Territory's tribal-national governments, the
Mayan people of Yucatán were living in an intolerable feudal state. Yucatán
was, like the rest of Mexico, on the cusp of a revolution.

Riggs was composing his plays in the same postrevolutionary decade
in which Downing was writing his novels, and the radical indigenismo
of the 1930s also provides part of the historical context for our understanding of the promising indigenous future that Riggs finds in Mexico.
However, dramatic changes in federal Mexican Indian policy had a much
greater impact on the daily lives of indigenous Mexicans than the attempt
by indigenistas to use their histories and material culture to invent a unified national identity. In his history of Cárdenas land reform in Yucatán,
Ben Fallaw explains that "as a presidential candidate in March 1934, Lázaro
Cárdenas pledged to carve dozens of collective henequen ejidos out of the
haciendas of Yucatán."[117] Cárdenas was elected later that year, and following his inauguration, he began slowly to institute his plan to return 20 to 25
percent of all hacienda land to indigenous people.[118] Fallaw calls Yucatán
one of "the two areas where Cárdenas tested land reform on the largest
scale."[119] "It is," Fallaw elaborates, "only a slight exaggeration to say that
Yucatán was Cárdenas' TVA; more resources were spent there on agrarian reform than in any other place except for La Laguna for most of his

presidency."[120] Yucatán was, in summary, "a Cardenista revolutionary laboratory."[121] The revolutionary narrative into which Riggs writes the Mayans
contrasts dramatically with the narratives that he plots in his other plays,
notably *The Cherokee Night*, that feature Cherokee or American Indian
characters: the legacy of invasion that contributes to Cherokee-against-
Cherokee violence in those plays becomes Mayan against Spanish in *Pilár*.
While the indigenistas in Mexico sought to utilize indigeneity as the foundation of national unity in 1920s and 1930s Mexico, Riggs, like Downing,
saw an opportunity for the revolution there to take another step toward
both retribution and indigenous autonomy. Though the official, national
Mexican revolution ends in 1920, Riggs boldly stages an indigenous one in
the late 1930s.

The Year of Pilár tells the story of the Crespos, a wealthy family that
owns a henequen plantation near Mérida in Yucatán but flees Mexico in
1917 during the revolution.[122] After living in New York for twenty years,
Pilár, the Crespo's oldest child, insists that the family now flee the cor-
rupting influences of New York and return to its hacienda in Yucatán. She
does not know that they will return immediately prior to the institution
of the agrarian reform measures. Riggs describes Pilár in the stage directions: "She is a vibrant girl, with the cool aristocratic authority and pride
of years of privilege. Her mind has the keenness and the violence of her
Conqueror forefathers; her emotions the fierce range that will devastate
others—or herself."[123] Riggs emphasizes the Crespo family's conquistador
ethic, as captured in the image of Pilár's keen and violent mind, by align-
ing the family with Porfirio Díaz, who visits the Crespo family and then
requests that they allow Pilár to spend a week with him. Don Severo Crespo, the hacendado and family patriarch, agrees to send Pilár with Díaz.
Díaz was the dictator of Mixtec and Spanish ancestry who ruled Mexico
from 1876 to 1880 and 1884 to 1911, and he gave his support to the hacendados, as well as to wealthy foreign investors and corporations, throughout
his career.[124] He was also the Mexican leader responsible for quelling the
Yaqui rebellion in the late 1880s in Sonora by forcibly relocating Yaquis to
Yucatán and enslaving them on the haciendas.

Though Riggs appears to take the titular Pilár's name from the Yucatecan revolutionary leader Pedro Crespo, she is the most explicit colonizer in
the catalog of Riggs's characters.[125] There is not a character so finely delineated as colonial oppressor in the Indian Territory plays. She is the "stone
post" of the Crespo family who relentlessly enforces her conception of the

dominant social, political, and racial status that the family's history confers upon them. Natividad Gutiérrez observes, "Spanish women were extremely efficient at introducing new fundamental structures and core values of colonial social organization based on the European model of the patriarchal family."[126] She adds, "The ideological basis of the caste system evolved from the Spanish concept of the nation, which involved beliefs concerned with racial purity, a 'community of blood,' and linguistic cohesion. Membership in such a community was given by an individual's ability to demonstrate 'purity of blood,' a concept tied to Christian ancestry and maintenance of a lineal pedigree by means of sexual honor. Women born in Spain played a significant role in preserving these core Spanish values and thus became synonymous with social status."[127] The Pilár of Riggs's play, like her historical cognates, stands for Spain, the mother country, as well as for the conquistador and his descendants. Pilár's zealous, dictatorial Catholicism produces a toxic family dynamic that drives her younger sister, Graziela, translated into English as *grace* and called *Chela*, into prostitution in Cuba. Her brother Fernando flees into the chicle forests to be a chiclero after he marries a woman from a family that does not satisfy Pilár's moral and social standards.[128] Her brother Trino also leaves the home to work in the fields with his Mayan half-brother, Beto, and live with him, perhaps incestuously, in his jacal. Her parents, Don Severo and Dona Candita, watch helplessly as Pilár destroys the family by trying to maintain the moral and social contours of the world that they inherited and helped to perpetuate.

Intrafamily resistance to Pilár comes primarily from Trino, short for Trinidad (Trinity), the most rebellious of the Crespo sons. Much like Downing portrays Madame Fournier in *The Cat Screams,* Riggs depicts Pilár as a foreign invader who maintains a discomfort for and displeasure with the country that she occupies. When the family first arrives at the hacienda, Trino shakes hands with Beto. Pilár reacts violently: "You don't have to give your hand to an Indian!"[129] Trino's threatening gesture of friendship and brotherhood with a Mayan, his assault on colonial decorum, has its origins in a view of family and colonial history that conflicts with Pilár's. Trino provides the most explicit denunciation of this colonial history: "My grandfather was a tyrant, an oppressor. It's no wonder he was at home here. Slaves to command—to torture if it please him—forcing them to work like beasts to fill his own money-bags. Women slaves to enjoy at night. The rich gluttonous old Spanish bastard! It's no wonder he was just like that with that old despot, Don Porfírio Díaz. They were birds

of a feather."[130] The outrage that Trino has at the abuses of his ancestors
and his immediate family, including the father that he shares with Beto,
leads him to establish an alliance with his half-brother.

Indigenous people and communities, like the colonizers, are more
readily identifiable in Riggs's Mexico than his Indian Territory. We know
from the moment that Riggs introduces Beto and the other indigenous
characters that they are Mayans, and they are not troubled by the kind of
blood politics in which the characters of *The Cherokee Night* are implicat-
ed. Though Beto has both indigenous and European heritage, like Riggs's
Cherokee characters in *The Cherokee Night*, there is no question that he is
Mayan. Beto is the dominant Mayan character in the play, and Riggs presents him as oppressed but dignified. When the scene shifts from New York
to Yucatán, "a little band of Indians," including Beto, awaits the arrival of
the Crespos.[131] The demand by Cuco Saldívar, the neighboring hacendado,
that Beto dance a jarana to celebrate the return of the Crespos makes legible and unequivocal the place of the hacendados and the Mayans in the
colonial social structure. In the first act of indigenous resistance in the play,
Beto refuses to perform Indian minstrelsy.

Riggs also depicts Beto as hardworking, philosophical, and immune,
almost stoically so, to Trino's outbursts of self-righteous anger. This representation of Mayans corresponds to Cárdenas's own view: "Cárdenas
himself clung to a romantic view of the Maya as a proud, stoic folk requir-
ing his government's paternalistic guidance for salvation."[132] Despite the
history of the Caste War, he shared with other Mexicans "the widespread
belief in the legendary peaceful and hardworking qualities of the Maya."[133]
Though the honorable Beto is Riggs's representative Mayan, one of the
omnipresent homicides of Riggs's Indian Territory suggests that Mayans
are prone to outbursts of violence: one Mayan character kills another with
a machete for obediently playing a song at the command of Fernando
Crespo. Riggs establishes this violence, though, as part of the colonial context: as with the Cherokees and Osages in his Indian Territory plays, the
oppressive interference of outsiders forces indigenous people into violent
conflict with each other.

Riggs suggests the possibility of an incestuous relationship between
Beto and Trino that represents not the nadir of a corrupt colonial history
but a promise of healing. In the two scenes that Riggs sets at Beto's jacal,
a stoic Beto and an outraged Trino discuss the region's colonial history.
When Trino's mother and sister arrive to reclaim Trino as a part of the

family, Pilár intuits what she thinks is an incestuous relationship. Though Trino explicitly denies it, the specter of incest allows Riggs to heighten Pilár's sense of horror that she first expressed when Trino shook Beto's hand. Beto and Trino's father then arrives to relinquish his position as patriarch. This seventh scene of *Pilár* is reminiscent of the seventh scene of *The Cherokee Night,* during which the outlaw Edgar Spench enters the elder John Gray-Wolf's home as he tries to escape from the authorities. Gray-Wolf encourages the injured Spench to "fight to live," and in an act of kinship with Spench, Gray-Wolf refuses to allow the authorities to enter his home and claims Spench as "*our* dead."[134] In *Pilár,* Trino rejects his family's legacy, after which a contrite Don Severo claims both Trino and Beto as his sons. Womack writes, "One of Riggs's themes is innocent youths in conflict with oppressive adults and restrictive social institutions that hold back natural and free impulses. Idealism, especially in youth, succumbs to convention."[135] The theme that Womack identifies in Riggs's Indian Territory and U.S. plays does not translate to the Mexican context, where social and political processes at work affirm Trino's idealism.

While the aforementioned Mayan-against-Mayan violence mirrors the Cherokee-against-Cherokee violence of *The Cherokee Night,* the Mayans in *Pilár* begin to direct their anger at the criollos. As the government begins the process of land redistribution, some Yucatecan Mayans begin to kill hacendados and their families. While the Mayan revolutionaries threatened Mérida in the early stages of the Caste War, in the later stages they fought primarily in the eastern and southern parts of the peninsula with a pacified frontier zone between them and the city. Thus Riggs brings his Mayan revolution closer to one of the main, urban colonial centers than it was historically. The radio delivers the news to the Crespos. The announcer reports, "On the *hacienda* of Don Ernesto Solis, the Indians, inflamed to passion against *Señor* Solis for his cruelties and abuses over the many years of their servitude, seized tonight the moment of their coming to power to raid the Solis house and to massacre all people within."[136] As Dona Candita fears the worst, Pilár says, "No, no, *mamacita!* For cruelties and abuses, the radio says. We've not been cruel."[137] Here, Pilár does not condemn the violence; she implies that those who commit cruelty and abuse deserve punishment for their crimes. At the same time, her denial of her own family's participation in the cruelty is absurd. These comments serve, therefore, to sanction the violence—killing one's oppressors is acceptable within the historical and moral universe Riggs creates—and seal Pilár's own fate.

The Spanish colonial world in the play, at least as represented in the contest over land, is approaching its end. Early upon their return to Yucatán, Cuco Saldívar compares the Crespo hacienda to the ruins at nearby Uxmal, and Trino repeats the comparison later in the play. The image of a colonial hacienda as similar to Mayan ruins recalls the abandoned towns and collapsed churches reclaimed by the jungle during the Caste War.[138] It foreshadows the end of colonial dominance, an end achieved by both friendship—between Trino and Beto—and violence. Trino tells Beto early in the play, "A little hate would have saved you."[139] Beto rejects hatred; instead, Trino and Beto work the fields and together help the government redistribute the land. As an employee of the government, Beto begins to take a role in a Mayan future that at this moment promises some self-government. Mayans on other plantations, however, express their outrage by killing the hacendados and their families. In the critical paradigm Justice presents in his literary history of the Cherokees, the different responses to colonial oppression taken by Beto and the neighboring Mayans are, respectively, the Beloved Path and Chickamauga consciousness. Indeed, the hope in the Beloved Path so conspicuously absent from *The Cherokee Night* appears as a powerful political principal in *The Year of Pilár*.

Yet it is a Chickamauga consciousness that will bring this colonial world to its end. As the Crespos prepare to flee, Trino and Pilár meet for the last time. Trino tells her, "The Mayans have always accepted authority from above, meekly. Now there's no authority above them—for the first time in centuries. There'll be abuses at first. It's inevitable. The *politico* crooks and dispossessed *hacendados* will scheme their guts out to get back what they've lost to ignorant Indians, accustomed only to the labor of the body. But the idea of the right to power goes to starving cells quickly. And it won't die so easily in their veins. *They'll learn to fight* [. . .] And to win."[140] Pilár follows Trino's speech with an apocalyptic vision: "There's a mist around me, everywhere I look—shapes of horror thrusting up with menacing eyes. [. . .] Trino's gone away forever to make our ruin complete—till the last of the Tueros and Crespos and all such people are slaughtered."[141] As Pilár's choice of words suggest, "The Last of the Tueros and Crespos" is an appropriate subtitle for the play. Following a final argument with Cuco Saldívar, to whom she is engaged, Pilár tells Beto that she is prepared to die, prepared to sacrifice herself to hasten the end of colonial domination:

"Not till I die—not till all such people as myself are dead—we, the ones who've lorded it over the weak and lowly—not till all of us are in the grave can a stricken people sing again, be free again!"[142] After she removes the family pictures from the wall and smashes them, and the history that they represent, she exits the hacienda and faces possible sexual assault and certain death. We hear the radio again as she walks to meet her fate: "*Buenos noches, señoras and señores.* You are listening to the Voice of Mexico!"[143] The revolution promises a good night for the Mayans and for the invaders another *noche triste,* the Spanish designation for the summer night in 1520 when the Mexicas drove them from Tenochtitlan. The voice of Mexico that Riggs celebrates is indigenous and revolutionary.

A World Elsewhere and *The Year of Pilár* are plays so surprising within the context of American Indian literary history of the interwar and early contemporary periods that they force us to wonder what else we have overlooked in Riggs's other plays and in the literary productions by other American Indian authors of this era. With its focus on the reclamation of indigenous land, as well as retribution against that land's foreign occupier, *Pilár* is a play that speaks directly to writers and activists of the civil rights and renaissance generations. Elizabeth Cook-Lynn laments that "there is little room for liberation literature, little use for nationalistic/tribal resistance" in much late twentieth century fiction by American Indian authors.[144] In *Pilár,* Riggs stages indigenous liberation and anticolonial resistance, as well as the retribution that Cook-Lynn applauds in Silko's *Almanac of the Dead.* This retribution, she argues, is "a matter of utmost importance to Silko, to indigenous peoples everywhere."[145] Following his own observations in *Red on Red* about land reclamation in *Almanac,* Craig Womack outlines a literary critical practice with similar politics to *World* and *Pilár*: "I will seek a literary criticism that emphasizes Native resistance movements against colonialism, confronts racism, discusses sovereignty and Native nationalism, seeks connections between literature and liberation struggles, and, finally, roots literature in land and culture."[146] The political consciousness that Riggs dramatizes in *Pilár* extends the genealogy of the American Indian literary renaissance back into the middle decades of the twentieth century and into Mexico.[147]

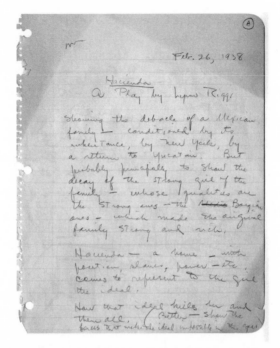

Figure 2.3. As his working notes for The Year of Pilár reveal, Riggs hoped to convey the utter exhaustion of the Spanish colonial model in the twentieth century. The last two paragraphs read, "Hacienda—a home—with position, slaves, power—etc comes to represent to the girl the ideal. How that ideal kills her and them all. (Better—show the forces that make the ideal impossible in the age)." From the Lynn Riggs Papers, 1971.004. Department of Special Collections and University Archives, McFarlin Library, University of Tulsa, Oklahoma.

The Return to Indian Territory

Immediately following his two published plays about Mexico, Riggs returns to the Big Lake setting in *The Cream in the Well*. This play is crucial to our understanding of how Riggs's visits to Mexico influenced his view of Indian Territory history and contemporary Cherokee and American Indian life. The play is set in Indian Territory, 1906, on a spring day and then at Thanksgiving at the home of a Cherokee family, the Sawters, on the shores of Big Lake, two miles from Verdigris. As in the other Indian Territory plays, including *Big Lake*, the significance of these contexts must not be underestimated in any reading of the play: the date and setting evoke the dispossession of the Osages and Cherokees at Big Lake and the imminent dissolution of Indian Territory. The frequent discussion of each family member's Cherokee allotment also reminds readers of the constant history of violence and dispossession that has produced this family. These histories, these acts of federal aggression, are intimately linked to the emotional, psychological, and sexual dynamics at work in the Sawter family, the only explicitly Cherokee family in Riggs's canon other than those in *The Cherokee Night*.

As in *Green Grow the Lilacs*, characters in *The Cream in the Well* discuss the new world of statehood that they will soon experience. Mrs. Lou Sawter says of statehood, "That'll just ruin everything," while Mr. Dave Sawter accepts it with resignation. His brief reference to the political and cultural battles over statehood disguises a repressed anxiety: "Only trouble is what to call it—Indianokla or Indiahoma."[148] This powerful anxiety emerges a few lines later: "I see only misery and trouble ahead."[149] The youngest child, Bina, is miserable, and in a letter that his family reads in the first scene, Clabe, the middle child, has written to say that his life is a mess and that there is "something awful and evil driving" his older sister, Julie.[150] A former seminary student, Julie is also tormented, mean, and temperamental. Julie and Clabe are both dark as well: Julie is "striking and dark," and Clabe is "dark and hefty."[151] As Justice argues, darkness in Riggs's dramatic world indicates a strong cultural connection to other people and the land. The troubled Sawter family dynamic is a response to the emotional and psychological threat of Oklahoma statehood to many Cherokees. As an act of witnessing to the legacy of a violent history of removal and dispossession, the dramatic staging of this landscape is also explicitly political.[152]

The incestuous feelings that Clabe and Julie share and Clabe's prostitution of himself with male sailors establish an emotional and sexual connection to the Indian Territory of Mexico in *The Year of Pilár*, in which Riggs hints at an incestuous relationship between the half-brothers Trino and Beto. The relationship between Trino and Beto helps to reconcile the Spanish and Mayan sides of the family and initiates a process of liberation from an oppressive history, while Clabe and Julie's feelings contribute to the toxic family dynamic but also represent an anxiety and desperation at this moment in Cherokee history. As statehood approaches, the Sawter family appears on the verge of imploding. After Clabe gets engaged to a neighbor, Opal, a jealous Julie encourages him to leave. Clabe joins the U.S. Navy, and Opal marries Gard Dunham, one of Julie's former suitors.

Opal knows Julie drove Clabe from Indian Territory and attacks Julie for believing that Clabe was too good for her: "Maw liked to died when I told her about Clabe and me. You should've saw her face! She thinks to be part Cherokee Indian is the same as bein' part nigger."[153] Act 1 shows Julie getting revenge against Opal. She spends the evening intentionally tormenting Opal until she flees the Sawter home, falls getting into a boat, and drowns in Big Lake.

While land reform comes to the Mayans in Yucatán in *The Year of Pilár*, the Cherokee land in *The Cream in the Well* is overburdened by the Sawter family and Cherokee national history. In his discussion of Riggs, Womack observes, "The land, more than a matter of ownership (which was inimical to a traditional Cherokee worldview anyway), is an identity marker, literally an indicator of Cherokee national citizenship."[154] In *The Cream in the Well*, the status of the land marks the Sawters as a particularly traumatized family. The family argues over it. Clabe liked to farm, according to Mr. Sawter, but left his father to do the impossible: work it alone. Julie says, on the other hand, that Clabe hated farm work and wanted to see the world. Indeed, we learn that he has never touched his allotment. Bina simply complains that they have too much land to work. As an expression of hope in a more self-determined indigenous future, Beto and Trino work the henequen fields in Yucatán. Back in Indian Territory, imminent statehood—a federal action that stands in striking opposition to Cárdenas land reform—paralyzes the Sawter family.

Yet the revolutionary politics, if not the revolutionary policies, that characterize the Indian Territory of *The Year of Pilár* are evident in *The Cream in the Well*. Clabe returns in act 2 as the most politically fervent Cherokee character in Riggs's canon: "Haven't you heard it yet—it's the millennium? The country's on fire with progress. Indian Territory's on the high road to statehood. Everybody's going to be rich and the old U.S.A.'s about to become heaven on earth. It must be so—because T.R. says it's so."[155] He then extends this mockery of discourses of progress to a critique of the U.S. imperialism that he witnessed firsthand as a sailor: "They can take over the little yellow people or the little brown people for the good of their heathen souls—but they can do it without me. *I've seen too much.* I've had enough."[156] Riggs gives to Clabe that which we can view in hindsight through the lens of Sean Teuton's work as a Red Power moment: he becomes conscious of his place in U.S. colonial history and vigorously condemns U.S. imperialism. Just as the shame that Teuton and his mother felt at their humiliating treatment by nurses and doctors during a hospital visit transforms into an empowering anger later that evening, the shame at the loss of his Cherokee culture that Gar experiences in *The Cherokee Night* transforms into the empowering anger that Clabe has in *The Cream in the Well*.[157] Teuton argues that a Red Power novel such as James Welch's *Winter in the Blood* (1974) "describes a procedure of political growth" in which "new knowledge about colonial relations of power develops one's own relationship to a community and history as well as to a dominating culture."[158] Welch's Blackfeet narrator finds this new knowledge at home, while Clabe finds it as a sailor in the U.S. Navy. As an artist, Riggs finds new knowledge about colonial relations of power in Mexico that enables him to imagine both a more politically outraged Cherokee and a more explicit critique of U.S. Indian and imperial policy than we see in the earlier plays, including *The Cherokee Night*.

Like Trino in *The Year of Pilár*, Clabe tries to heal the rupture within his family. He tells Julie, "Let's say it out plain [. . .] We're in love with each other."[159] Julie refuses to say it plainly, however, and says that she will kill herself. Clabe resists initially but then says he cannot and does not want to stop her, and Julie leaves to drown herself in Big Lake. Julie's walk to her death from the Sawter home recalls Pilár's walk to her death from the Crespo hacienda at the end of *The Year of Pilár*. These deeply troubling sacrifices of vicious women, an expression of the misogyny that Riggs shares with Oskison, establish an optimistic path into the future for indigenous families—Mayan and Cherokee, respectively. The play ends with Clabe telling Bina "tomorrow will be clear and bright" and Bina happily playing a hymn on the organ.[160] Though Riggs does not take his audience anywhere close to the revolution of *Pilár*, he places Clabe in the same position as Beto and Trino: looking to the day after unthinkable horrors, rather than being consumed by the trauma.

While both the threat and promise of indigenous revolution run like an underground current throughout many of Downing's detective novels, the same promise erupts only once and quite violently within the context of Riggs's canon. Yet Riggs prepares the narrative foundation for the Mayan revolution in *The Year of Pilár* in the preceding plays. With remarkable consistency, Riggs dramatizes the lives of impoverished Indian Territory families and communities in the midst of struggles over the relative merits of ranching, farming, or emigrating to more populous regions. Indeed, Oklahoma statehood for Riggs stands as not only a disruption of Cherokee sovereignty but also an attendant disruption of traditional land use in the late nineteenth century in Indian Territory. Riggs gives this struggle its most dramatic and violent treatment in *The Year of Pilár*. Looking backward and forward from *Pilár* to the other plays allows readers to see the Cherokee and Indian Territory historical contexts on which Riggs consistently constructs his dramatic narratives. While the sexual, familial, cultural, and historical contexts of Riggs's Yucatán give that dramatic geographic space a distinctly Indian Territory identity, Riggs finds in Yucatán a possible resolution, unavailable or perhaps too difficult to imagine in the Indian Territory of his youth, to the conflicts and traumas that define these contexts. The frustrated desires of Cherokees throughout *The Cherokee Night* are affirmed and acted upon in the Mexico plays. Like the Lost Cherokees, Duwali's Texas Cherokees, Richard Fields, Sequoyah, and Redbird Smith, Riggs went to Mexico to find an American Indian past and hope for an American Indian future. Unlike Oskison's Sequoyah, as we saw in chapter 1, Riggs returns, still troubled but invigorated.

· CHAPTER 3 ·

"Mexico Is an Indian Country"

American Indian Diplomacy in Native Nonfiction and
Todd Downing's *The Mexican Earth*

HE PERIOD FROM THE 1920S to the 1960s was an era of diplomacy in American Indian literature and politics, and the work of
this era's diplomats, in literary and political circles, prepared the ground
for a more politically assertive generation of writers and activists. While
Lynn Riggs was not involved in organized political efforts on behalf of
American Indians, Todd Downing, Will Rogers, and many of the authors
from this period model and document in their writing the diplomacy in
which they engaged. John Oskison was an active member of the Society
of American Indians (SAI) in the 1910s and an advocate for practitioners
of the peyote religion.[1] Rogers brought his considerable influence in the
1920s to the successful effort to raise funds to build in Claremore the first
Indian hospital in the United States. His son, Will Rogers Jr., followed in
his father's footsteps: he created the American Citizens League to provide aid to urban Indians and a tax-exempt organization to help fund the
National Congress of American Indians (NCAI) in its early years in the
mid-1940s.[2] As an Osage tribal councilman, John Joseph Mathews helped
to establish in 1938 the Osage Tribal Museum, the oldest tribally owned
museum in the United States. He also describes in *Talking to the Moon*
(1945) his annual travels to Washington, D.C., to meet with House and
Senate committees on behalf of the Osage Nation. Ruth Muskrat Bronson
and D'Arcy McNickle were founding members of the NCAI in the early
1940s. The preamble that they helped to write at a planning conference
in May 1944 in Chicago "stressed both civil and tribal rights by declaring
that the common welfare of Native Americans required the preservation
of cultural values, the defense of legal rights, and the education of the public."[3] Historian Thomas Cowger praises Bronson's critical contributions:

"Bronson served as executive secretary, editor of the NCAI *Washington Bulletin*, lobbyist, and jack-of-all-trades. Her tireless efforts, usually without pay, kept the organization afloat in its initial years."[4] In his history of American Indian activism from 1945 to 1968, historian Daniel M. Cobb describes McNickle's equally resolute dedication to the NCAI and many other Native organizations and causes. Downing, who like Rogers was the son of an elected tribal nation politician, was an important contributor to the Choctaw Bilingual Education Program (CBEP) in the early 1970s.

These authors represented American Indians in tribal nation, intertribal, pan-Indian, U.S., and settler-colonial and indigenous transnational political arenas and cultivated good relations among individual indigenous people, tribal nations, intertribal and pan-Indian organizations, and the United States. The urgency of maintaining good relations within and among these groups is consistently evident in the writing by Downing, Oskison, and Riggs discussed in previous chapters and in the nonfiction by Rogers, Mathews, Luther Standing Bear, Downing, and Oskison under consideration here. Natives and non-Natives risk social unrest and possibly revolution, these authors warn, if diplomacy fails.

The frequently slow, cautious, and tedious negotiation that characterized American Indian political work of the middle decades of the twentieth century contrasts with popular depictions of the direct action of the Red Power period. Yet even Vine Deloria Jr., often represented and honored as the quintessential Red Power intellectual voice, favored diplomacy—or what Cobb calls the NCAI's "incremental approach"—over direct action.[5] Deloria Jr. was opposed, for example, to Native participation in the Poor People's Campaign in 1968. In an interview with Cobb, Deloria Jr. recalls:

> What I objected to very strongly on the Poor People's March was that they went in and hassled government officials [. . .] You go into those higher level federal officials, all they can possibly do is blow smoke up your ass for an hour and send you on your way. [. . .] I thought, "Jesus, after we worked, I mean, finally after three years we'd gotten to the point where we could make suggestions . . . [and] these guys come in with all this ill will." I didn't have anything against working with blacks and Chicanos and Asians or whatever. But after we'd done all this work? And these guys would resent it personally—the people in Congress and the people in the Bureau.[6]

Within the context of this study, the march on the Mexican Embassy during the Poor People's Campaign, in which Native people participated in substantial numbers, resonates within the revolutionary political register to which Deloria is objecting.[7] The lives and writings of the American Indian authors of the previous decades inform and establish continuity with the diplomacy to which Deloria Jr. and others within the NCAI devoted themselves.

Downing fashions himself a diplomat at several key moments in *The Mexican Earth*, which upon publication in March of 1940 received a laudatory review from the archaeologist and historian Philip Ainsworth Means in the *New York Times*. Downing identifies himself as an American Indian early in the book, and it is clear from the narrative that follows that this strategic revelation implies a political and cultural alliance with the indigenous peoples of Mexico. Indeed, as he tours Mexico and relates its history, Downing practices a diplomacy that foregrounds an indigenous-to-indigenous transnational relationship among indigenous nations and communities in Mexico and the United States. By working like Rogers as a self-made diplomat to reestablish the political, historical, and cultural ties among American Indian and indigenous Mexican peoples, Downing foregrounds the geographies of both settler-colonial nations as politically, historically, and culturally indigenous.

The result is one of the most radical or revolutionary pieces of writing by an American Indian in the interwar and early contemporary periods. Within a history of indigenous Mexico thinly disguised as a travelogue, Downing promotes an antiracist, anticolonial transindigenous American politics.[8] Similarly, though more explicitly than the two published Mexico plays by Riggs, *The Mexican Earth* anticipates late twentieth- and early twenty-first-century coalitions between indigenous people in the United States and Mexico. It also anticipates the current disciplinary interest in tribal nation–specific literary criticism and American Indian literary nationalism, both of which encourage the foregrounding of indigenous creative and intellectual traditions in readings of indigenous literatures and histories. Downing highlights the diverse histories, worldviews, and landscapes that define indigenous nations, privileges tribal specificity in a reading of the histories of the Americas, and encourages indigenous solidarity against colonial dominance. He also emphasizes, however, the shared experience of originating and continuously residing in the Americas that establishes a kinship between all indigenous American people.

The diplomacy that he practices while traveling in Mexico is the key to reinvigorating and sustaining that kinship.

In addition to its concern with American Indian diplomacy in the literature of this era and, more specifically, Downing's self-made role as an American Indian diplomat in indigenous Mexico, this chapter situates *The Mexican Earth* in the American Indian nonfiction context of the mid-twentieth century. The nonfiction of this era is rich in generic diversity. There are pan-Indian and tribal nation–specific histories; autobiographies that are both personal and tribal-nation histories; biographies of celebrated American Indian leaders, such as Tecumseh and John Ross; biographies of non-Native men, such as McNickle's book on Oliver La Farge; biographies of non-Native men such as Sam Houston and E. W. Marland embedded by Oskison and Mathews, respectively, in tribal nation histories; and, in the case of Downing, a serious contemplation of a perpetual indigenous anti-colonial revolution. Downing's *The Mexican Earth* is more overtly political than his own novels and the rest of the era's nonfiction, but reading these other works with and against *The Mexican Earth* allows us to continue to map the era's dynamic literary politics.

Native Nonfiction and the Diplomatic Arts

Downing published his history of Mexico in an era of American Indian writing dominated by nonfiction. Robert Warrior makes the case for the historical significance but critical neglect of American Indian nonfiction in *The People and the Word: Reading Native Nonfiction* (2005): "Though contemporary fiction and poetry receive the lion's share of scholarly attention in studies of Native literature, the historical centrality of nonfiction in Native writing in English since the late eighteenth century is inarguable."[9] The neglect of this nonfiction, Warrior argues, drastically impoverishes our understanding of American Indian intellectual and literary traditions:

> Nonfiction writers have brought us impassioned pleas on behalf of Native peoples, accounts of crucial moments in Native history, profiles of people in contemporary Native communities, and explorations of dysfunctions, like substance abuse, in the Native world. The Native nonfiction tradition, thus, is vibrant, complex, and worthy, in and of itself, of serious critical attention. This tradition of writing is the oldest and most robust type of modern

writing that Native people in North America have produced as they have sought literate means through which to engage themselves and others in a discourse on the possibilities of a Native future. Scholarly attention to the novel, as I figure things here, has told us more about the preoccupations of literary studies than about the history of the critical contributions of Native writers.[10]

With scholars such as Daniel F. Littlefield Jr. and James Parins and more recently Chadwick Allen, Lisa Brooks, Maureen Konkle, and Bernd Peyer, Warrior contributes to the recovery of the American Indian nonfiction tradition by focusing on William Apess's work; the Osage Constitution; a leaflet produced by students at the Santee Normal Training School and dated 1888–89; and Momaday's "The Man Made of Words," one of the three keynote addresses at the First Convocation of American Indian Scholars in 1970 at Princeton University.[11] D'Arcy McNickle was one of the few participants over forty years old to participate in the convocation. His presence there is another reminder of the continuity in American Indian politics from the interwar and early contemporary to the civil rights era, though it is also a reminder of the dramatic generational shift toward younger leaders that began most conspicuously with the founding of the National Indian Youth Council (NIYC) between August 10 and August 13, 1961, in Gallup, New Mexico.[12] The NIYC's origins are also traceable to the NCAI and McNickle's American Indian Development (AID), the organizations that beginning in 1956 sponsored the Workshop on American Indian Affairs out of which the NIYC emerged.[13]

This section takes as its purview the nonfiction of Luther Standing Bear and John Joseph Mathews but introduces their work through Rogers. All three produced multiple and successful book-length works of nonfiction in the same era, but scholars rarely discuss them at the same time. Standing Bear has maintained a consistent presence in literary scholarship, most recently and prominently in Lucy Maddox's *Citizen Indians* and Lee Schweninger's *Listening to the Land* (2008). Mathews's place has been more uncertain, while the Cherokee-specific contexts of Rogers's life and work have only recently attracted the attention of scholars. In an effort to establish a literary and political context for the discussion of Downing's work, as well as to elucidate a connection among these ostensibly disparate authors, the discussion that follows will foreground the diplomatic positions and strategies that they model in their writing.

This focus on diplomacy as a consciously critical and theoretical paradigm derives from the literary productions and political lives of the authors under my consideration in this chapter. This paradigm helps illuminate the interwar and early contemporary era of American Indian literary history and its politics. A more detailed, tribal nation–specific reading of Rogers and Standing Bear would provide a differently complex, nuanced portrait of American Indian life from the late nineteenth to the early twentieth century. My main interests here, though, are those diplomatic moments that run throughout the lives of both authors and their work and what those moments tell us about this literary historical era as well as Downing's place in it.

This approach also addresses the concerns of scholars such as Jace Weaver and Craig Womack about the limits of a critical practice that privileges mediation.[14] Diplomacy involves the patient, tactful advocacy of an idea, a policy, or a plan. It is distinct, therefore, from direct action but also from mediation—a social, cultural, and political act on which a familiar critical paradigm in American Indian literary studies has been constructed. James Ruppert describes mediation as understood and practiced in American Indian literary studies in his scholarship on novels of the early renaissance era:

> By mediation, I mean an artistic and conceptual standpoint,
> constantly flexible, which uses the epistemological frameworks
> of Native American and Western cultural traditions to illuminate
> and enrich each other. In working toward an understanding of
> Native American writers' texts, it is more useful to see them not as
> between two cultures (a romantic and victimist perspective) but
> as participants in two rich cultural traditions. While some may say
> these writers are apologists for one side or the other, or that their
> texts inhabit a no-man's-land, a mediational approach explores how
> their texts create a dynamic that brings differing cultural codes into
> confluence to reinforce and re-create the structures of human life:
> the self, community, spirit, and the world we perceive.[15]

Mediation has a primarily cultural orientation, while the act of diplomacy is more explicitly political, and mediators must attend to and try to reconcile the desires and expectations of multiple audiences. Ruppert explains, "Contemporary Native American writers insist on their freedom to use the forms and expectations of both Native and Western cultural codes to achieve the goals of each as well as to satisfy the epistemological expectations of both audiences."[16] A diplomat also must not alienate her audience, but she has one goal: to advocate for a specific position. Thus while "no one ever has the last word" in the cultural conversations managed by mediators, by American Indian authors in this context, diplomacy has an end game: stronger horses and fresh food for the reservation community, the deed to an allotment, better roles for American Indian actors in Hollywood films, and the freedom to practice indigenous religions.[17]

Rogers helps to introduce this section as a prolific Cherokee author of nonfiction and a self-identified "self-made diplomat" who eventually traveled with Charles Lindbergh to Mexico on an official diplomatic mission.[18] Historian Andrew Denson establishes the Cherokee-specific context for Rogers's diplomacy:

> The Cherokee National Council began to appoint official emissaries to the United States in the 1820s, as pressure mounted for the tribe to move west. These were Cherokee leaders, often members of the National Council itself, whose duty it was to watch over the federal government and to convey to American authorities Cherokee opposition to removal. While in the past, leaders had met with federal officials only when called, the growing threat of forced migration inspired them to send representatives to the capital whether they were invited or not. Cherokees maintained the practice after the Trail of Tears, and by the post-Civil War era, appointing delegates had become a standard part of each year's business in the tribal government.[19]

"In essence," Denson summarizes, "their job was to monitor the activities of the United States government."[20] Rogers fulfills this job description of a Cherokee diplomat in his daily and weekly newspaper columns, in which he constantly monitors the federal government for his audience. Rogers, like his official diplomatic forbears, was also a member of the Cherokee elite.[21] His father, Clement Vann Rogers, was the owner of a ranch worked in part by two slaves before the Civil War and a founding member and vice president of the First National Bank of Claremore. He was also a judge and an elected member of the Cherokee Nation senate from the Cooweescoowee District and a delegate to the Oklahoma Constitutional

Convention. His son Will was not elected to or appointed by the Cherokee national government, though his unofficial status within this historical
context makes him a self-made diplomat for Cherokees as much as he is a
self-made representative of the United States. Rogers moves between these
two usually oppositional roles during his travels: he is both a Cherokee
diplomat representing Claremore, the Cherokee Nation, or Indian Territory and a Cherokee diplomat representing the United States. Indeed, his
diplomacy on behalf of Cherokees and American Indians threatens to subvert his other diplomatic role and informs his consistently satirical view of
an absurd and even futile diplomacy on behalf of the United States.

For his first mission, Rogers adopts the guise of a diplomat working
on behalf of President Calvin Coolidge and the United States and visits
Europe from April to September 1926. In his letters to Coolidge, first published in the *New York Post* and then in the international bestseller *Letters
of a Self-Made Diplomat to His President* (1926), Rogers uses the code name
"WILLROG" and reports on his diplomatic activities.[22] His primary goal,
he explains, is to help the United States recoup some of the loans it made
to European nations during the Great War. He is representing U.S. rather
than Cherokee interests; he is reporting to the U.S president rather than a
tribal government.

As in his weekly articles and daily telegrams, however, Rogers identifies himself as a Cherokee from Indian Territory and positions himself as
a self-made diplomat representing Cherokees and other American Indians. The difficulty he has getting a passport without a birth certificate
is familiar satire of incompetent government bureaucracy. His struggle
is also embedded, though, in a long history of American Indians trying to gain the recognition of U.S. federal authorities. Rogers explains
in the second letter: "You see, in the early days of the Indian Territory where I was born there was no such things as birth certificates. You
being there was certificate enough. We generally took it for granted if
you were there you must have at some time been born."[23] This common
sense that characterizes Indian Territory is nearly absent in the United
States from which he departs and in the Europe where he arrives. After
Rogers notes that the only time he needed a passport as a child was to
visit Kansas, a journey that constituted international travel from the
Cherokee Nation to the United States, he explains, "Here my Father and
Mother were both one-eighth Cherokee Indians and I have been on the
Cherokee rolls since I was named, and my family had lived on one ranch

for 75 years. But just offhand, how was I going to show that I was born in America?"[24] Rogers alludes here to the always shifting legal status of Cherokees and American Indians, especially in Indian Territory, as well as the also always shifting boundaries of tribal nations. He introduces into his diplomatic mission for the United States, therefore, a history of settler-colonial aggression poorly disguised as diplomacy under the Dawes Commission.

Similarly to Riggs in his plays, Rogers roots his diplomacy in the landscape of the Cherokee Nation, particularly the town of Claremore. As a first step in an ultimately successful attempt to get into the House of Commons, Rogers goes to the foreign press office in London and shows his press credentials for the *Claremore Progress* of Claremore, Oklahoma. Claremore then remains a key point of reference in his travels, including in his next book, *There's Not a Bathing Suit in Russia* (1927).[25] Rogers catalogs in *Letters* the relative merits of Claremore and Paris, for example, by comparing the Tiber unfavorably to the Grand or Verdigris Rivers, suggesting Claremore as a summer vacation spot, or preparing to meet Mussolini by giving himself the following pep talk: "Come on, Claremore, les see what Rome has got. I am going to treat this fellow like he was nobody but Hiram Johnson. Get your Lions ready for a foot race, in case I dissplease."[26] The use of metonymy—the substitution of Claremore for Rogers—demonstrates the powerful association Rogers experiences between himself and his hometown. While his definition of a diplomat is facetious—"a Diplomat is a fellow to keep you from settling on a thing so everybody can understand it"—his observations in *Letters*, as on the questionable logic of military men negotiating for disarmament and the unlikelihood that Europe will ever repay its debts, comprise serious political commentary.[27] In his role as a diplomat in Europe, he also continues to monitor the U.S. federal government, and he repeatedly advises President Coolidge to tend only to the business of the United States. The Rogers diplomatic doctrine of noninterference becomes a staple of his later journalism.

Rogers's visit with Spanish premier Miguel Primo de Rivera demonstrates that this doctrine of noninterference, while related to the politics of isolationism between the two world wars, is also embedded in Cherokee Nation and European New World colonial histories. Rogers was grateful, in this era of Prohibition, to have the Spanish premier summon a servant to bring him a glass of sherry. The description of this moment reveals Rogers occupying simultaneously two distinct and possibly incommensurable diplomatic roles as he solidifies ties between the United States and Spain by drinking with the Spanish premier while mocking U.S. law and Spanish colonial history: "He explained to us that it was some stuff that Queen Isabella, I believe it was, had put these few bottles away for Columbus when he come in from a hard trip exploring. It was supposed to have some kind of spices in it, they said. I slipped my glass over to be reloaded. I says if I can just inveigle this old General out of a couple of more jolts of this Discovery medicine I will go out and hide America where no one can find it."[28] Rogers's wishful thinking for a reversal of European colonial history anticipates the nostalgia for Indian Territory that becomes part of his regular newspaper columns. As he returns to the United States, Rogers comments that as a result of their nation's unpopular status in the world, many of the other passengers are traveling incognito—and hiding liquor in their luggage. From the evidence of his later weekly articles and daily telegrams, Rogers likely wished that he was returning to Indian Territory instead.

As a diplomat from Claremore, the Cherokee Nation, and Indian Territory, Rogers thus occupies an oppositional political space from which he also comments on settler-colonial diplomacy between the United States and other nations such as Mexico. From this third political space, U.S. diplomacy in Mexico looks distinctly undiplomatic.[29] Rogers made an official trip to Mexico with Charles Lindbergh in 1927 at the request of Dwight Morrow, the new U.S. ambassador to Mexico. The two settler-colonial nations were in conflict primarily over the rights of U.S. oil companies in Mexico.[30] Rogers published his articles in the *Saturday Evening Post* in 1928. As he does in *Letters*, Rogers addresses his reports from Mexico to President Coolidge. He observes in the first letter that U.S. diplomacy in Mexico leans toward the aggressive: "Up to now our calling card to Mexico or Central America had been a gunboat or a bunch of Violets shaped like Marines."[31] He then comments wryly on the desire of some U.S. citizens simply to conquer their southern neighbor. Rogers believes President Coolidge sent Morrow on a diplomatic mission defined instead by "kindness and common sense."[32] Though he praises Morrow's work, Rogers is still suspicious of conventional U.S. diplomacy: "Diplomats, when they get to a Country, they figure they must first meet the rich people of their own Country who are living there, and then the rich ones who belong in the Country. But as far as the Government officials are concerned, why, they will perhaps know them at some time through the exchange of official visits."[33] His subsequent comments on bullfighting include the self-deprecating comment: "No sir, I had been butted enough in a branding corral by snorty old calves to know that Clem Rogers' boy Willie of Oolagah, Oklahoma, wasent carved out to meet any Bull in combat."[34] By once again insisting that his readers recognize his Indian Territory homeland, Rogers reminds them of the multiple constituencies that he is representing.

His satire of U.S. international relations, therefore, always has Cherokee or indigenous American roots. On his Mexico diplomatic mission, Rogers gives a speech on diplomacy to Morrow and President Plutarco Elías Calles at a dinner at the American Embassy in which he mocks diplomats and diplomacy and then encourages Mexico to invest in itself. "A Diplomat," jokes Rogers, "is a man that tells you what he don't believe himself, and the man that he is telling it too don't believe it any more than he does. So Diplomacy is always equal. It's like good bookkeeping. He don't believe you and you don't believe him, so it always balances."[35] He follows this observation with a series of one-liners about diplomats that includes, "Diplomats are just as essential to starting a war as Soldiers are for finishing it."[36] Mexico does not need diplomacy, Rogers suggests, or the United States. It needs, instead, Mexican capital and Mexican confidence. He claims that Mexico also needs to pay attention to its indigenous populations: "Make your rich, every time they send a Child to Paris to learn 'em to talk French—make them send one to Sonora to learn to talk Yaqui. They are the ones you have to live and get along with, not the French."[37] Rogers makes this observation at the end of a year in which the Mexican military had finished a campaign, complete with aerial bombing, against the Yaquis in Sonora. Thus in a speech to the Mexican president who authorized and directed the war and to the U.S. ambassador to Mexico, Rogers suggests learning Yoeme, the Uto-Aztecan Yaqui language, is more diplomatic than bombing. As the Yaquis are also a tribal nation split by the Mexican-U.S. border, this piece of advice, similarly to Downing's observations on the Yaquis in *The Mexican Earth*, resonates historically and politically in both settler-colonial nations.

Luther Standing Bear, one of Gerald Vizenor's representative examples of a post-Indian warrior of survivance, became, like Rogers, a writer in the mid-1920s after a career in performance in Buffalo Bill's Wild West show and as a lecturer, rather than on vaudeville, led to roles in Hollywood films.[38]

In his autobiography *My People the Sioux* (1928), Standing Bear provides a view of late nineteenth-century American Indian life in the Great Sioux Nation in Dakota Territory (1861–89) and then in South Dakota. Standing Bear's representation of Lakota life within these polities and territories offers a rich contrast to the contemporaneous representations of the Cherokee Nation, Indian Territory, and Oklahoma in John Milton Oskison's novels or Rogers's newspaper columns. The early chapters depict the daily life of the Lakota world in ethnographic detail: Standing Bear describes making tipis, working with porcupine quills, hunting for buffalo and tanning the hides, moving camps, making runners for sleighs out of buffalo ribs, playing games such as pa-in-yan-ka-pi, getting government rations, capturing wild horses, and preparing for and watching a sun dance. Standing Bear also situates this daily Lakota life in a context more legible to consumers of conventional U.S. histories. He reports, for example, on the Battle of the Little Big Horn, a meeting with Crazy Horse, and, later in the autobiography, the massacre at Wounded Knee in 1890.

When Standing Bear shifts the focus from tribal nation–specific ethnographic detail to the social, economic, and cultural changes in his own and his tribal nation's life, the content of the autobiography begins to converge with the literary productions of other American Indian authors under consideration in this study. While Oskison, Rogers, and Riggs represent the farming and ranching economy of Indian Territory in the late nineteenth century, Standing Bear describes the cattle sent to the Lakotas by the federal government as repulsive: "What a terrible odor met us! It was awful! We had to hold our noses. Then I asked my father what was the matter around there, as the stench was more than I could stand. He told me it was the odor of the spotted buffalo. Then I asked him if we were going to be obliged to eat those terrible animals."[39] He indicates, too, that at the time the Lakotas had no interest in farming: "What did we care— or know—about farming at that time? We did not need to. Everything necessary for our comfort and needs grew wild in our own land."[40] Following his return from Carlisle, though, Standing Bear briefly ranches and opens a store. His career trajectory then closely resembles Rogers, as they both arrive in Southern California in the 1910s—Standing Bear in 1912 and Rogers in 1919.

After he joins the first class at Carlisle in the fall of 1879, Standing Bear describes his successful attempts to follow his father's oft-repeated advice: learn the ways of white men. Learning these ways helps position Standing Bear to serve officially and unofficially throughout his life in the role of a diplomat. The diplomatic moments in Standing Bear's autobiography are also some of the most urgent moments in his life, the lives of the people he represents, and the life of his tribal nation. Richard Henry Pratt, the founder and superintendent of Carlisle, sends Standing Bear as an emissary to the Lakotas, for example, to recruit more students. Many children have died at the school, however, so Standing Bear meets considerable resistance from parents. Standing Bear explains that after trying "to create a good impression upon the other Indians [. . .] it was decided to hold a big council." There, he adds, "I was delegated to speak."[41] Standing Bear's talk, which his own father supplements, is successful: he returns to Carlisle with fifty-two students. A second recruiting trip is equally successful. When Standing Bear returns home as a diplomat sent by Pratt to represent Carlisle, the ensuing interaction with his fellow tribal-nation citizens reveals some of the excruciating questions that Lakotas faced in the late nineteenth century: Do we send our children to a place where they might die? Do we send them and hope that they return like this young man, Luther Standing Bear? Do we keep them at home under difficult conditions created by the same government that runs the schools?

Standing Bear describes diplomatic moments such as these throughout the autobiography, though, as in the case of Rogers, Standing Bear's constituencies constantly shift. He represents American Indians, for example, when he goes to work at John Wanamaker's eponymous store in Philadelphia. "My boy," Pratt tells him, "you are going away from us to work for this school, in fact, for your whole race."[42] Once he returns to his home community, he helps to settle a dispute over rations between Agent George Wright and a band leader named Wooden Knife. Later his father, following Standing Bear's council, advocates for allotment. Agent Wright also sends him to his father's band during the turmoil that culminated in the massacre at Wounded Knee. Standing Bear describes his diplomatic efforts: "I told my people that I wanted to help them, and that was the reason I had come. I said it would not be right for them to join the ghost dancers, as the Government was going to stop it, and it would not be best for them to be found there. I told them the Government would use soldiers to enforce the order if it became necessary."[43] As the interpreter for and a performer in Buffalo Bill's Wild West show, Standing Bear also constantly worked as a diplomat representing the needs and desires of the performers either to Cody or to the non-Native cowboys.

Once he is made chief, Standing Bear's diplomatic status becomes official. "A chief receives no salary," he explains, "and at gatherings it is up to

him to see that everything is done properly. We have no more war councils, but if a Commissioner is sent from Washington to make any sort of
contract with the tribe, it is up to the chief to be present and investigate
the matter."[44] When Standing Bear begins to lecture in New York, his
transformation into a diplomat, first self-made and then official, is complete: "While lecturing I met many people who were really interested in
learning the truth in regard to the Indians. I determined that, if I could
only get the right sort of people interested, I might be able to do more for
my own race off the reservation than to remain there under the iron rule of
the white agent."[45] He is here, again, a representative of his race, as he was
earlier at Wanamaker's store. One of his last acts of diplomacy is on behalf
of the city of Los Angeles, which sends Standing Bear to Oklahoma to
invite American Indians there to come to California: "I went to Tulsa, and
the day of the parade I hired an automobile, dressed myself carefully in
full Indian regalia and represented the city of Los Angeles."[46] This focus on
diplomacy in his autobiography emphasizes the stakes of Standing Bear's
representation of himself, Lakotas, and American Indians. These representations are always political and always charged with immediate relevance
and urgency to the daily lives of American Indians in this era.

In the books published after *My People the Sioux*, the children's book
My Indian Boyhood (1931) and *Land of the Spotted Eagle* (1933), Standing
Bear situates himself first as a diplomat and then as an outraged partisan
for the Lakotas. Both books cover much of the same, often idealized autobiographical, ethnographical, and tribal-nation historical ground. The
content is so similar that we can read both books as revisions of *My People
the Sioux* and as attempts by Standing Bear to make the same material tell
different stories about the Lakotas. Standing Bear begins *My Indian Boyhood* with a statement to readers: "Note: I write this book with the hope
that the hearts of the white boys and girls who read these pages will be
made kinder toward the little Indian boys and girls."[47] The author's note
introduces the book itself as a diplomatic act and indicates that Standing
Bear envisioned *My Indian Boyhood* as a tactful gesture toward maintaining peaceful relations between American Indians and what he calls "white
boys and girls." However, *Land* shifts the emphasis of the first two books
toward tribal-nation history rather than autobiography and from a com-
paratively accommodating view of U.S. federal policy to a much more
critical view of it. Lucy Maddox observes of *Land*: "The voice of this
book is defiant, oppositional, often angry, and distrustful of institutions

and practices that he had accepted with equanimity in the former book. Repeatedly he contrasts Indian ways of doing things with the ways that whites have forced on Indians, or with practices that whites have held up as models for the Indians, and repeatedly he declares the Indian ways superior."[48] *Land* is, therefore, less diplomatic than the first two books, and accordingly, the diplomatic moments disappear from the narrative. Rather than recurring episodes of diplomacy, Standing Bear provides recurring episodes of resistance and the celebration of it. When he shifts from a historical to an autobiographical mode in the penultimate chapter, he establishes a nearly militant rather than diplomatic subject position. The positions that he takes in these chapters on colonialism, assimilation, and federal policy appear remarkably similar to the politics of the Red Power era and the early literary renaissance.

Standing Bear's condemnation of colonial practice in all its manifestations is thorough and unequivocal and related within a narrative of loss. In his assessment of the loss of the buffalo and the Black Hills, Standing Bear elegizes:

> The white man will never know the horror and the utter bewilderment of the Lakota at the wanton destruction of the buffalo. What cruelty has not been glossed over with the white man's word— enterprise! If the Lakotas had been relinquishing any part of their territory voluntarily, the Black Hills would have been the last from the standpoint of traditional sentiment. So when by false treaties and trickery the Black Hills were forever lost, they were a broken people. [...] But could the Lakota braves have foreseen the ignominy they were destined to endure, every man would have died fighting rather than give up his homeland to live in subjection and helplessness.[49]

The U.S. government and its citizens are responsible for the many other losses that Standing Bear subsequently documents. Lakota medicine people have lost the sacred powers that Standing Bear presents as one who believes in them. After relating the story of a train wreck about which he was forewarned and in which he sustained serious injuries, he asks, "Where are our prophets and wonder workers today?"[50] A comment immediately following on the Thunder Dreamers emphasizes the sense of loss: "Today the potency of song and ceremony are gone; our youth are scornful; our medicine-men can no longer cure. There is no solidarity of faith to work its magic wonders."[51] On the production of material culture, Standing Bear observes, "Today the only means whereby native designs might be kept alive is through the use of the white man's beads. The Lakota woman no longer pounds out earth paints, porcupine quills are scarcer, and the process of dyeing and sewing them seems tedious to the younger generation, and the plants from which once were brewed lovely colors grow no more."[52] He also laments the loss of the social power of women, though in this case in both Lakota and white cultures: "Today mother-power is weak, scattered to many places—taken over by the teacher, preacher, nurse, lawyer, and others who superimpose their will. This loss applies also to the white mother, for she, too, is blinded and confused by the intricacies of society in which she lives."[53] In perhaps the most explicit statement on the decline of the Lakotas, Standing Bear claims that the surrender of Crazy Horse meant "the doom of his race."[54] While *My People* shares with Oskison's novels a qualified optimism, *Land* shares Rogers's nostalgia for an American Indian past, though a past much different than the one Rogers remembers and represents. At these moments of pathos, *Land* also shares with Riggs's *The Cherokee Night* a tremendous sense of sorrow at this loss.

Yet Standing Bear tells readers at other places in *Land* that the loss is not complete and that there is still considerable resistance to the forces that cause the destruction. Of the official federal policy of assimilation, which the Indian Reorganization Act of 1934 rejects soon after the publication of *Land*, Standing Bear comments, "Maybe they are kind and altruistic motives that prompt the white brother to seek to remake the red man in his own likeness, and even some red men themselves hope they are 'progressive,' having donned the white collar for breechclout and outrageous boots for the comfortable and beautiful moccasins; nevertheless, Mother Nature and Wakan Tanka rule, and the last drop of Indian blood will disappear in white veins before man can remake his brother man."[55] In another extended condemnation of assimilation, Standing Bear implicitly repudiates his father's advice to learn the ways of white men by calling those who have done so "weak," "traitorous," and "deluded."[56] Standing Bear makes explicit the necessity of resistance to the coercive remaking of the Lakotas: "'going back to the blanket' is the factor that has saved him from, or at least stayed, his final destruction. Had the Indian been as completely subdued in spirit as he was in body he would have perished within the century of his subjection. But it is the unquenchable spirit that has saved him—his clinging to Indian ways, Indian thought, and tradition, that has kept him and is keeping him today."[57] He then entreats Indians to continue to wear their tribal dress. Standing Bear's plea to maintain American Indian ways of knowing and being possibly emerges from an evaluation of his own good-faith diplomacy as ineffective. Representatives of the U.S. federal government would have perceived this advocacy as ungrateful militancy rather than diplomacy.

Standing Bear even rewrites his life story as a narrative of resistance rather than diplomacy. Though a student in the first class of Carlisle, which was a key part of the official federal policy of assimilation, he returns to his home still a Lakota. "Outwardly," Standing Bear asserts, "I lived the life of the white man, yet all the while I kept in direct contact with tribal life. [. . .] I kept the language, tribal manners and usages, sang the songs and danced the dances. I still listened to and respected the advice of the older people of the tribe. I did not come home so 'progressive' that I could not speak the language of my father and mother."[58] Once back home, he begins what he calls the battle of his life against the Bureau of Indian Affairs' Indian agents "to retain my individuality and my life as a Lakota."[59] Thus doom and hope coexist in *Land*, and Standing Bear refigures his diplomacy as activism.

This battle with the agents leads to his arrest for participating in a Fox Lodge dance that he did not know had been banned. Standing Bear became one of the members of this lodge, who are "the peace keepers for all Lakota gatherings," when he was ten years old.[60] The older members of the lodge teach the younger "that in the performance of duty the tribe comes first." "The Fox men," Standing Bear adds, "must perform such duties of correction as fall to their lot and allow neither ties of family nor sentiment to interfere with tribal justice. Furthermore they are doubly bound, for when a young man has once accepted the vows and pledges of the lodge he can never break them. He remains with the lodge for life."[61] The diplomacy in his first book is embedded in this social context: Standing Bear was required by his lifetime membership in this lodge to try to keep the peace. His arrest for participating in a ritual that contributed to social harmony must have made Standing Bear reconsider his dedication to diplomacy.

By the time he was writing *Land*, Standing Bear had powerful doubts about his diplomatic efforts, at least between the Lakota Nation and the

United States. He had already chosen a different kind of diplomacy than his brother, Henry Standing Bear, who was a founding member of the Society of American Indians; Luther Standing Bear never participated in this organization. Indeed, as Maddox argues, *Land* is a repudiation of the reform efforts of progressives, both Native and non-Native. "He encouraged cultural entrenchment, a reappropriation of the highly symbolic and much-reviled blanket," Maddox comments. She then provocatively asserts, "The new chapter in the history of Indian reform that Standing Bear anticipated would not be about acceptance or assimilation but about cultural and political sovereignty."[62] Like Riggs's *The Cream in the Well*, *Land* has the characteristics of Red Power literature as defined by Sean Teuton. While it does not necessarily represent the most successful or productive American Indian politics, Red Power and its vocabulary of self-determination, sovereignty, subversion, and activism have become de facto touchstones of value and credibility in renaissance era literary criticism. These works by Riggs and Standing Bear, as well as many others under consideration in this study, stand on their own politically but also, surprisingly, establish continuity and share a political consciousness with the literature of the Red Power era.

This continuity is also evident in the nonfiction of John Joseph Mathews, whose work has been recovered primarily due to the efforts of Robert Warrior and Susan Kalter. Mathews, like his contemporaries Rogers and Standing Bear, published a successful work of nonfiction that reached a broad audience during the interwar period. *Wah'Kon-Tah*, a history of the Osage Nation in the late nineteenth century, was a Book-of-the-Month Club selection upon its publication on November 1, 1932. It was the first book published by a university press and a Native author to earn this distinction.[63] The reviewer in *Time* observes, "A first book, his work reads like the matured wisdom of a man civilized but unspoiled."[64] The *New York Times* review, which was published the same day as the book, implies incommensurability between the Osages and modernity and focuses on the loss that Mathews laments throughout the work: "Mr. Mathews tells how the Osages live today when they have more money than they quite know how to spend and with their old culture doomed."[65] The reviewer then notes that though President Herbert Hoover lived briefly at the Osage agency with the Indian agent, Major Laban J. Miles, Mathews does not mention him. The rest of the review focuses on a single episode of diplomacy in the book, when Wah Ti An Kah, "a dangerous man, for he was a great orator, with what they regarded as dangerous ideas," visits the commissioner of Indian affairs in Washington, D.C. Wah Ti An Kah impressed the reviewer as vain and haughty. The *New York Times* also published advertisements for the book that included praise from Oliver La Farge, the 1930 Pulitzer Prize winner in the novel category for *Laughing Boy*, and Mary Austin, the Illinois born author of mostly Native-themed books.

Wah'Kon-Tah is one of several books under consideration in this study, such as Oskison's *The Singing Bird*, in which American Indian authors relate American Indian histories through the perspective of non-Natives. *Wah'Kon-Tah* also represents an effort to imagine and recreate a non-Native view of Native peoples, cultures, and nations. Mathews tells most of his story through free indirect narration from the perspective of Miles, who earned the title "Major" upon his appointment to the Indian service. Mathews inherited the Indian agent's journals and papers from Miles.[66] *Wah'Kon-Tah* covers the history of the Osage Nation from the late 1870s to several weeks after Miles's death in 1931. Mathews depicts the daily life of the nation and offers the perspective of Miles and the Osages on topics that would be familiar to many readers: rations, day and boarding schools, squatters, horse theft, allotment, smallpox, religion (Wah'Kon-Tah, Christianity, peyote worship, the ghost dance), and the ranch and oil economies. Mathews spends considerable time on the mourning dance, which on occasion culminated in the fatal scalping of a man unfortunate enough to encounter a party of grieving warriors. Intertribal nation and Osage-U.S. diplomacy also figure prominently in *Wah'Kon-Tah*. At these diplomatic moments, as in Standing Bear's *My People the Sioux*, Mathews dramatizes the most urgent political, social, and cultural issues in this era for the Osages.

Wah'Kon-Tah, like many of the literary productions of this time period, has been curiously neglected. Susan Kalter suggests that the generic challenge of the book, which she calls a novel, is in part to blame, as is Mathews's reliance on the work of a non-Osage writer, Miles.[67] Kalter initiates a recovery of *Wah'Kon-Tah* by identifying its value as a "reverse ethnography of white sympathizers," and she argues, "Mathews fabricates through *Wah'Kon-Tah* an experience for his non-Osage readers of celebratory biography and intimate ethnography while in fact performing a sympathetic parody of Agent Miles, a structural critique of the agency system, and a refusal and reversal of the ethnographic impulse in its comprehensive trajectory."[68] Kalter presents the same defense of

Wah'Kon-Tah that Timothy Powell and Melinda Smith Mullikin offer of Oskison's *The Singing Bird*. Kalter concludes that "despite significant gestures towards the tragic, *Wah'Kon-Tah* confirms [Louis] Owens' and [Robert] Warrior's arguments that Mathews privileges a comic view of Osage cultural survival."[69] Mathews is a challenging author in a contemporary literary critical context that places a political value on subversion, sovereignty, and self-determination. This same context, however, with its emphasis on tribal-nation specificity, also provides the tools to assess Mathews without dismissing him for failing to represent a particular kind of Indianness, promote a particular Indian identity, or meet a political litmus test. Indeed, we must not mistake political strategy for political belief; diplomats, as well as intellectuals, often share political beliefs with activists and militants.

In *Wah'Kon-Tah* Mathews celebrates tactful and good faith negotiation as a group effort and encourages readers to condemn diplomacy that does not fulfill these criteria. Mathews establishes the significance of politics and diplomacy at the beginning of *Wah'Kon-Tah* in his description of the agency: "Dominating the valley, standing brusquely above the post-oaks was the native sandstone Council House."[70] Yet politics and diplomacy occurred in more than just official, Osage national contexts. As Mathews continues to describe the organization of the buildings at the agency, he identifies "a dusty area, dotted with great post-oaks" that is "the center and the heart of the Reservation."[71] Here, everyone who resides on or visits the reservation gathers to talk. However, Mathews initially withholds any optimism about what diplomacy might accomplish. Miles has difficulty understanding the Osages upon his arrival: "It seemed to the Major that the two races would never meet, and that there would be no one with sympathy and understanding sufficient to interpret the Indian."[72] Thus in the next chapter, when Miles must discuss with the Osages their concerns about poor rations, readers do not anticipate diplomatic success. Miles tells the gathered Osages that he is powerless, explains why he is powerless, then advises them just to accept the poor rations.

The Osages challenge Miles with a more productive diplomatic style. A man rises and says that white men just talk and lie. Before he finishes, he adds that Osages know how to die. An interpreter relates the man's speech, but "he thought it discreet to leave out the threat."[73] After several other chiefs speak, We Eh Sah Ki (Hard Robe) takes his turn and suggests that the Osages take the rations and give Miles the opportunity to prove that he talks straight. Hard Robe's speech ends the council. The contrast

among the speeches by the two Osages and Miles demonstrates a dramatic diplomatic gulf in experience, motivation, and strategy. Miles is helpless
and, as a diplomat representing the United States, reduced to talking in
circles and saying he cannot accomplish anything; the Osages are clear in
their desires, direct in speech, tactful in translation, and pragmatic, though
perhaps reluctantly, in the end. Mathews then informs readers that the
government does not address the Osages' concerns about the rations.

The conflict, therefore, persists, and further diplomatic effort must be
exerted. One of the most important diplomatic figures in *Wah'Kon-Tah* is
Wah Ti An Kah, the Osage leader who did not impress the *Times* critic.
Mathews describes him carefully:

> He was very handsome and extremely proud. He was well over six
> feet and always dressed in the finest buck-skin moccasins and leg-
> gings. He wore a great beaver-skin bandeau and bear-claw necklace,
> and affected a red blanket, in the folds of which he carried a long
> knife. His face was like that of a bronze Dante. His voice was loud
> but beautiful, and he was a great orator. He swayed the people by
> his personality and his voice, but he usually had things to say. He
> would not tolerate inattention to his harangues.[74]

This characterization is crucial to how we read Wah Ti An Kah's diplomatic efforts and the general political character of this era as depicted in
American Indian writing. Wah Ti An Kah is an influential tribal-nation
leader devoted to that nation's interest and fiercely proud of his Osage
identity and citizenship. Mathews presents to readers in the segregated
1930s, prior to the repudiation of assimilation as federal policy in the 1934
Indian Reorganization Act, a man who values himself as an Osage. In his
desire to mark himself explicitly as Osage, Wah Ti An Kah also marks
himself as a literary ancestor to the more vocal members of the younger
generation of American Indian activists in the 1960s. He would not have
appeared anomalous in the Red Power and renaissance era.

As Mathews demonstrates, different eras, and different moments
within those eras, demand different diplomatic strategies. The Osages
of *Wah'Kon-Tah* operate accordingly. When tribal leaders plan to go to
Washington to discuss the rations with federal officials, they do not put
Wah Ti An Kah on their list. "They were afraid," Mathews explains, "that
he would harm the cause by undiplomatic speeches."[75] Wah Ti An Kah
learns of the diplomatic mission, though, and convinces the other Osage

leaders to let him go. They remain fearful, however, of what he will say. As the delegation waits to meet with the commissioner of Indian affairs, Wah Ti An Kah makes a grand entrance: "Soon they saw him coming, moving across the floor quickly, though silently and with great dignity. He was wrapped almost to the eyes in a great red blanket, and they could see that his face was painted like one who goes to war."[76] When the commissioner arrives, he is fascinated with Wah Ti An Kah to the point of insulting the Osage leader with his staring. Wah Ti An Kah apparently frightens the commissioner, who while still staring at him says he has another meeting to attend. Wah Ti An Kah stops him at the door and drops his blanket to reveal his breech clout, moccasins, tattoos, beaver-skin bandeau, and bear-claw necklace. He then demands that the commissioner sit and talk with them about the rations.

The interpreter translates the demand as a request, but the commissioner at this point is not interested in diplomacy of any kind. He uses Wah Ti An Kah's actions as an excuse not to continue the talk by telling Wah Ti An Kah that by appearing in this way, he just proves that the Osages are savages and deserve only rations rather than the money to buy their own. Wah Ti An Kah's assertive diplomatic strategy appears to have failed, but he responds, "Wah'Kon-Tah has made me as I am. I am glad, I am not ashamed of my body. I do not wear clothes to hide body that Wah'Kon-Tah gave me."[77] He then demands again that they discuss the rations and the commissioner relents: he says other arrangements will be made after the rations already purchased are used. With his more aggressive, uncompromising defense of the Osages and their nation, Wah Ti An Kah stands out in the 1870s setting that Mathews imagines in *Wah'Kon-Tah*; he stands out for the same reason in the 1930s present in which Mathews published the book.

In his diplomatic victory, Wah Ti An Kah teaches Miles the stakes of these negotiations with the federal government. Lamenting that "the two races would never meet" is not an option for the Osages; it is imperative to the survival of the Osages that the races do meet. The stakes for the non-Osages involved are not nearly as dramatic. For the commissioner, for example, the primary stake is his wounded ego. Following his capitulation to Wah Ti An Kah, the commissioner "wished to vindicate his dignity," but Wah Ti An Kah rises again and dismisses the commissioner before he has a chance to speak.[78] The interpreter translates Wah Ti An Kah's words "tell this man it is all right now—he can go now" as "he said his people have said all that they came to say."[79] Thus the interpreter makes Wah Ti

An Kah appear more diplomatic to the commissioner. While stopping the rations causes some suffering at first, that suffering is the result of intrusive non-Osages, primarily the cattlemen who have such a significant presence in the work of Oskison and Riggs and who kill the wildlife intended to replace, in part, the rations. But the payments to the Osages grow, and the issue is eventually settled. Wah Ti An Kah's diplomatic strategy, therefore, works, though with the help of a tactful interpreter.

Miles never again so carelessly assumes the hopelessness of diplomacy. He comes to "[believe] that the swarming European who thought of gold and land, and razed forests, would eventually come to an understanding of the Indian people; they need only understand them as he understood them, to experience the same emotions he experienced."[80] Yet he makes at least one egregious mistake. He "[loathes] to interfere" in a Kaw child marriage case but does so by illegally cutting the rations.[81] "Here was the iron hand of the conquering race," observes Mathews.[82] But he learns quickly to attend to conflict and negotiation with more care. When traders claim that Osages have stolen some of their horses, Miles proceeds with patience. In his investigation, he visits a friend but does not ask about the horses. The next morning after breakfast, he carefully broaches the topic. The approach works, and he learns the identities of the culprits. Later that morning, he approaches a second camp and enters before realizing that it is in the process of mourning: "He felt a little annoyed with himself that he had been so discourteous in coming at this time."[83] He says he will go but relents after the camp residents insist he can stay. Though Mathews leads readers to believe that Miles will raise the issue of the horse theft, he instead encourages them to alter slightly their mourning ceremonies to avoid more of the fatalities that had occurred recently. Only later does Miles, after waiting patiently, raise the issue. Miles later takes a similar approach, with the additional step of obtaining the help of a skilled intermediary, to earn an exemption from allotment for the Osages and, again, to have overturned a government order demanding that the Osages remove all cattle from within the boundaries of their reservation. Mathews shows Miles learning diplomacy in an Osage-specific historical and contemporary context; in a diplomatic context, Miles is indigenized or Osaginized. Craig Womack, among other contemporary American Indian intellectuals, contends that assimilation works both ways. *Wah'Kon-Tah* illustrates one example of the process by which a non-Native begins to assimilate into a Native world.

Mathews then provides examples of successful Osage-Wichita and Osage-Pawnee diplomacy, following the murder of a Wichita chief by Osages during a mourning ceremony and the theft of horses by the Pawnees from the Osages. In the council with the Wichitas, an unidentified Osage speaker indicates that he thinks the Wichitas are weaker than the Osages and, therefore, will accept ponies, instead of the murderer, as restitution. After a Wichita speaker requests that the Osages give them the murderer, Three Striker, the council continues through the day. Three Striker even takes the opportunity to inform the audience that he does not intend to go with the Wichitas and that he was not afraid to die. Finally, Pawnee No Pah rises, suggests that the other Osage speakers are weak, and announces that the Wichitas will take ponies. The council then ends: "On the Osage side of the circle there were many how's and oh-oooooo's, and several arose to go, indicating that this was the end of the council. A Wichita arose and almost trembled with anger, but he spoke only a few seconds then sat down. Already the council had begun to break up."[84] The other conflict over the stolen horses ends with the Pawnees hosting a feast for the Osages from whom their fellow tribal-nation citizens stole the horses. In both cases, the diplomats involved avert further crime and violence.[85]

As he continues to adjust to the structure of Osage social and political life, Miles becomes increasingly exasperated by the perpetual assaults on Osage land, property, and bodies, and the "invasions" of the Osage Nation by squatters and unscrupulous businessmen. "As from the beginning," he observes, "the so-called civilized white man gave more trouble than the savage Indian."[86] Eventually, his political and historical perspective completes a dramatic shift: "The Indian problem had become a white problem, and the day of barbarism and outlawry began in the Reservation of the Osages."[87] Yet life in the Osage Nation continues with Wah Ti An Kah's nephew as one of the next generation's leaders: "Standing much as his fathers stood, he at once commands the attention of his hearers, then in flowing Osage talks of what is on his mind. Fortunately he has a very intelligent, diplomatic and discreet interpreter, and his speeches are usually accepted as being in harmony with the bigger and better spirit."[88] Miles insists that Wah Ti An Kah was a great leader but not a real Indian, not a real Osage, because he was "too noisy."[89] Mathews conveys to readers, however, the absolute necessity of having leaders like Wah Ti An Kah. "Too noisy" in this context more precisely means "too Osage": too devoted to the Osage Nation, past and present; too proud of being Osage; too unwilling to adapt. Diplomats like Wah Ti An Kah held the line against political, cultural, and socioeconomic incursions. As diplomats, they constantly took risks by testing the political landscape to see what and how much the Osages could demand from the federal government.

While Miles ends his life bitter and once again feeling impotent, the Osage leader Eagle That Dreams faces his own imminent death by chanting at sunrise: "Wah Tze Go, Wah Tze Go, may my feet go along road that is straight; may my lodge be filled with meat, may my lodge be filled with children; may I live long on earth, that my feet may travel straight in roads of earth."[90] *Wah'Kon-Tah* has been read often as a tragic narrative, as Kalter notes. However, readers only need to focus on Mathews's examples of Osage diplomacy to infer that he sees the Osages as capable of advocating for and securing their political autonomy as well as maintaining their dignity. The retired Indian agent Major Miles is the helpless one at the end of the book.

Like Wah Ti An Kah, Mathews represented the Osage Nation in Washington, D.C. He served two four-year terms, from 1934 to 1938 and from 1938 to 1942, as an elected member of the Osage tribal council. Mathews's Osage national service coincides with his residence in rural Osage County from the early 1930s to the early 1940s. While serving the nation and living at the Blackjacks, Mathews was also writing the memoir *Talking to the Moon*. Robert Warrior observes of *Talking*, "At first glance it might seem a simple telling of interesting anecdotes, along with a few sections of social commentary about World War II. Its subtlety, perhaps, explains the neglect it has suffered among those who read American Indian literature."[91] Warrior then argues, "More than simple nature writing, *Talking to the Moon* is an interpretation of the ecological and social history of the Osage land and people."[92] *Talking* is also a production informed by a particular political and diplomatic moment in Osage history. Oil was discovered on Osage land in the 1890s, and production increased dramatically into the 1930s.[93] The discovery of oil raised the socioeconomic status of some Osages, and Mathews's diplomatic work in Washington, D.C., was often related to the distribution of royalties. The Osages divide themselves, Mathews explains, into *Chesho*, or sky people, and *Hunkah*, or earth people. The former is the peace and the latter the war division of the nation. Throughout the memoir, he speaks of his Chesho thoughts and, therefore, as a diplomat he speaks as a member of the tribal nation's peace division.

The tragic tone of *Talking*, which also might account for its neglect by scholars of American Indian literatures, should also be considered within this context. Mathews laments cultural loss, the passing of a generation of Osages, throughout the book. Within the context of his discussion of the blood/land/memory complex in the work of Bronson, Ella Deloria, and McNickle, Chadwick Allen assesses *Talking*:

> I focus [. . .] on an aspect of this text scholars largely have avoided, namely, Mathews's unshakable sense that he had witnessed the demise of distinctly Osage people and lifeways. He did not share Bronson's or [Ella] Deloria's confidence in national movements— whether they were Christian missions or Indian rights organizations—to ameliorate such radical change or to help retain a sense of indigeneity. Nor did he share Deloria's confidence in the power of writing to maintain vital links with the past. In Mathews's "organic" formulation, indigenous survival is possible only at the level of the local and only at a significant remove from U.S. "civilization": that is, only with Osage land intact and flourishing and only with the Osage memory fully operative across the generations. At the end of World War II, he considered the prospects for such survival at best grim.[94]

A representative example of this lament comes as he travels with an artist who is making portraits of Osage leaders for the new tribal museum. Mathews thinks of "the old men of the tribe who feared the missing of their immortality." The portraits are, he thinks, "real conservation, since these old men would soon pass away and with them the Osage as he was, the era and the type passing with the individuals."[95] The lament, here as it is elsewhere in *Talking*, is for a particular religious and cultural view of the world. Mathews says earlier that the old religion will pass with the old men. His additional reflections are more dramatic: "I feel that I have been extremely fortunate to be a witness to the last struggle of a native religion, and certainly my daily life in the blackjacks has been influenced as much by this struggle as by any other struggle for survival. The passing of a concept of God seems to be almost as poignant as the passing of a species."[96] It is apparently little consolation to Mathews, but the Osage Nation endures, even beyond the Oklahoma statehood that figures so devastatingly for the Cherokees in Riggs's plays. Even as he produces an elegy for the Osage religious worldview, Mathews serves the Osage Nation and contributes to national continuity.

Mathews devotes only a few pages in the memoir to the details of his diplomatic efforts. He reports, "I usually spend several weeks or a month in Washington, D.C., attending to the business of the Osage. They have bills in Congress to be guided, and because they have oil royalties they are, as a tribe, ever on the defensive, so that there are always matters under litigation as well. It seems that they must be constantly protecting themselves against those who sincerely believe them to be a vested interest."[97] Mathews is not in Washington, D.C., alone: "Sometimes some of the older men of the tribe make the trip along with the members of the business committee and members of the agency staff in order to be company for the chief. [. . .] Their presence before the Indian committees of both houses is quite effective, as the older men talk with dignity and formality."[98] Mathews's subsequent description of the men in "blankets, bandeaux, or black Stetson hats" evokes the image of Wah Ti An Kah from *Wah'Kon-Tah*.[99] Though Mathews does not see the kind of cultural and religious continuity that he desires, there is still Osage national continuity. He was clearly saddened by the cultural and religious losses but was determined to contribute to the maintenance and continuity of the Osage Nation as a politican and diplomat. During the 1950s, he also devoted himself to writing his magnum opus, *The Osages: Children of the Middle Waters*, which was published in 1961. In a letter to Oliver La Farge dated June 27, 1960, Mathews requests the use of a passage from one of La Farge's books and writes excitedly: "I am just finishing an overwhelming story of the Osages. This ought to be definitive."[100] As a historian, Mathews also served the Osage Nation.

Warrior also identifies a powerful anticolonial sentiment in *Talking*. He asserts, "More than any American Indian writer up to his time and until Deloria, Mathews saw through the presuppositions of the culture that had come to dominate both the land and the people of this continent, and was able to speak with great power about the destructive defects of it."[101] As discussed in chapter 2, Warrior uses this reading of *Talking* to recover *Sundown* from prevailing scholarly interpretations of that novel as tragic. By connecting Mathews to Vine Deloria Jr., Warrior establishes another link between two eras generally understood as dramatically different in literary and political character. Mathews's commentary on the legacy of colonial invasion and destruction also reads like a nonfiction translation of Lynn Riggs's *Dark Encounter*, which was published just a year earlier than *Talking to the Moon* in 1944. We can, therefore, identify a political kinship between Riggs and Deloria Jr., as well. More explicitly than Riggs, however, and as Warrior argues, Mathews situates his anticolonial politics in an indigenous, specifically Osage, social and historical context.

From October 1939 to August 1940, Mathews also spent a year in Mexico on a Guggenheim Fellowship. Susan Kalter has discovered in his letters and diaries that Mathews worked on *Talking to the Moon* while he was there. In addition, in 1940, along with D'Arcy McNickle, Mathews attended the first Inter-American Congress on Indian Life in Patzcuaro, Michoacan, Mexico, as a U.S. representative.[102] In his discussion of Mathews's childhood, John Hunt describes a frightened boy listening to a song or chant, of a wolf, perhaps, or a wapiti, in the Osage country outside his home: "As Mathews would later write, this prayer-song was Neolithic man talking to God in a chant that always ended, before it was finished, in a sob of frustration. For the rest of his life, Mathews would search for its continuation—in the cathedrals of Europe, in desert mosques, in pre-Columbian Mexico, and finally once again in the Osage hills."[103] Mexico is a hidden part of Mathews's political and intellectual enterprise. If his time there influenced the writing of *Talking to the Moon*, that influence is not perceptible. For Downing, however, as for Riggs and, in the following chapter, McNickle, Mexico was the center stage for international American Indian diplomacy and for the most radically anticolonial indigenous politics in the literature of this era.

Downing: From Detective to Diplomat

One week before Mathews and McNickle attended the Inter-American Congress on Indian Life, Downing published *The Mexican Earth*. President Lázaro Cárdenas's term also came to an end that year, and his agrarian reform program stalled.[104] While American Indian authors such as Rogers, Mathews, and Standing Bear engaged in diplomacy among American Indians as well as between American Indians and non-Native people, the diplomatic moments in their writing primarily involve indigenous people negotiating with more socially and politically powerful non-Natives. Downing demonstrates in *The Mexican Earth* an approach that is more indigenous-centric in this literary diplomatic context. *The Mexican Earth* is a well-reviewed history of Mexico that celebrates Mexico as an unconquered geography of indigenous communities.[105] He posits explicit connections between those polities and American Indian nations in the United States and makes frequent, direct assertions of indigenous Mexican cultural, political, and social potency in the present. By writing the history of Mexico as a statement on the continuous centrality of strong indigenous communities to the life of that nation, Downing produces a Native-centric political and historical work that anticipates renaissance-era nonfiction by writers such as McNickle and Deloria Jr.[106] The careful scrutiny of the writing careers of Downing and his contemporaries forces a reconsideration of the conventional understanding of the origins of the Native American literary renaissance. This scrutiny reveals those origins have deeper roots in the literary work of the middle of the century than scholars have acknowledged. Some of these roots are multiply international and transnational, as writers such as Riggs, Rogers, Standing Bear, Mathews, and Downing situate tribal nations in opposition to or alliance with other tribal nations, settler-colonial nations, or colonial nations. While writers such as Riggs, Downing, and McNickle also position settler-colonial nations in opposition to or alliance with other settler-colonial nations, they also imagine an indigenous American transnation that vitiates settler-colonial borders and prepares the political ground for the creation of an indigenous transnational coalition.

Downing opens *The Mexican Earth* with the first of two key acts of diplomacy in which he presents himself as an Indian of Oklahoma establishing friendly relations with indigenous Mexicans. Downing enters Mexico from the International Bridge at Laredo, Texas, and cites a recent example of border violence only to reject that "wild-West" representation of Mexico: "Mexico is safe to the point of monotony."[107] He then describes the country and its people as he moves from Vallecillo to Monterrey, Saltillo, Victoria, Valles, and Tamazunchale to the Otomi region around Zimapan. Here, he comments on the "alien" presence of the hacienda, the church, and the nearby "Monument of Friendly Relations, erected by the American Colony of Mexico City"; these foreign buildings and monuments are cognates of the domesticated animals, "the other, latecoming things" that have in Momaday's *House Made of Dawn* "an alien and inferior aspect, a poverty of vision and instinct."[108] Downing collapses the Spanish and U.S. presence in Mexico in this passage. They are equally foreign and, as readers will see, both unfriendly despite the guise of benevolence and diplomacy.

While Downing is also foreign, he distinguishes himself from other visitors through the practice of Choctaw diplomacy. As he travels through this Otomi region on the Pan-American Highway and on what he calls the downward slope of the pyramid of the Mexican landscape, he sees many Otomies walking home along the highway from their work in the fields. Some wear maguey sandals; others wear sandals made from tire rubber. Downing claims that their distinctive walk, an "Indian trot," does not change with the change in footwear.[109] Indeed, the tracks of the rubber sandals "look so much like the prints of the snake's scales."[110] After Downing demonstrates that adaptation does not alter a person's indigeneity—their footprints suggest the presence of Quetzalcoatl, the feathered serpent—a man steps from behind a cactus. He requests a ride to Mexico City for an older man standing behind him, and moments later, the older man's two sons ask to come as well. Downing explains, "We looked up at the Monument of Friendly Relations and acquiesced."[111] More workers clearly desire rides, but "we drove on, leaving to the next of our countrymen who should pass the responsibility for carrying on friendly relations."[112] As they drive away, the crowd cheers and waves pieces of red cloth either to celebrate Downing's generous offer of a ride or to honor the man who talked Downing into providing the ride for his friends.

Other U.S. visitors to Mexico do not follow Downing's model of kind and generous diplomacy. Prior to describing his gesture of goodwill to the Otomies, Downing relates the story of a young Californian in Mexico City who "was ecstatic about Indians" and "was studying indigenous art and folk dances and the Aztec language in the summer school of the National University of Mexico."[113] She had, Downing observes, "horned in on" an Indian family during lunch and "eaten their *tortillas*."[114] Following this example of intrusive behavior, she irritates Downing further by implying that there are no Indians in California. Downing asks, "You have Indians out in California, don't you?"[115] Her hesitant, uncertain response suggests that she has been conditioned not to see the Native people in her own region of the United States. One of Downing's projects in *The Mexican Earth* is to make indigenous people in the United States more visible by highlighting their ties to indigenous Mexicans, as he does several pages later when he comments on the Uto-Aztecan languages spoken in southern and central Mexico, the U.S. Southwest, the Great Basin, and the young woman's home state of California.

The young woman's clumsy diplomacy, however, fares better in comparison to what Downing witnesses after he leaves the Otomies at Venta del Carpio. There, Downing sees "other cars with United States license plates going by at great speed. I caught glimpses of startled faces turned in our direction."[116] "In Mexico City the next morning," he continues, "I was hailed by a gentleman who had had a great deal to say, in the Valles hotel where we both stayed, about the recent expropriation of oil properties."[117] This gentleman, who reads the red pieces of cloth as signs of Communist sympathy, was under the impression that Downing had been held up by Communist agitators.[118] In particular, he was annoyed that Mexicans were ungrateful for Americans who came to their country to spend money and improve the Mexican economy. Downing's plan for his fellow U.S. citizens to cultivate friendly relations fails—for his countrymen, at least as represented by this gentleman, have a paranoia about Communism that leads them to see a man who needs a ride home from work as a threat to capitalism and U.S. economic interests. However, good relations between the Choctaw author and the Otomies have been assured.

The diplomacy that Downing practices in *The Mexican Earth* occurs in a shared indigenous American history and homeland, and it has at once precolonial roots and a transnational configuration. While an open wound in the earth at Claremore Mound represents a history of unsuccessful Osage and Cherokee diplomacy in Riggs's *The Cherokee Night*, the definitively indigenous Mexican earth produces beauty and sustains its people. The title *The Mexican Earth* expresses the integral connection between the health of indigenous polities and land tenure that Downing develops throughout the work. This history does not tell the story of a Mexico founded in colonial documents and validated by international law, treaty, or diplomacy, though Downing's argument is compatible with McNickle's position in the renaissance-era *Native American Tribalism: Indian Survivals and Renewals* (1973) that there was loss but not defeat and that an always coherent, sovereign, and legally recognized indigenous presence can be traced from contact into the present.[119] Rather, the book is about the Mexican land, or the land of the Mexicas (pronounced "Meshicas"), and the self-identification of the Aztecs.[120] As Burr Cartwright Brundage explains, the name *Mexica* derives from a deity named Mecitli or Mexitli who told the group that rose to power in Anáhuac to break from the rest of its people. Brundage believes that the translation of Mexitli is "the Maguey Grandmother." Mexico means *Mexitli's Place*; a Mexican in an indigenous

context is a person from Mexitli's Place, a person with a divine relationship to the maguey.[121]

The land and what emerges from it, including the maguey, sustains
indigenous Mexicans but also, Downing eventually claims, Choctaws and
other American Indians. It takes precedence over the human world both
in the book's title and in the title of the first chapter, "Cactus, Orchids,
Maguey." Indigenous Mexicans use parts of the maguey, also called agave,
to make thread, rope, shampoo, cloth, shoes, medicine, paper, aguamiel,
pulque, and mezcal, and they use the thorns, for example, for sewing. The
maguey clothes, cleanses, heals, and feeds indigenous Mexicans and provides the means to write and draw their history. Downing adds that Otomi
infants ride in *ayates* made of maguey fibers on the backs of their moth-
ers, and Otomi markets still contain many items made from the cactus:
"bags, sashes, hats, baskets, cordage."[122] Even human-made structures such
as the pyramids are, in Downing's view, explicitly of this Mexican earth:
"A Mexican pyramid is an imitation of a mountain."[123] In this section of
the first chapter, he uses as his specific example the pyramid of the sun at
Teotihuacan, a popular tourist destination for which John Joseph Mathews
expressed his admiration after his visit in 1940.

The historical and political kinship of indigenous people in the Americas that Downing describes and attempts to cultivate as a diplomat also
derives from the land. In a discussion of the men who governed the
Mexica world, Downing insists that calling them kings or emperors, the
titles of European rulers, is not accurate. "Beneath the gold and silver and
quetzal feathers this was an American ruler and these American institutions," Downing says of the last Moctezuma, "whose background was not
the minarets of Bagdad but the cornfields which had produced as well the
Muskogean Confederacy and the League of the Iroquois."[124] By virtue of
this common parent, corn, or *teocentli*, these indigenous people have kinship: the Mexicas, the Muskogeans, and the Iroquois. This constellation of
confederacies evokes a vast indigenous network of related peoples from
Central America through Mexico, the U.S. Southeast and Northeast, and
into eastern Canada.

Downing's people, the Choctaws, speak a Muskogean language in which
he was fluent. Anthropologist Charles Hudson observes, "The Muskogean
family [...] was the most important language family in the Southeast. Once
spoken in Louisiana, Mississippi, Alabama, Georgia, and adjacent areas,
it includes five closely related groups of languages: Choctaw-Chickasaw,

Apalachee, Alabama-Koasati, Mikasuki-Hitchiti, and Muskogee-Seminole."[125] Muskogean peoples had first contact with the Spanish not long after indigenous Mexicans and the Incans in Peru. In May of 1539, Hernándo de Soto landed on the western coast of Florida at what is now the town of Bradenton. De Soto's journey through the Southeast, until his death on May 21, 1542, parallels Hernán Cortés's journey into Anáhuac in many of the most brutal ways, including his meeting with Muskogean people under the leadership of Tuscaloosa at Mabila.[126] However, Downing recognizes that the Muskogeans and Mexicas have a different, deeper, much older common bond produced by the land and corn, and this common bond does not subvert the political organization of any group or the confederacies into which these individual Native polities formed.

As a Choctaw traveler and chronicler rather than a tourist, and as a cartographer mapping both the indigenous land throughout North America and a relationship among the indigenous communities that reside in that land, Downing writes through dominant narratives of Mexico to foreground an indigenous past, present, and future. He reads, for example, the Mexican revolution—or more precisely the Mexican revolutions, including the war for independence from Spain—as indigenous attempts to reclaim the land. In the middle of his narrative of Cortés's invasion, Downing stops to consider Pedro de Alvarado, Cortés's second in command, as an archetypal colonizer: "Mexican history falls into periods during which foreigners like him have come to make personal fortunes out of first one and then another of the country's resources: yellow gold, silver, green gold, black gold. The Mexican Revolution, in the last analysis, is a repudiation of these exploiters—yellow beards, blue eyes, smiles and all—and of the alien institutions which they brought with them."[127] Even in the earliest moments of Cortés's invasion of Anáhuac, Downing always sees indigenous history at work; from the point of initial contact with the indigenous people of Mexico, the Spanish were in indigenous history.

Mexica imperialism in Anáhuac was one of the prominent features of this indigenous history. When Cortés made alliances with the Mexica Empire's tributaries, these alliances were, Downing insists, motivated by anti-imperial designs: from the moment these alliances were solidified, voluntarily or under coercion following a military surrender, "the conquest of Anáhuac was really a conquest by its Indian enemies led by the Spaniards."[128] Although this anti-imperial design left Cortés in power,

Downing explains that a conquistador and writer such as Bernal Díaz del Castillo, who wrote *Verdadera Historia de la Conquista de Nueva España*, or *The True History of the Conquest of New Spain* (1632), "could never have understood the assertion that [. . .] they failed to destroy Tenochtitlán. It remained as a beautiful consoling memory, an Aztec Tula, and that memory could never fade because—literally—Tenochtitlan has kept coming up out of the ground."[129] Just as it gives birth to corn, the maguey, and orchids, the Mexican earth gives birth to indigenous cities. In addition, the Spanish used the bricks and stones of Tenochtitlan in the construction of Mexico City. The buildings look different than the pyramids and apartments, the former plazas and markets and causeways, but the same building materials are a part of the places of worship, shelter, and trade in the new city. The labor devoted to the construction of Mexico City was also indigenous.

Downing's narrative of continuous indigenous Mexican revolution is a savvy political appropriation of what historian Enrique Florescano calls Mexican national narratives. As Florescano explains, supporters of Francisco Madero constructed a revolutionary genealogy from Hidalgo's "Grito de Dolores" in 1810 to the plan of Ayutla and the War of Reform from 1854 to 1861 under Benito Juárez, the Zapotec leader from Oaxaca, to the uprising led by Madero against the Porfiriato in 1910.[130] Downing adopts this feature of Mexican revolutionary discourse, but his narrative of revolution begins much earlier than 1810 and has specifically indigenous roots. The indigenous Mexican revolution begins for Downing in Toxcatl (Dryness), the fifth month of the Mexicas' calendar, or on May 19, 1520, the day that Pedro de Alvarado slaughtered celebrants of a festival for Huitzilopochtli, the hummingbird god of the south and the Mexicas' god of war and the sun. Following this date, the Mexicas drove the Spanish from Tenochtitlan on July 1, 1520, only to lose the city again on August 31, 1521, following a long battle with the Spanish, their allies, and a smallpox epidemic. The Spanish occupation of Anáhuac as well as Central and South America then began in earnest. Downing expresses dismay at the brutality of the conquistadors, but he argues, "Not by killing [. . .] did they make their rule intolerable [. . .] but by violating—with the *encomienda* system—the relationship between the Indian and the land."[131] The encomienda system involved the granting of Native villages to conquistadors, who then ran the villages and used the residents as slave labor. The attempt to end this violation defines the indigenous revolution that follows the first arrows sent against the Spanish in the defense of those who were celebrating the festival for Huitzilopochtli. While revolution flourishes in Mexico, it threatens to spread throughout the homeland that the Choctaws share with indigenous Mexicans.

Almost four hundred years after the beginning of the revolution, the Mexican nation wrote article 27 into its Constitution of 1917, and as Downing explains, the Expropriation Law of 1936 put this article into effect. Article 27 vests in the nation original ownership of Mexican territory and resources. This ownership is inalienable, and only Mexican citizens can obtain ownership as well as mineral or water concessions. Will Rogers's observations on U.S. resistance to Mexican plans to nationalize its oil reserves occur within this particular historical context. The attempt to restore Mexican sovereignty over the land and resources controlled by other nations and foreign corporations has eighteen sections that define the provisions governing land rights. Section VIII declares the following null and void:

a. All transfers of the lands, waters, and forests of villages, rancherías, groups, or communities made by local officials (jefes políticos), state governors, or other local authorities in violation of the provisions of the Law of June 25, 1856, and other related laws and rulings.

b. All concessions, deals or sales of lands, waters, and forests made by the Secretariat of Development, the Secretariat of Finance, or any other federal authority from December 1, 1876 to date, which encroach upon or illegally occupy communal lands (ejidos), lands allotted in common, or lands of any other kind belonging to villages, rancherías, groups or communities, and centers of population.

c. All survey or demarcation-of-boundary proceedings, transfers, alienations, or auction sales effected during the period of time referred to in the preceding sub-clause, by companies, judges, or other federal or state authorities entailing encroachments on or illegal occupation of the lands, waters, or forests of communal holdings (ejidos), lands held in common, or other holdings belonging to centers of population.[132]

In the historical moment that Riggs dramatizes in *The Year of Pilár*, President Lázaro Cárdenas began returning the ejidos to indigenous people and communities in the 1930s. This attempt at land reform was consistently compromised by counterreforms, amendments to article 27, and

the resistance of the hacendados and their political allies, such as anar-
chists and urban labor. The hacendados in Yucatán, as historian Ben Fallaw
explains, obstructed reform: "Their employees routinely sabotaged rasp-
ing machinery and overcut their henequen fields rather than turn them
over to the ejidatarios. Another favorite tactic, when forced to transfer
land, was to turn over newly sown, immature fields instead of mature ones.
Many landowners threatened not to plant new henequen and refused to
hire workers unless agrarian reform was suspended."[133] They also mobilized the peons—the workers on the hacienda that stayed after they were
allowed to leave in 1915 and were then excluded by federal policy from the
reforms—against Cárdenas's policy.[134]

Yet Downing still has reason for optimism in the late 1930s. To Downing, article 27 "was an expression of the fundamental Mexican tenet sung
by Nezahualcoyotl in the fifteenth century."[135] Nezahualcoyotl, or Hungry
Coyote, was a poet and the ruler of the Acolhua city of Texcoco in the
fifteenth century. He wrote "gently melancholic poems on the hollowness
of human vanity brightened now and then by some good old Epicurean-
ism."[136] Meyer and Sherman call him "one of the most remarkable figures
in the history of Mexico" and explain that he was known as "a wise legisla-
tor and an impartial judge."[137] Downing reads a constitutional act of the
Mexican nation as an explicit expression of an indigenous philosophy, and
he interprets Emiliano Zapata's revolutionary philosophy of land reform
as an attempt to enforce "Nezahualcoyotl's law."[138] In the late nineteenth
and early twentieth centuries, indigenous Mexican legal principles are still
shaping the nation and the lives of indigenous, mestizo, and nonindigenous people.

Downing also foregrounds indigenous histories and epistemologies in
his comments about Native people in the United States. During his discussion of the Mexican Constitution of 1917 and the ejidos, for example, he
writes, "In 1492 Amerindian life from Cape Horn to Bering [sic] Sea was
characterized by communal ownership of real estate, based on the family
group. [. . .] Yet today, when a commissioner of Indian affairs encourages
Indian tribes to return to a degree of communal organization, politicians,
missionaries and others with axes to grind raise the cry of Russian influence."[139] Downing does not mention John Collier by name in this passage,
but his disdain for the criticism of Collier's policies, with their own roots
in the Bureau of Indian Affairs commissioner's interest in Mexican federal Indian policy, indicates that Downing supported them. The implied

comparison of U.S. federal Indian policy with Cárdenas's policy in Mexico also indicates that Downing conceived of indigenous futures in the United States and Mexico as shared and perhaps even interdependent.

Downing's historical narrative of Mexico as an indigenous nation, and the indigenous Mexican revolution motivated to recover and reassert social, cultural, and political power, is not a romantic gesture toward the return of Mexica hegemony. Following his discussion of human sacrifice in Anáhuac, a practice that he later compares to the Spanish Inquisition, Downing describes the Mexica empire as "a reasonably successful experiment in democracy."[140] This satirical observation is reminiscent of Will Rogers's political commentary. It suggests that the Mexicas practiced domination similarly to Europeans and some of their colonial descendants, who call this domination the spread of democracy, while the communities dominated by the Mexicas started the anti-imperial revolution that Downing celebrates. That the Mexicas practiced human sacrifice did not justify Cortés's attempt to destroy their empire; that Cortés attempted to destroy the empire, in turn, does not justify romantically longing for its return.[141] Instead, Downing points readers to an indigenous anti-imperial movement with origins in Anáhuac long before the Spanish arrive, and it is in that anti-imperial movement that he roots his historical perspective of contemporary indigenous communities within U.S. and Mexican borders.

Downing also situates Mexican national events in local indigenous contexts. In the late 1860s and early 1870s, the Zapotec land reformer, president, and revolutionary Benito Juárez engaged in a political struggle with Porfirio Díaz, whose mother was Mixtec. The battle between the two men culminated in a presidential campaign in 1870–71, accusations of fraud after Juárez was reelected, and a Díaz rebellion in Oaxaca.[142] The Zapotecs and Mixtecs were ancient antagonists, and Downing sees the conflict between Juárez and Díaz as part of this continuous history. Downing suggests that their antagonism can be understood, too, in the context of Díaz's rejection of his own Mixtec family: "Porfirio Díaz tried to bleach his Mixtec skin with chemicals."[143] Díaz and Juárez restage the old battle between the Mexica Empire and its tributaries. While Downing must elide the complexities of indigenous Mexican politics and identities to draw this comparison, Juárez and Díaz inarguably had indigenous Mexican families that shaped their lives, political careers, and by extension, the Mexican nation.

In addition to reading Mexican history as indigenous, Downing sees the indigenous prevailing in Mexican religious beliefs and practices. In "Towards a National Indian Literature: Cultural Authenticity in Nationalism," Simon Ortiz describes his Uncle Steve's celebration of Catholic saints' days at Acqumeh:

> Obviously, there is an overtone that this is a Catholic Christian ritual celebration because of the significance of the saints' names and days on the Catholic calendar. But just as obviously, when the celebration is held within the Acqumeh community, it is an Acqumeh ceremony. It is Acqumeh and Indian (or Native American or American Indian if one prefers those terms) in the truest and most authentic sense. This is so because this celebration speaks of the creative ability of Indian people to gather in many forms of the socio-political colonizing force which beset them and to make these forms meaningful in their own terms. In fact, it is a celebration of the human spirit and the Indian struggle for liberation.[144]

Downing sees the same process in indigenous Mexican communities that Ortiz describes at Acqumeh. Though Downing explains that in Spanish colonial practice "a policy of terrorism was adopted to stamp out idolatrous practices," the mass conversions were superficial.[145] He offers as his primary example the history of the Virgin of Guadalupe, the patron saint of Mexico. In the Mexica month of Atemoztli (The Descent of Water) just before the winter solstice, December 1531 in the Gregorian calendar, a Chichimec named Juan Diego Cuauhtlatoatzin had a vision of Mary the mother of Christ and, therefore, Christianity. Downing argues, as have many commentators before and after him, that Cuauhtlatoatzin saw Tonantzin, an indigenous mother goddess.[146] The Virgin of Guadalupe is a subversive disguise that indigenous people use to maintain their beliefs. Downing says that even Bernardino de Sahagún, the missionary and historian, knew what he was seeing when he looked at La Guadalupana: a Native woman standing in the cup of Tonantzin's moon. To emphasize that the Virgin was Tonantzin in disguise, Downing discusses the virgins that represented the competing factions fighting for Mexican independence: the white Our Lady of the Remedies of the criollo conservatives and the brown Our Lady of Guadalupe of the indigenous and mestizo revolutionaries. The indigenous virgin lost this battle, but as the patron saint of Mexico, she maintains her stature as one of the most powerful religious figures in Greater Mexico.[147]

Downing interprets the miracles that occurred throughout Mexico following the sighting of Tonantzin at Tepeyac as the work of Native people using Christianity to revitalize their indigenous beliefs: a miracle in Ocotlan corresponds to the old spring fiesta of the Tlaxcalans; in Amacameca, the goddess of ripe maize, Teteoinan, returns; and the cave once belonging to Tlaloc becomes the site where a local indigenous population pays reverence to an image of Christ made from corn stalks. Downing notes that the Tlaxcalans call Saint Anna "Toci," our grandmother, and adds that Sahagún knew that the pilgrimages to her are made on the days of the old sacrifices.[148] The clergy surrenders to this affirmation of indigenous religious beliefs and practices and, finally, "by the end of the first century of New Spain's existence the clergy as a whole had given up missionizing and was reaching out for real estate as avidly as the *encomenderos* for gold."[149] Downing's interpretation of these events foregrounds the indigenizing force of the land and people of Mexico: "Christ and all his saints had to follow the example of the Virgin of Guadalupe and change their complexions if they were to live in Mexico."[150] In comparison to the works of fiction by American Indian authors in the first half of the twentieth century, *The Mexican Earth* much more forcibly asserts that indigenous people had a profound influence on European beliefs and practices. Native Mexicans, just as the people at Acqumeh, incorporated Catholicism into their world and indigenized it.

The indigenizing of alien cultural and religious institutions is part of the centuries of resistance to the Spanish invasion that Downing documents. For Downing, in fact, there has never been a conquest of Mexico: "The great conquest of the Revolution was a return to Indian values, concretely expressed in that pre-Conquest institution, the *ejido*. There is no wall around Mexico, of course, but whatever form its national life ultimately assumes it is going to have its roots in Mexican soil, like corn and the maguey. The issue was decided during the days of Cortés and the viceroys, when the Spaniards failed to annihilate either the Indian or his culture. Now Mexico is an Indian country, where the white man is rapidly being bred out."[151] When Downing ends the penultimate chapter with an image of Quetzalcoatl returning to live among his people, readers understand that this returning has always been in process.[152] Indigenous people in Mexico have made it happen by their preparations, their resistance.

From Downing's perspective, the belief that Cortés was a returning Quetzalcoatl is fallacious. Quetzalcoatl, the Mexica god that did not demand
human sacrifice, is still on his way home to a nation that is still indigenous.

The promise of Quetzalcoatl's return resonates within Choctaw and
Native southeastern U.S. history, as indigenous Mexicans share traditions
of feathered or horned serpents with the culture groups of this region.
Susan C. Power observes in her study of the history of winged serpents in
the art of the Native southeast: "Many theories have suggested that Mesoamerica and South America were the sources of major artistic influences
on the early Southeast. The prehistoric parallels in art and architecture,
especially the iconography and artistic processes, are difficult to dismiss."[153]
After she provides a catalog of cultural links between North America and
Mesoamerica, Power identifies some of the similarities between winged
serpents in these regions: "The arts from both areas depict individuals
wearing uniquely comparable ensembles: large shell-bead necklaces with
gorgets, shell ear flares, and bird-wing capes. In fact, the Mayan Eagle Lord
in art wears an identical feather cloak and carries the same *tumi*, or knife,
and severed head as the southeastern Winged Beings. The figures in *Rogan
Copper Plates* [. . .], for example, have been compared to Aztec figures
of the Codex Borbonicus. The two regions share the Long-Nosed God,
feathered serpent (the Toltec/Aztec god Quetzalcoatl), underwater cou-
gar, and Winged Beings with common regalia and accessories."[154] Finally,
after asserting that "archaeology and oral traditions show that the worldview and belief systems of Mesoamerica and the eastern United States
were quite close over a period of many centuries, perhaps millennia,"
Power also notes the similarities between the Choctaw and Mexica origin
stories.[155] Like the main character Salt in D'Arcy McNickle's novel *Runner
in the Sun* (1954), Downing's journey into Mexico was not to a foreign land
but through an extended homeland. The homecoming of the powerful
god, the winged serpent Quetzalcoatl, promises revitalization not just for
indigenous Mexicans but for Choctaws and other indigenous nations that
shared with them a long residence in the Southeast before removal and
continue to share eastern Oklahoma with them.

This revitalization depends on the maintenance of good diplomatic
relations among these indigenous polities. Thus in the closing chapter
of *The Mexican Earth*, the second key moment of diplomacy, which with
the first in the opening chapter frames the history, is crucial to Downing's
optimism for indigenous American futures. Downing ends his history on

indigenous ground in Benito Juárez's home state of Oaxaca in the Zapotec town of San Pablo Villa de Mitla. Of the local residents of Mitla, Downing observes: "Two Mitleyenos will not join in the Spanish *abrazo* at meeting, although they may give the forward movement of the body, first on one side, then on the other, without actually touching each other. If they shake hands palm will barely meet palm—exactly in the manner of two Choctaws."[156] This handshake is the embodiment of the indigenous diplomacy that Downing pursues: careful and noninvasive. He provides a historical and contemporary profile of the town then spends Día de los Muertos with Luis, a native Mitleyeno whose brother has died. Downing gives the last pages of his book to Luis, who tells a story of the souls of the dead residing with us in our homes. Luis's story mirrors Downing's narrative of the town by collapsing the indigenous past with the indigenous modern present. The bureaucratic and academic Mexican indigenistas valued cultural productions over indigenous producers.[157] The final image of Downing's history is, in contrast, of two indigenous Americans, a Choctaw and a Zapotec, simultaneously within this indigenous past and modern present and simultaneously within indigenous history as actors and authors—as producers—rather than objects of indigenismo. They are also residents of a shared homeland, the southern part of which is in the midst of enduring indigenous revolution.

In addition to anticipating the more assertive politics of the Red Power and renaissance era in *The Mexican Earth*, Downing takes a political position that has striking similarities to the contemporary critical mode called American Indian literary nationalism. Warrior's *Tribal Secrets* (1995), Weaver's *That the People Might Live* (1997), Womack's *Red on Red* (1999), and their coauthored study *American Indian Literary Nationalism* (2006) build on the work of Ortiz and Cook-Lynn, for example, and provide the most explicit definitions of contemporary American Indian literary nationalism.[158] Warrior, Weaver, and Womack use literary nationalism to describe the efforts to do anticolonial academic work in the field of Native studies; to foreground Native histories, epistemologies, and intellectual traditions in discussions of Native American literature; and to affirm the status of Native nations as sovereign bodies of people with basic human and civil rights protected by the law. "At its most profound," Weaver explains, "literary nationalism is not a confrontation, not a tearing down, but an upbuilding," and though confrontation and disagreement are unavoidable, he continues, "we would rather commit considerable energy to the explication of specific Native values, readings, and knowledges and their relevance to our contemporary lives."[159] Womack and Warrior reiterate these sentiments: Womack outlines ten steps toward a compassionate American Indian literary nationalism, while Warrior discusses what he learned from Edward Said about nationalism and the role that secular criticism, "a critical discourse that is willing and able to stand against the tide, calling into question the moral and ethical basis of the assumed authority of every and any claim to power," can play in tempering its possible abuses.[160] Throughout their work, all three theorists encourage the privileging of Native lives, voices, and histories in critical practice, just as Downing does in *The Mexican Earth*.

The Revolution Comes to Oklahoma

The Mexican Earth is an extraordinary example of revolutionary American Indian history in the interwar era. There were many other works of book-length nonfiction than those by Rogers, Standing Bear, Mathews, and Downing, including two works of pan-Indian and intertribal nation history—Bronson's *Indians Are People, Too* and McNickle's *They Came Here First*—that were produced by authors who served as key diplomatic figures of the era as members of the National Congress of American Indians. Yet it is John Milton Oskison's *Tecumseh and His Times: The Story of a Great Indian* (1938) that best approximates the revolutionary narrative of Downing's *The Mexican Earth*. Oskison is widely regarded as proassimilation. Though his work suggests a much more complicated figure, any resistance to settler colonialism in his many short stories and the three novels published during his lifetime is muted. His biography of Tecumseh, however, is extraordinary in its celebration of military resistance and the suggestion that this resistance has contemporary—that is, late 1930s—relevance. Oskison dedicates the book "to all Dreamers and Strivers for the integrity of the Indian race, some of whose blood flows in my veins; and especially to the Oklahoma Shawnee friends of my boyhood."[161] These Oklahoma Shawnees are the ancestors of the Shawnee kin, neighbors, and close friends of the Cherokees in the early nineteenth century. Oskison asserts that the alliance between the Cherokees and Shawnees "has continued to this day." "Now," he continues, "the larger number of surviving Shawnees are living on land in Oklahoma allotted to them out of Cherokee holdings."[162] Of their ancestor, Tecumseh, Oskison observes,

"Like other champions of the ideal of Indian sovereignty before him, he stored his mind with the details of tribal history."[163] These are the same details of tribal history that Oskison takes as his own task to relate to readers in the 1930s.

The biography is a narrative of Tecumseh's valiant but ultimately unsuccessful efforts to fight for this Indian sovereignty following the invasions of the old Northwest Territory and the hunting grounds of Kentucky shared by the region's Native nations. Oskison takes readers through the American Revolution, William Henry Harrison's attack on Tippecanoe, and Tecumseh's alliance with the British and defeat of Fort Dearborn. Tecumseh fights against these intruders, Oskison informs us, with Cherokee warriors. As settlers pour west following the Treaty of Greenville in 1795, Tecumseh knew "their wisest course was one of peaceful and diplomatic resistance."[164] Oskison's Tecumseh wants to fight, but he knows it might not be the most productive course of action. He chooses peace but still hopes to recover their lost lands. His nemesis, Harrison, who Oskison argues was enabled by Thomas Jefferson, leaves him no choice.

As Tecumseh's brother seeks what Oskison calls an emotional answer in religion, Tecumseh seeks practical answers by recruiting a confederacy: "Meanwhile, Tecumseh went about the work of organizing the Indians to rebellion in a much less spectacular and more effective manner."[165] In addition to the Creeks, his recruiting tour takes him to Rogers's, Oskison's, and Riggs's Cherokee ancestors; Downing's Choctaw ancestors; and Mathews's Osage ancestors.[166] In a statement that evokes Mexico as a site of indigenous resistance, Oskison comments of Tecumseh: "Now Harrison began to think of him as a putative Montezuma, or a North American Inca chief."[167] The specter of indigenous Mexico, at least, frightened Harrison. Tecumseh's diplomatic efforts are not successful, however, though Oskison says this failure is the result of the incompetent, untrustworthy British leader, Major-General Henry Proctor. The Trail of Tears was the reward, argues Oskison, for the aid the Cherokees provided Andrew Jackson at the Battle of Horseshoe Bend in March of 1814 against Tecumseh's Creek followers.

But this end—for the Shawnees and the Cherokees—is not final. As Oskison reports, "Tecumseh's dream persists even today. Among the Oklahoma Shawnees the prophecy is current that Tecumseh will be born again and will achieve his great purpose in some glorious spring-to-fall season of the future."[168] It is in the peyote church where the dream persists:

"In these long sessions, the modern reservation Indians recapture a dream; they reach for—at the least—a spiritual union of the race, seek to preserve that which is distinctively Indian."[169] Oskison even ponders, though cautiously, the activist potential of the Native American Church: "So far, no individual has emerged as a leader strong enough to fuse the movement into one of active protest against a rubber-stamp Christian civilization. It is unlikely that anyone will, for the leaders are well enough read in Indian history to know that the sure way to extinction for the peyote religion is to bring it into the open."[170] As some indigenous Mexicans, and at least one Choctaw, await the return of Quetzalcoatl, peyotists in Oklahoma engage in a social and religious practice with roots in northern Mexico and await the return of Tecumseh. Downing and Oskison do their part to summon both into the present.

CHAPTER 4

The Red Land of the South

Indigenous Kinship in D'Arcy McNickle's *Runner in the Sun*

D'ARCY MCNICKLE WAS A TIRELESS advocate for American Indian self-determination as an employee of the Bureau of Indian Affairs (BIA) and a founding member of the National Congress of American Indians (NCAI) in the early 1940s. In the early 1950s, he also raised funds for and founded American Indian Development Inc. (AID), a community development organization. Dorothy Parker describes the AID approach: "Participants devoted the first week to a discussion of basic problems encountered by everyone who lived on Indian reservations. They were often surprised to discover how many difficulties they shared with other Indian groups. [...] During the second week the focus shifted to identifying the options available for dealing with some of those problems. They learned how other communities, facing similar problems, worked together to develop effective programs."[1] As the author of *The Surrounded*, which holds a canonical place in American Indian literary studies, as well as a second novel, *Runner in the Sun*, and several works of nonfiction published during his lifetime, McNickle is also the principal literary bridge between the progressive era, in which he was born in 1904, and the American Indian civil rights era, during which he died in 1977. It is, therefore, predictable and appropriate to complete this study's discussion of the middle decades of the twentieth century with a consideration of McNickle's contribution to American Indian writing about Mexico and his role in the development of a potentially revolutionary indigenous American transnational imaginary.

Rather than a touchstone author, however, the McNickle of *The Red Land to the South* is one in a chorus of many American Indian literary voices from the interwar and early contemporary era. He follows other American Indian authors to Mexico and with them finds an Indian country in Mexico with strong historical, cultural, and political ties to the north. This study's focus on Mexico establishes deeper literary and political links among McNickle and the other writers of the era. Todd Downing in *The Mexican Earth* implies a kinship among indigenous Mexicans and American Indians and practices an American Indian diplomacy, while McNickle honors this diplomatic relationship in *Runner in the Sun* and makes indigenous Mexican/American Indian kinship explicit. The recurring affirmation of this kinship is a crucial component of the creation of a new, peaceful, healthy indigenous community in the novel.

McNickle was born at the mission town of St. Ignatius on the Flathead Reservation in Montana in 1904, two years after Downing was born in Atoka, Choctaw Nation, Indian Territory, and five years after Lynn Riggs. McNickle's mother was from a Métis community at Batoche on the Saskatchewan River in present-day Saskatchewan. The Métis fought the Canadian government for legal title to their lands, and following the Riel rebellion of 1885, Riel sympathizers Isidore and Judith Parenteau, McNickle's grandfather and grandmother, fled to St. Ignatius in what was then still Montana Territory. McNickle's mother, Philomene, was with them; she was three years old. As a young adult in 1899, Philomene married McNickle's father, William James McNickle, whose parents were Irish immigrants. When the government compiled the tribal rolls for allotment in 1905, Philomene McNickle and her three children were adopted by the Confederated Tribes of the Flathead Reservation (Bitterroot Salish, Kootenai, Pend d'Oreille) and assigned eighty-acre parcels of land. McNickle attended the mission school at St. Ignatius until 1913 and then the Salem Indian Training School in Chemawa, Oregon, until 1916. After high school first in Washington and then back in Montana, he enrolled at Montana State University in 1921. Downing and Riggs were at the University of Oklahoma at the time, and John Joseph Mathews had just graduated. Similarly to Downing, who wrote for the *Oklahoma Daily* as an undergraduate and, after earning his MA, served as the business manager and a book reviewer for *Books Abroad*, McNickle served on the editorial staff of a periodical, *Frontier: A Literary Magazine*. He left for Oxford in 1925 before graduating from Montana State, but after only a few months went to Paris and then back to New York. His ten-year stay in New York overlapped with Downing's arrival; like Downing, these were the years in which McNickle began to devote himself more seriously to his writing. He started the novel that became *The Surrounded* in the late 1920s, and after many rejections and revisions, had the novel accepted in December of 1935 and published in February of 1936.[2] Work with the Federal Writers Project in Washington, D.C., in 1935 led to a job offer from the BIA immediately after *The Surrounded* was released.[3]

During this same period of the mid-1930s, he also wrote a biographical piece on William Gates for the *National Cyclopedia of American Biography* and exchanged four letters with the anthropologist. Gates's specialty was Mayan language and culture. As Parker explains, McNickle's first letter to Gates included the veiled proposal that he could "[do] some kind of translation or interpretation of Mayan material."[4] Despite the brevity of their correspondence, Parker argues that "it reveals the direction of D'Arcy's thoughts about the essential nature of Indian-white conflict."[5] Thus Mexico and specifically the Mayans occupy a foundational place in McNickle's developing views of a conflict between two groups with distinct worldviews trying, often unsuccessfully, to communicate.

McNickle published the novel *Runner in the Sun: A Story of Indian Maize* in 1954, the same year in which Riggs succumbed to cancer in his lungs, stomach, and throat.[6] According to historian Donald Fixico, that year also "marked the climax of the termination years when a deluge of termination bills, affecting many tribal groups, flooded Congress."[7] Those tribal nations included McNickle's own Confederated Salish and Kootenai. Like many other authors of this period, McNickle was born into a tribal-national world dramatically shaped by allotment. As historian Daniel Cobb explains, the U.S. Congress passed the Flathead Allotment Act in the year of McNickle's birth. The act, Cobb argues, "destroyed the reservation, leaving tribal members with only a fifth of the original land base and opening much of the rest to non-Native homesteaders."[8] He continues, "Whites flooded in to lay claim to the rich interior farmlands along the Jocko River, forcing Salish-Kootenai peoples to marginally productive areas at the base of the majestic Bitterroot Mountains and Mission Range. McNickle later recalled that he came of age at a time when the federal government attempted to "rip the guts out" of Native communities by annihilating tribal cultures and undermining traditional social, religious, and political institutions—a process he graphically depicted in his 1936 semiautobiographical novel, *The Surrounded*.[9] Like his contemporary Riggs, McNickle sold his allotment to pay for his education, specifically at Oxford.[10] McNickle feared that termination would prove equally destructive, and as a powerful member of the NCAI he fought vigorously against the policy.

The publication of *Runner in the Sun* was fourteen years removed from 1940, when McNickle, along with Mathews, attended the first Inter-American Congress on Indian Life in Patzcuaro, Michoacan, Mexico.[11] John Collier, who participated in the planning for the congress in 1938 at the Eighth International Conference of American States in Lima, Peru, refers to McNickle and Mathews by tribal nation rather than name in his report on the conference published in *Indians at Work*: "Our Indian delegates, named by the Secretary of the Interior, represented the Papagos, the Jicarilla and San Carlos Apaches, Isleta Pueblo, Santa Clara Pueblo, Taos Pueblo, the Hopi tribes, the Flatheads and the Osages; and none did better work than they."[12] McNickle authored "La Re-edificatión del gobierno tribal bajo la ley de reorganización," a piece on the Indian Reorganization Act, as part of the U.S. delegation's contribution to the conference.[13] The materials either submitted or presented by representatives of the United States include an eighty-page coauthored piece called "Indians and the Land" and Felix S. Cohen's "The Legal Status of the Indian in the United States" as well as, in Spanish, short works on the Sun Dance, the BIA, the Cherokees, and the economic rehabilitation of Native Alaskan communities.[14]

McNickle, Mathews, and the representatives from the seven other American Indian tribal communities witnessed the meeting of prominent figures in federal Indian policy in Mexico and the United States, as well as from the rest of the hemisphere. In the diary he kept while in Mexico, Mathews reports meeting Collier, who was apparently displeased that Mathews arrived late, as well as BIA officials Walter Woehlke and Allan Harper. He also roomed with future BIA commissioner William Brophy. In the entry from Sunday, April 20, he notes, "With D'Arcy McNickle, Woelke, and Kirchoff, whom I recognized today, to the municipal building to attend a Posada. Native dances, and much fun. I can't get all the confetti out of my pants-cuffs, my pockets, my hair."[15] McNickle and Mathews, two of the most prominent American Indian writers in the mid-twentieth century, therefore had at least one opportunity to converse about what American Indians could learn from indigenous Mexicans and Mexican Indian policy.

While American Indians and indigenous Mexicans contributed to the conference, the program was dominated by non-Natives. Lázaro Cárdenas, in the final months of his presidency, gave an opening address titled "Los Indígenas: Factores de Progreso." Natividad Gutiérrez describes the conference as an expression of "a new form of indigenism":

John Joseph Mathews

Pátzcuaro, Michoacan.
April 19, 1940.

Dibbers,

I have just now realized that I have been gone from home a
week. It seems very much more like a month. I have virtually
been on the fly. I stopped in Mexico City long enough to
read my mail (two letters from you), and then after a nights
rest, left for Patzcuaro, arriving yesterday.

Collier was very busy, running about, when I reported, and
he seemed abrupt and a little cool. I am not sure whether it
was coolness due to my delayed arrival, or whether he was so
preoccupied that he was scarcely conscious of me. The latter
possibility is certainly in harmony with his nature. But, what
ever the reason, it makes no difference to me. If there is not
some recognition of my presence by tomorrow, I shall leave for
Guadalajara and Mazatlan for a visit to these places, since I
am so near. Conferences of this sort give me a slight belly-ache
any way. I sat all the morning in the Socio-Economico Section,
and my mind went back to the days in Geneva, when I listened to
the delegates to the League of Nations. Each Nation with his
own little axe to grind coupled with personal ambitions.

This morning Mexico proposed the establishment of Indian Credit
Banks, and Peru and Chile wanted none of them, and later Ecuador
joined in. It later developed that one of the Chileans was a
private banker, etc, etc, ############# ad nauseum. Mexico, under
the leadership of the mass-leader, Toledano, is attempting to
run the Socio-Economico #### show and get the other delegates to
accept the principles of the "Plan Sesenal" (The Six Year Plan
of Mexico) in solving the "Indian problem". However, I was very
much interested in the discussions, and sat from 9 a.m. until
2 p.m. listening.

Pátzcuaro is picture-bookish. One of the most interesting markets
I have seen, with ################# startling color filling a
spacious Plaza. The Indians are the Tarascans; the tribe of the
present President, Cardenas. Leading to this village on the lake
is one of the best roads in Mexico. Roads were needed elswhere
in Mexico of course. Oaxaca has no communication with the outside world except by a rather uncertain narrow-gage railroad---
Oaxaca, one of the treasure houses of the Nation, yet this road
---this almost perfect road must be built to a little village
on a lake.

A little Tarascan boy became president of his country, and the
road therefore is a Tarascan dream. And, I approve.

Love,

Jo

P.S. ____ d letters to the Carltan ____ you hear from
me to the contrary. J/M.

Figure 4.1. John Joseph Mathews attended the first Inter-American Congress on Indian
Life in Patzcuaro, Michoacan, Mexico, April 18–25, 1940. In this letter to Elizabeth Hunt
dated April 19, 1940, Mathews expresses irritation at BIA Commissioner John Collier's
tepid welcome. He also identifies President Lázaro Cárdenas as Tarascan (P'urhépecha),
an indigenous people in Michoacan, though Cárdenas was a mestizo in Mexican social and
racial contexts. After several days, Mathews became more excited about the conference.
Courtesy of the Western History Collections, University of Oklahoma Libraries, John
Joseph Mathews Collection, box 1, folder 13.

"The Indians were now to be regarded as potential promoters of development rather than mere obstacles to modernization."[16] This revised indigenism, she explains, "[assumed] that integration was to be encouraged, while at the same time respecting the 'race,' 'consciousness,' and 'identity' of the Indian peoples."[17] The excerpts Collier published in the August 1941 *Indians at Work* from the "Acta Final," "the authorized version of all the resolutions and actions taken at the Inter-American Conference," confirm Gutiérrez's general assessment of the conference's politics.[18] A *New York Times* article on the conference interpreted, perhaps with some suspicion, the contemporary status of indigenous Mexicans as auspicious: "In Mexico, with its leftist reform program, Indianism has been an increasingly popular political movement since the Revolution of 1910, and under President Cardenas the Indian has become the only privileged class in the nation."[19] The author comments that, in contrast, "The Indian cult in the United States has assumed chiefly a cultural pattern, since the proportion of the aborigine to the white population is so small."[20] An Inter-American Indian Institute was also formed at the conference by founders including the indigenistas Manual Gamio and John Collier, who, Parker observes, "had dreamed for years about creating such a body."[21] Gamio was the institute's first director. Goals of the congress and the institute consist of cooperation between member governments on the formulation of Indian policy as well as a commitment to supporting indigenous peoples, histories, and cultures.

McNickle maintained his interest in indigenous peoples in Mexico and elsewhere in the hemisphere following the congress. He was appointed the "mandated Indian member" and later served as the director of the National Indian Institute (NII), the U.S. branch of the organization, and published at least three articles in *América Indígena*, the organization's journal.[22] The first two of these articles describe and express dismay at the policy of termination, while the third provides an overview of the culture areas in the United States before again discussing the dangers of termination. He also attended the second and fourth Inter-American Indian Institute Conferences in Cuzco, Peru, in 1949 and Guatemala City in 1959.[23] The focus of *They Came Here First* (1949), his sweeping history of indigenous America, is primarily north of Mexico, but he emphasizes several times the trade routes that connect Mexico to the north. He is also careful to emphasize that indigenous agriculture, and especially maize, has its origins in Mexico. *They Came Here First* was published in the same year that McNickle appeared before the House Appropriations Committee to defend the NII.[24]

McNickle's visit to Mexico occurred during a busy season of conferences that took him in 1939 and 1940 to Minneapolis, Billings, Carson City, Phoenix, and Toronto, according to historian Thomas Cowger.[25] The seeds of the NCAI were planted during these conferences. That it is to Mexico that McNickle's characters travel in his novel suggests that he also saw rich possibilities in Mexican federal Indian policy and contemporary indigenous life in that nation. As the NCAI, the influential and successful intertribal organization that he helped to found, approached its tenth anniversary during a confrontation with the federal government over termination, McNickle returns to Mexico again—this time imaginatively and narratively. *Runner in the Sun* is a reimagined Inter-American Congress on Indian Life with indigenous people exclusively as the actors. In addition to a narrative model of the peaceful establishment of new, healthy American Indian nations, it is an emphatic appropriation of indigenismo and an equally emphatic assertion of autonomous indigenous political expression. It also recovers the region from the U.S. Southwest to central Mesoamerica as a Greater Indigenous Mexico.

"Be Friendly" and "Show No Fear"

While Downing's American Indian diplomacy in *The Mexican Earth* implies a kinship among American Indians and indigenous Mexicans, McNickle is preoccupied with kinship in general and with a specific U.S. Southwest/Mesoamerica relationship in particular in *Runner in the Sun*.[26] McNickle develops a direct link between the recognition and cultivation of this kinship relationship with Mesoamerica and the social and political health of Native communities in what is now the United States. McNickle, similarly to Gerald Vizenor in his quincentennial era novel *The Heirs of Columbus* (1991), makes indigenous Mexico in *Runner in the Sun* a crucial component in the founding of a new Native community following a natural disaster: drought in *Runner* and a thunderstorm in *Heirs*. The kinship in McNickle's novel, like the diplomacy in Downing's *The Mexican Earth*, has roots in the land and the cultivation of maize. McNickle asserts the strength and legitimacy of American Indian communities and nations with deep roots in the land and oral histories. This assertion occurs within a historical context in which tribal nationhood is once again, following just over a decade of federal policy under the Indian Reorganization Act, under attack—this time by termination and relocation legislation. By demonstrating that the recognition of intertribal kinship contributes to the peaceful establishment of new indigenous communities, McNickle critiques the violent nationalism that motivates military, religious, and economic aggression in the quest for dominance. His novel is a guide to Native community relationships that preserve the social and political integrity of Native communities and reject all violations of it. When viewed from mid-twentieth- and early twenty-first-century perspectives, these relationships register as transnational, too, in exclusively indigenous as well as settler-colonial contexts.

Runner in the Sun tells the story of Salt, a young man from a cliff-dwelling community north of Chaco Canyon in what is now northwestern New Mexico. His community, the Village of the White Rocks, which McNickle might have imagined as Mesa Verde in what is now southwestern Colorado, is threatened by increasingly smaller yields of corn, the loss of its water source, and internal discord.[27] The community's leader, the Holy One, chooses Salt to journey to Culhuacan in central Mexico. The Holy One explains, "I can only tell you that somewhere in the south lies a land our fathers called the Land of Fable. We know nothing about it, but we are told that our songs, our dances, and our Mother Corn came from there."[28] The Holy One's explanation of the relationship between White Rocks and Culhuacan foregrounds the way that the land and what it produces, in addition to the beliefs and traditions that emerge as a result of the central presence that corn has in indigenous American life, bind these communities together.

McNickle's strategy recalls Downing's approach in *The Mexican Earth*, in which Downing presents corn as the common parent of the Mexicas, the Muskogeans, and the Iroquois. The kinship that the Holy One proposes also has roots in the land rather than blood or biology: "Mother Corn" is the common ancestor of the people in the Land of Fable and in the Village of the White Rocks.[29] There is biological kinship, albeit a distant one, and it is more important to the Holy One that the residents of the Village of the White Rocks and central Mexico sustain themselves with the same product—Mesoamerican maize. Once he arrives in Culhuacan, Salt tells Quail, a young woman designated as a sacrifice to Mother Corn: "Corn! I came to find corn."[30] He then adds, "I have come to find the Mother Corn from which ours came."[31] Salt's people have migrated to a geographically

distant region, and human memory no longer retains a sense of that homeland. Communal memory has become fable, but the connection between
the two peoples maintains in the single word that Salt uses to describe his
journey. Similarly to his reorientation of kinship to a shared history in the
land rather than a shared genetic inheritance, McNickle demonstrates a
connection between fable and nationhood that is much different than
the connection between the two for the Spanish and its conquistadors.
The stories about the Land of Fable promise survival for the people of
White Rocks rather than the wealth promised by the fable of the Seven
Cities of Gold that some Spaniards, such as Francisco Vásquez de
Coronado, pursued in the Southwest.

These ties of history and tradition do not imply a pan-Indian hemisphere
in the fourteenth or fifteenth centuries. Instead, McNickle celebrates indigenous American people committed to the "ethic of respect for particularity
and sameness" that defines intertribalism.[32] The Village of the White Rocks
is a community with a clearly defined territory and political organization
and only limited contact with other indigenous communities. However,
Salt practices an indigenous citizenship that values intertribal sociality,
acknowledges both a kinship with near and distant neighbors and a shared
history in the land, and respects the boundaries and beliefs of other indigenous communities. McNickle contrasts Salt's intertribal practice explicitly
to Mexican imperialism in the central Valley of Mexico and implicitly to the
federal policy of termination in the 1950s. The novel imagines in indigenous
American kinship an antidote to the kind of nationalism that motivates military aggression, land seizure, and genocide and all that follows these acts of
violence in a colonial context: the denial of basic human rights; the denial
of political, cultural, and educational sovereignty; and the persistence of
the many forms of racial terrorism. Salt's goal on his journey is to save his
people, not to discover new worlds to dominate. His people will not survive
at the expense of others.

Corn plays a central role in McNickle's demonstration of an intertribal
kinship with literal roots in the land. In addition to her role as common
ancestor, Mother Corn is the source of the cultural value of peaceful relations. After the novel's villain Dark Dealer takes control of White Rocks by
stopping the flow of the village's spring, Trailing Cloud lectures him: "You
must know, since you were born among us, that when our Mother Corn
came to our elders, we were told to keep peace in our minds and in all
our actions. Those who remember this and live accordingly will never be

destroyed."[33] The corn on which Salt's community relies has been isolated from other varieties for so long that the yields are smaller each year, and McNickle connects this weakening of the corn to the animosity and violence between clans in the village. In addition, the Holy One tells Salt: "A field of corn is like a village of people—so my father would say. If people stay too long among themselves, they weaken themselves, some families die out entirely. He encouraged young men from other villages to come among us, marry our girls, and become part of us. He also encouraged our men to go elsewhere to find wives. On your journey south, you will find some of our people." After he establishes the necessity and even urgency of a perpetually renewed kinship with the people to the south, he adds, "A race of corn will become weak in the same way. No man among us can say how long we have had our corn. It has been too long."[34] The Holy One asserts a similarity, though not quite an equivalence, between the life of a field of corn and the life of a human village.

The Holy One's comparison of corn fields to villages conveys a lesson in social responsibility within and without one's community. The health and stability of each community requires the organized, permanent immigration of young men between villages. This shared descent from Mother Corn makes possible, therefore, a kind of social interaction between related people that without contradiction has deep roots in the land and can adapt to different environments and recover from natural and social disasters. Salt's village has central Mexican roots, as represented by the central Mexican corn that they plant every year to sustain themselves. At the same time, by migrating from central Mexico and transplanting central Mexican corn, Salt's village establishes new roots. The village has simultaneously both one origin—central Mexico—and two origins—central Mexico and, perhaps, Mesa Verde. However, there is no hierarchy of origins. These origins exist in a lateral relationship to each other.

At the same time that McNickle connects the health of the corn fields to the health of the village, he correlates the health of the village to the willingness of its residents to balance honoring origins with the necessity of renewing and adapting traditions. McNickle's concern for the Village of the White Rock's social and political health in the novel coincides with one of his projects after he left the BIA in 1952. Dorothy Parker explains, "McNickle established a health education and community development project among the Navajos at Crownspoint, New Mexico. This project, which lasted from 1953 to 1960, was funded through the National Congress of American Indians (NCAI)."[35] In addition, as several scholars have noted, McNickle was writing the novel during the termination and relocation era.[36] If the novel is a response to either contemporary Native health crises or the threat of termination, then McNickle is urging American Indians to recognize that solutions can come from within their communities or, more specifically, from the deliberations of Native governing bodies.

The recognition of kinship with other indigenous communities is equally important and empowering. This recognition is at the foundation of Salt's model of self-determination that is not militant or defined by the desire to dominate. Before Salt leaves on his journey, the Holy One gives him two pieces of advice: "be friendly" and "show no fear."[37] As Salt travels from White Rocks to Culhuacan, he follows an unbroken path of kinship, although this kinship has many manifestations. Initially, he encounters friendly people, including some who speak his language and some from his own village. In response to their inquiries about his journey, Salt "thanked them for their kindness and remarked that he had a long way to go and must not delay."[38] Salt's willingness to decline hospitality early in the journey introduces one of the novels' primary lessons in international relations. The closer Salt is to home, the more flexibility he has about how much he follows social conventions of hospitality. The farther he is from home, however, the less flexibility he has: he must be more polite, more attentive to social conventions, more gracious in accepting hospitality. Leaving home is not a license to ignore rules about right action or to act, for example, violently.[39] The farther he travels, the more he must fulfill the ideals of his home village. In fact, before he leaves, readers see Salt negligent in the performance of some of his duties, such as attending to crops and arriving on time to meetings in his Turquoise Clan's kiva. The village tolerates this kind of negligence to a limited extent while Salt is at home, but the same kind of negligence would put him in grave danger while he is on the road.

Four days from White Rocks, then, Salt must become more accommodating to his hosts. After he arrives at another village, McNickle explains, "Salt found the people of his village and was made welcome, as if he had been a younger brother. He must stay to be feasted. Indeed, he was feasted by each of the headmen in turn."[40] Delaying his journey directly benefits Salt, for the imminent summer rains to the south make travel dangerous. However, McNickle uses the coincidence of right action (accepting hospitality) with safety (avoiding the storms) to remind readers of the correlation between good international relations and the health of Salt's community. That is, any mistake by Salt threatens to leave White Rocks without the gifts with which Salt might return. After fulfilling these social obligations, a clan leader sends his own son, River Fighter, "to accompany Salt as far as certain kinsmen living many days' journey to the south."[41] After four days of travel, Salt still finds himself with kin—he is their "younger brother," and they even live on the same corn that Salt and his people do at White Rocks. The journey from White Rocks involves travel from a home but also through a homeland. It is also not a journey away from family.

Once River Fighter returns to his people, Salt continues, like Downing in *The Mexican Earth*, to practice the art of friendly international relations. When he sees shrines by the paths that he follows, "he never failed to take up a rock from the roadside, breathe upon it, and, as taught him in childhood, lay it atop the pile."[42] McNickle observes, "This practice, unwittingly on his part, had several times saved his life. Men of strange tribes had followed him, distrusting him as they distrusted any stranger. [...] They saw him perform his act of grace; thereafter he went on unmolested."[43] There is more in these passages than the glaring contrast between Salt's worship at the shrines of geographically distant indigenous communities and the violence of what George Tinker calls the "missionary conquest" of the Americas.[44] Salt's actions are not calculated to keep himself safe. Instead, he acts "unwittingly"; he worships because he has been taught that it is right to do so. Respect for foreign religious beliefs in the context of intertribal relationships is a social ideal that Salt succeeds in practicing.

Even when the world begins to look more unfamiliar and "alien" to Salt, he finds kinship with other people.[45] The first large, foreign city that Salt reaches is Culiacan, through which Coronado passed in the sixteenth century on his way north toward the indigenous cities of New Mexico.[46] Upon Salt's arrival in the city of Culiacán, which is now in northwestern Mexico in the state of Sinaloa, two men lead him to a judge-priest and his two assistants. Following several failed attempts to find someone who speaks Salt's language, a woman speaks to him in his own language, though "with a strange accent," and explains that the judge-priest suspects Salt of being a spy. Salt tells the woman his story carefully. He situates himself geographically in the north and cosmologically as a member of the Turquoise Clan protected by the gods. The judge-priest accepts Salt's explanation, and the woman leads Salt home: "She took him to her house. [...] She gave orders, and the children brought cook pots, blew life into the fire in the outdoors cooking place, and fetched articles of clothing. That was like his mother." While the woman washes his hair, Salt thinks, "This too was like being home again. Surely he was now safe with these people."[47] The Turquoise Clan then makes him an "honored guest" at a feast.[48] Salt's experience of kinship has shifted from the biological relationship he had with his earliest hosts to the linguistic kinship with Yucca Flower Woman and the cosmological clan kinship with the judge-priest of Culiacan. No one kind of kinship is more important than the other; there are all kinds of families and family obligations in the indigenous world that McNickle depicts.

Voluntary acculturation can also be the first step toward establishing a new kinship relationship. Salt's next stop is the city of Tzintzuntzan, where he meets a young man named Ocelot at the edge of Lake Patzcuaro. McNickle had been a visitor here as well in 1940 at the Inter-American Congress on Indian Life, and Downing notes that the Tarascan capital city "had one of the most beautiful names in Mexico: Tzintzuntzan—the sound of the hummingbird's wings."[49] During this initial meeting, Salt decides to learn the language of his new friend, and he begins the process immediately by asking Ocelot the names of his boat and fish. The scene is brief, but within the context of the entire narrative, Salt's behavior is part of a broad pattern of acting according to the idea that everyone is or could be family. The world in Tzintzuntzan and in central Mexico more broadly is much different than White Rocks. There is class stratification and an economy in which men have specialized skills. To Salt, the religious ceremonies are large and "solemn spectacles."[50] Though this world is unfamiliar and intimidating, "Salt [. . .] became a member of a family."[51] McNickle emphasizes later the development of this familial relationship: "[Salt] and Ocelot had come to be as close as brothers."[52] Ocelot takes Salt on the final leg of the journey to Culhuacan, where the two boys stay with Tula, a friend of Ocelot's family. Thus Salt is with family from the geographic beginning to the geographic end of his journey. A map of the route Salt takes on his journey would represent a long branch—spatial and temporal—of a single indigenous family. The kinship network is unbroken between these two places.

However, there are people in, between, and around both places, White Rocks and Culhuacan, who do not recognize this kinship. Discord fomented by Dark Dealer within the community at White Rocks motivates Salt's journey, and White Rocks faces raids on their corn fields by neighboring nations. Yet the recognition of kinship is necessary for the maintenance of individual, communal, national, and international health. By refusing to practice the ideals of peaceful relations at all levels of social interaction, people like Dark Dealer figuratively, and perhaps literally, leave the family. In central Mexico, as Salt learns from Tula, an entire region has come under the control of people like Dark Dealer. The fact of kinship does not guarantee peace, though the careful, sincere practice of it does.

McNickle demonstrates that a disregard for kinship correlates to a disregard for human life in his depiction of Quail, the young slave woman of Culhuacan that Salt and Ocelot save from sacrifice. Salt tells Quail, "Here you will never have your own life. You will have no family, no people of your own."[53] Proximity to one's homeland does not guarantee that one has a family or, even, a home. Although Salt is the traveler and Quail is from central Mexico, Salt is more at home: he is with family. Quail must travel with Salt back to White Rocks to find a home, to find welcome as kin. Following Salt's suggestion that she does not have any family, their conversation turns to the corn that Salt seeks. Quail sings a song about Mother Corn for Salt, and when Salt helps her to escape, she brings this corn with her. The corn is the primary connection that she has to her home, just as it is Salt's primary connection to both central Mexico and White Rocks. Upon their return to White Rocks, the Holy One says, "We will call her Red Corn Woman, honoring the south, which sent her to us. With this name we make her one of us, and her strength will be ours."[54] The entire community then accepts her as a new member of the family. When White Rocks finally must move to new land, they do so without displacing another community. The corn grows abundantly, and in the new land they develop a new ceremony, the Red Corn Dance. Peace has been reestablished, and it is Salt's recognition of his kinship with everyone on his journey that makes it a success.

McNickle correlates this peace explicitly to the village's reconnection, through the corn, Quail / Red Corn Woman, and the Red Corn Dance, with their central Mexican homeland. Peace within the context of the novel emerges from the recognition of the correlation between kinship, community health, and the practice of good international relations. The development of this kinship / community health / international diplomacy complex requires McNickle to eschew the predominant fascination with the Aztecs or Mexicas. Salt does not journey to Tenochtitlan but to Culhuacan, which was founded at the beginning of the tenth century CE by Mixcoatl, or Cloud Serpent.[55] On his way there, Salt passes through

Tenayuca, which was founded in 1244 CE by Xolotl, or Monster, who also conquered Culhuacan in 1246 CE.[56] He travels through Atzcapotzalco, a Tepenac city that initially recognized Xolotl's rule before it became in the fourteenth and early fifteenth centuries the region's dominant power: Atzcapotzalco, led by Tezozomoc, conquered Tenayuca and Culhuacan.[57] Meyer and Sherman explain, "Through politics of terror, Tezozómoc had succeeded in unifying under one government most of central Mexico."[58] This description of central Mexico in the fourteenth and early fifteenth centuries parallels McNickle's description of the world through which Salt travels. When Salt asks Tula for advice about the rest of his journey, Tula responds: "It is the Valley of Mexico of which you speak. A sorry land it is. Once the gods smiled upon it, and in gratitude the people built temples, cities of stone. If you go, you will see all these, but you will see them in ruins. Jaguars come out of the hills and walk the ruined streets. Thieves and murderers too roam the streets. What was once great is so no more."[59] Tula's description of the Valley of Mexico as a "sorry land" suggests that Salt has arrived during this era of struggle among rival urban centers. At the same time, McNickle challenges the sense of Mexica exceptionalism that permeates conventional histories of indigenous Mexico. The Mexicas were simply the people in power when Cortez arrived in 1519. In addition, as McNickle suggests, empires always have their internal critics, such as Tula.

Tula's people, in fact, had once been the region's most powerful. He tells Salt, "My name is the name of my race."[60] Tula is, therefore, a Toltec, the founders of the city from which Tula takes his name. Tula refers to this homeland as "a great dead city."[61] Meyer and Sherman relate that after Mixcoatl's brother assassinated him, his pregnant wife escaped and gave birth to a son, Ce Acatl Topiltzin, or One Reed / Our Prince. When Ce Acatl Topiltzin was a young man, he killed his father's assassin, his uncle, and became the Toltec ruler. "Topiltzin-Quetzalcóatl eventually removed his capital some fifty miles northwest of the present Mexico City to a remote site on the frontier," Meyer and Sherman explain. "There, around A.D. 968, he founded the splendid city of Tula, the most important city in the long interim between the fall of Teotihuacán and the later rise of Aztec Tenochtitlán."[62] As the leader of Tula, Ce Acatl Topiltzin became known as Topiltzin-Quetzalcóatl: "According to tradition, Topiltzin-Quetzalcóatl, as the great leader of infinite knowledge, showed his people how to plant the 'miraculous' corn, and under his tutelage all cultivated plant life yielded produce of gigantic size. [. . .] The ruler was also responsible for writing, the ritual calendar, and the architectural wonders of Tula."[63] Tula and the Toltecs, however, experienced the same threats, though on a much larger scale, as the Village of the White Rocks: "From the late eleventh century to 1156, drought and famine struck the Toltecs. Wars further weakened the state until, in desperation, the people even turned to the worship of their enemies' alien deities."[64] The histories of Culhuacan and Tula, including in the latter a fratricide and the retaliatory murder of an uncle, demonstrate the potential consequences of valuing political and military power over kinship. Tula and Culhuacan fall to other powers as the violence in their own histories turns against them.

Peace, therefore, is only a memory to Salt's new friend. At his ancestral city, Tula says, the god Quetzalcoatl came to them. He tells Salt, in passages that precisely follow Toltec history, "I cannot tell you everything that came to us through Quetzalcoatl. I only say this, that the breath which is life, which is seen as a feather on the face of still water, and again in the movement of the Evening Star through the night sky—that is Quetzalcoatl. The least thing, and at once the greatest also. Through his help, our people learned to write upon paper and upon stone. They were told about corn, our Mother."[65] Tula continues, "Quetzalcoatl [. . .] is not fashionable now. [. . .] We now have coming from all corners of the world, it seems, a race of men who have neither reason nor shame. [. . .] These later comers, these men without reason and without shame, are devouring our people. You tell me that your small village is faced with destruction. What if I should tell you that my country, great as it is in people and in land, is destroying itself!"[66] While the Quetzalcoatl religion required only the small blood sacrifice from the scratch of a thorn, the new religion requires human sacrifice: "They turn the simple ceremonies of our fathers into spectacles of horror."[67] Tula's narrative blames a foreign race of men for what occurred in his people's home city, though historically what Meyer and Sherman call "dissident factions" at Tula overthrew Topiltzin-Quetzalcoatl and his religion in favor of Tezcatlipoca, "the ancestral supreme deity of the Toltecs [. . .] [who] demanded human hearts."[68] Now in central Mexico, new corn requires the decapitation of a young woman; corn has become connected not with peace but with death. Like Todd Downing in *The Mexican Earth*, Tula is awaiting the return of peace in the form of Quetzalcoatl.

McNickle appears to combine the fall of Topiltzin-Quetzalcoatl and his exile to the Yucatán in the late tenth century with the collapse of Tula in the twelfth century and the rise of the Mexicas in the early fifteenth. The Mexicas begin to assert their influence in Anáhuac ("near the water"), the Valley of Mexico, following the waning of Atzcapotzalco's power, and they formed what is called the Triple Alliance of their own city, Tenochtitlan, with Texcoco and Tlacopan, in 1428.[69] Salt passes through Tlacopan as well as two cities to its south, Chapultepec and Coyoacan, and he crosses Lake Xochimilco, which separates Coyoacan from Culhuacan. After establishing this alliance, the empire began to grow. However, Salt's destination is Culhuacan, not Tenochtitlan. Therefore, the most likely setting for the novel is prior to the ascendancy of the Mexicas or during it in the early fifteenth century.

McNickle situates the novel in this early fifteenth-century context, or more specifically in the 1420s and 1430s of emerging Aztecan or Mexican imperialism, in order to position Salt's journey as explicitly anti-imperial. White Rocks does not face the threat of conquest by an emerging empire, but Dark Dealer's actions are a microcosm of the process that might lead to their village becoming one. McNickle suggests that the violence that Dark Dealer commits against, for example, Elder Woman, is the kind of affront to family and life that when embraced collectively drives the violent excesses of imperialism and colonialism. Historians call the era in which Salt is traveling in central Mexico the postclassic or historical period. One of the characteristics of this period, according to Meyer and Sherman, is, following a period with little warfare, "the emergence of conquest states."[70] This description corresponds to what Tula says about the region. Central Mexico needs healing, that is, renewal, too: their corn, their life has grown weak with violence. Central Mexico represents a possible future for Salt's village, and the renewal of the White Rocks community without the proliferation of violence shows what central Mexico could have avoided. Perhaps the exodus of Salt's people was a result of this kind of intertribal and interfamily fighting in central Mexico.

Thus McNickle uses a specifically indigenous American context to critique imperialism. Tzintzuntzan registers as a particularly compelling example of this history of indigenous resistance to imperialism prior to the arrival of Europeans. The home city of Salt's ally Ocelot, which was also the site of the Inter-American Congress on Indian Life in 1940, successfully resisted an Aztec invasion in 1478. McNickle gives no indication that there has been an invasion of the city, which provides further evidence that the novel is set in the earlier fifteenth century. Salt, whose homeland is vulnerable to internal and external attacks, thus makes alliances with Ocelot, whose land will soon be invaded, and Tula, whose land has already been conquered. The meeting of these three young men ties together their shared and divergent histories and recreates the Inter-American Congress on Indian Life but as an exclusively indigenous event. The plan that emerges from the Inter-American Congress in *Runner in the Sun* involves affirming kinship, honoring intertribal nation differences, establishing intertribal nation coalitions, and resisting colonial and imperial violence.

The Missing Border: American Indian Maps of Indigenous Mexico

McNickle chose the celebrated Apache artist Allan Houser to illustrate his novel. McNickle met Houser, a Chiricahua Apache born Allyn Capron Haozous, in Utah in 1950, when Houser was teaching at the Inter-Mountain Indian School in Brigham Young, Utah.[71] Houser's drawings include a sketch at the beginning of each chapter and a map of the American Southwest and Mesoamerica. Leslie Marmon Silko, whose father, photographer Lee Marmon, did a photographic documentary on Houser in April 1991 titled *A Day with Allan Houser,* draws a straight line to indicate a border between the United States and Mexico in the map in her novel *Almanac of the Dead*.[72] In contrast, Houser's map, titled "Land of the Runner in the Sun," shows no borders between the two regions. Houser's choice reflects the pre-Columbian setting of the novel, though the map includes designations such as the Gulf of California and Pacific Ocean, and river names such as Colorado, Gila, Salt, Little Colorado, and Rio Grande. On Houser's map, however, the Rio Grande River stops flowing in what is now southern New Mexico. Instead, a drawing representing a scene in the novel occupies what would be New Mexico, Texas, and the northern states of Mexico. In this scene, Dark Dealer's men stop the flow of the village's spring while Salt watches from his hiding place. Thus Houser erases even the "natural" boundary, the river, between the two colonial nations. The only explicit border in the drawing is the stylized frame with a pattern of black squares like steps.

Houser's map complements McNickle's narrative about a world in which everyone is related in some way. When the Holy One begins to prepare Salt for his role in saving the village, he explains, "Three different times I have had a certain dream. Each time a sacred person talks about our village and tells me that our troubles will not be solved by ourselves alone, that we must go outside of ourselves to find help."[73] Yet this going "outside of ourselves" involves having the capacity and willingness to recognize that what is outside one's world—the village of White Rocks—is also a part of that world, that community, that family. Political and religious divisions, for example, are always a threat, though they can be resisted by foregrounding one's familial relationship with others. The failure to see this relationship is the first dangerous step toward community discord and violence, but the acceptance of a familial relationship with all people, with all one's relations, and a willingness

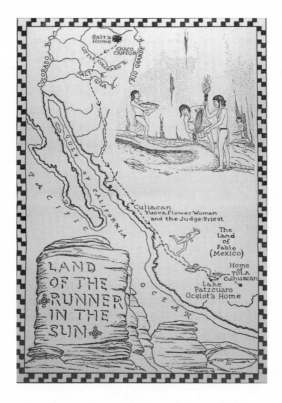

Figure 4.2. Allan Houser's illustration "Land of the Runner in the Sun" from the first edition of the novel shows no border between the U.S. Southwest and Mexico. On this map, Salt's home is northern Mesoamerica. Reproduction of the image used by permission of Chinde LLC. Photo by Johannah Hochhalter.

to fulfill all the obligations to maintain it, collapses all distances—of geography, language, religion—and ensures the health or healing of a community.[74]

Salt embodies a kinship and diplomatic ideal that many if not most readers will struggle to reconcile to the real-world U.S.–Mexican borderlands. Houser's drawings for the novel indicate that he read it very carefully, but McNickle's idealism must have challenged him, too. Similarly to McNickle's mother's family, Houser's father's family members lived a bi–settler colonial nation life as they fled from U.S. and Mexican federal authorities. Houser's parents were Sam Haozous and Blossom Wratten. Barbara H. Perlman describes Houser's genealogy: "Sam Haozous traced his lineage to the Bedonkohe and Warm Springs-Mimbreños bands. [. . .] His father, Goonah-hleenah, was a member of the Warm Springs-Mimbreños Apaches and great-grandson of the important Bedonkohe chief Mahko. Sam, a nephew of Geronimo, never knew his father [. . .] Sam's mother, Nah-ke-de-sah, was a daughter of the hereditary chief Mangas Coloradas ('Red Sleeves' or 'Roan Shirt') and full sister of the chief's son, Mangus."[75] Perlman relates a story that the elder Haozous tells about Geronimo threatening people at Warm Springs with death if they did not leave the reservation with him. Geronimo led his men and the others from Warm Springs into Sonora, where Haozous recalls fighting with both the Mexican and U.S. armies.[76]

Following Geronimo's surrender at Skeleton Canon on September 4, 1886, more than five hundred Apaches, including Sam's father and mother, were imprisoned in Florida at either Fort Pickens or Fort Marion. After an initial relocation to Mount Vernon Barracks in Alabama, Perlman explains, "On October 4, 1894, the Chiricahuas were relocated again, this time to the Fort Sill Military Reserve in southwestern Oklahoma. By then, approximately three hundred remained of the more than five hundred Apaches sent to Florida in 1886."[77] Sam met Blossom, the daughter of the interpreter George Wratten and Annie White, a Chiracahua Apache, at Fort Sill, where they were married in 1910. They had two daughters while still in captivity, then Blossom gave birth to Allan on July 30, 1914, at Apache in Caddo County, Oklahoma. Perlman notes, "The baby, named for Army captain Allyn Capron, was one of the first Chiricahua children born in freedom, after the long captivity."[78] Thus Houser was born into a family and tribal-nation history in which Mexico promised possible refuge but also more danger. In addition, some of Houser's family members appear to have been unwilling participants in Geronimo's flight from the U.S. Army, while the U.S. Army had employed Apaches from various bands as scouts. The Haozous family's flight into Mexico, then, occurs in a context of deep familial and communal discord.

The sight of a young boy running south on Houser's map between Culiacan and Lake Patzcuaro evokes Salt but also Geronimo, Houser's parents, and the Warm Springs Apaches. It evokes as well Hugh Rennert and the many characters from Downing's fiction and the Crespo and Bodine families from Riggs's plays. It is a reminder, too, of Sequoyah, Downing, McNickle, Mathews, Riggs, and Will Rogers. Houser's map contains this southward movement within the drawing's frame and both the western coast of Mexico and the looming land formations that rise out of and dominate the Pacific Ocean. In the map by Howard Willard on the front and rear end papers of Downing's *The Mexican Earth*, the landscape appears a little more ominous from a mainstream political U.S. perspective. A pictorial representation of the founding of Tenochtitlan rises out of the Gulf of Mexico. An eagle perched atop a cactus holds a serpent in its mouth, and the serpent's mouth appears on the verge of striking in the region of Mississippi and Alabama. In the west, Quetzalcoatl occupies the Pacific Ocean. Willard includes a southern border of long and short dashes to California, Arizona, and New Mexico and traces the path of the Rio Grande, but the eastern coast of Texas and the entire U.S. Southeast are in maroon shadow. In both maps, the entire south is indigenous.

The path that Salt takes into indigenous Mexico is well worn. He moves along "a broad avenue." "The pounding feet of many generations of men had," McNickle writes, "kept it clear of growth, its direction certain. Here, trade and communication flourish."[79] McNickle, with Downing, Mathews, Riggs, Rogers, and many other indigenous Americans from the land that is now the United States, also traveled this broad avenue. Downing in particular but also Riggs were looking for their own figurative Red Corn Woman, or Red Corn Man, with which to return to the United States. Alfonso Ortiz retells what he calls "one of D'Arcy McNickle's favorite stories" in the afterword to the University of New Mexico Press edition of *Runner in the Sun*. McNickle taught a survey course on indigenous America in the Department of Anthropology at the University of Saskatchewan's Regina campus. Following the completion of the section on Mesoamerica, a Cree student disappeared for several weeks. McNickle learned that the student had become so fascinated with Mesoamerican architecture that he had hitchhiked to central Mexico and back to Regina. Ortiz insists that the story is not apocryphal. Nor is the content of the story anomalous. Whether as the source of desirable revolution through indigenous religious beliefs, language revitalization, agricultural practice, or the fieldworker's machete, or, on occasion and more conventionally, as a threatening, premodern presence on the southern border of the United States, indigenous Mexico occupies a powerful place in American Indian literary history. It also opens for early twenty-first-century readers a new avenue of inquiry running from the civil rights and renaissance era into the middle decades of the twentieth century. The avenue is broad, and its direction is certain. Whether diplomacy, trade, and communication flourish depends on remembering the path and cultivating kinship as one travels along it.

CHAPTER 5

The Return to Mexico

Gerald Vizenor and Leslie Marmon Silko
at the Quincentennial

GREATER INDIAN TERRITORY, AN INDIGENOUS American homeland that subsumes the settler-colonial nations of the United States
and Mexico, makes a dramatic return to American Indian literature in
1991 and expands into Canada, the Caribbean, and Central and South
America with the publication of Gerald Vizenor's *The Heirs of Columbus*
and Leslie Marmon Silko's *Almanac of the Dead*.[1] As celebrations of and
protests against the Columbian quincentennial approached, their novels
converged in an indigenous Mexico with the same revolutionary potential
that captured the imaginations of Todd Downing, Lynn Riggs, and D'Arcy
McNickle. McNickle's story of Salt, intratribal conflict at the Village of the
White Rocks, and the creation of a new community anticipates Vizenor's
story of Stone Columbus, intratribal conflict at the White Earth Reservation, and the creation of a new, sovereign nation. In McNickle's and
Vizenor's novels, indigenous Mexican bodies, and in *Heirs* Mayan texts, are
required components of the communal or national health of the people.
Silko's novel has a more direct revolutionary kinship with Riggs's Mexico
plays, as Craig Womack observes, and Downing's *The Mexican Earth*.[2]
While McNickle and Vizenor imagine imminent eras of peace generated
from within tribal communities and histories, Riggs, Downing, and Silko
envision armed indigenous revolution. This revolution is distinctly Mayan
for Riggs and Silko. His play ends with Mayans killing the hacendados of
Yucatán as Cárdenas land reforms begin; her novel ends with an enor-
mous army led by three Mayans approaching the Mexican–U.S. border in
fulfillment of the prophecy of an ancient Mayan codex or almanac. Silko
and Vizenor follow Downing, Riggs, and McNickle in appropriating an
indigenous Mexico with a perceived political strength and revolutionary

promise from which American Indians can draw. These shared visions of indigenous Mexico establish literary and political continuity between the writing of the twentieth century's middle decades and the renaissance.

These shared visions also constitute a point of convergence in the work of two first-generation renaissance writers whom scholars rarely pair with each other and, more often, whom they place in dramatic contrast. Silko is, with N. Scott Momaday, the most celebrated of the early renaissance fiction writers. Her novel *Ceremony* (1977) is a critical touchstone that receives an uninterrupted amount of attention from scholars of American Indian and American literatures. Robert Dale Parker captures the wonderful dilemma in which scholars find themselves when writing about *Ceremony*: they must read an imposing amount of secondary material.[3] PEN/Malamud, PEN/Faulkner, and National Book Award winner Sherman Alexie (Spokane and Coeur d'Alene), the most well-known and celebrated contemporary American Indian author, calls *Ceremony* "the greatest novel in Native American literature [. . .] [and] one of the greatest novels of any time and place," even though Spokane writer Gloria Bird uses it, as well as Momaday's *House Made of Dawn*, as the standard against which she condemns his own *Reservation Blues*.[4]

Vizenor is, in contrast, an anomalous and polarizing figure. He was involved in American Indian politics at local levels prior to and during the rise of Red Power in the 1960s as the executive director of the American Indian Employment and Guidance Center in Minneapolis, a staff writer covering contemporary American Indian life for the *Minneapolis Tribune*, and a board member of the Minneapolis chapter of the ACLU.[5] In editorials for the *Tribune* published in the early 1970s, he publicly expressed frustration with the tactics of the leaders of the American Indian Movement. However, he directs much of his criticism at the press, which covers the public confrontations but not the private negotiations that lead to institutional change. He also expresses some admiration of the American Indian Movement (AIM) leadership as well as some hope that the organization will develop more productive strategies.[6] While with the ACLU, Vizenor wrote and distributed pamphlets about the case of Thomas James White Hawk, a nineteen-year-old Dakota man condemned to death for killing a jeweler and raping the jeweler's wife in 1967.[7] The governor of South Dakota commuted White Hawk's death sentence in October 1969.[8] Vizenor's work is also more consistently tribal-nation specific than Silko's, and he contributed to the drafting of a new constitution for the

White Earth Band of Anishinabe. The constitution was ratified in April 2009.[9] However, the influence of poststructuralism and deconstruction on his idiosyncratic prose, in fictional and theoretical work, frustrates many scholars who would otherwise likely embrace the Anishinabe politics, history, and culture in which he embeds most of his writing. Even when he turns to Mexico, Vizenor centers his narrative within specific Anishinabe historical and cultural contexts.

Mayans at the Place of Stones

Vizenor's *The Heirs of Columbus* is a narrative of migration and the creation of a new, sovereign Anishinabe tribal nation with significant Mayan origins. Vizenor does not identify the region or language of the Mayan ancestors of the heirs, though they connect themselves to the Itza, a Mayan group that speaks Yucatecan.[10] The novel, which Vizenor sets in 1992, tells the story of an Anishinabe family descended from Samana, an Anishinabe hand talker or healer, and Christopher Columbus, the explorer and, in the novel, a descendant of Mayan adventurers to the Old World.[11] The protagonist Stone Columbus establishes a floating reservation in the boundary waters on the international border between Minnesota and Ontario on the Santa María, the Nína, and the Pinta, a casino, restaurant, and tax free market, respectively. He is married to Felipa Flowers, a former fashion model who poaches tribal human remains and ceremonial objects from museums and repatriates them and with whom he has a daughter named Miigis. The heirs, similarly to the people of Salt's clan in McNickle's *Runner in the Sun*, face the envy and suspicion of other tribal-nation citizens. After a storm destroys their reservation ships, Felipa Flowers becomes involved in attempts to repatriate medicine pouches and the remains of Columbus and Pocahontas. Immediately following her recovery of Pocahontas's remains in a small London church, Felipa is abducted and later found dead. Stone's grief and his frustration with reservation politicians motivate him to establish both a new tribal nation, Point Assinika, in the Strait of Georgia between Washington and Vancouver, and a new casino, again on the international border. The presence in the story of Mayans as well as indigenous Caribbean peoples and the Métis resistance leader Louis Riel links Native worlds in North America within a Greater Indian Territory, implies the possibility of a continent-wide indigenous coalition of tribal nations, effaces settler-colonial borders, and challenges the legal and political hegemony of settler-colonial nations.

Vizenor grounds the novel's support of Anishinabe sovereignty and cultural continuity in specific geographical, political, historical, and cosmological contexts. He sets the novel on the White Earth Reservation and at the headwaters of the Mississippi River. As in many contemporary American Indian novels, such as Sherman Alexie's *Reservation Blues* (1995) or Choctaw author LeAnne Howe's *Shell Shaker* (2001), the depiction of tribal leaders in *Heirs* is not flattering. Rather than invalidating White Earth sovereignty, however, the novel depicts the heirs of Columbus acting as citizens of White Earth, either on the Santa Maria Casino, in federal court, or at Point Assinika, to develop a model of sovereignty distinct from the practices of the tribal government. As Leech Lake Ojibwe scholar Scott Richard Lyons insists, "Like the *nation*, citizenship is a good x-mark to make; but like *sovereignty*, one must claim it in order to have it. As for the criteria used to grant it, I offer a simple maxim: *require what you want to produce*."[12] As citizens of White Earth and then Point Assinika, the heirs require, for themselves, an understanding of their Mayan heritage and, for others, a commitment to healing the people damaged by colonial and settler-colonial practice.

The heirs base the model for this sovereignty and citizenship on Anishinabe storytelling and ceremonial traditions. Sovereignty and citizenship are thus, in Vizenor's conception, at once indigenous transnational and tribal-nation specific. These Anishinabe traditions include the trickster Naanabozho, a particularly malevolent windigo, the Anishinabe story of origin and creation that Vizenor recounts in the novel's opening pages, and the midéwiwin ceremonies.[13] The midéwiwin society, explains Anishinabe scholar Basil Johnston, "refers to a society of medicine men and women that was formed to preserve and advance the knowledge of plants and healing and to establish the relationship between health and upright living, known as walking in balance."[14] American Indian studies scholar Benjamin Burgess suggests that *The Heirs of Columbus* works similarly to a midéwiwin ceremony in which a midé healer tells the Anishinabe origin story. "The level of the healer will be reflected in his or her ability to elaborate on the origin story," Burgess explains. "The greater the Mide healer, the more pieces of the story he or she will know."[15] Burgess draws other parallels between the midéwiwin and the traditions of the heirs of

Columbus, including that both groups have "an annual gathering to tell their origin stories and heal. [. . .] The heirs recite the story of Columbus's arrival along with the elaborations; the Midewiwin recite the creation story of the Anishinaabe and the migration from the shores of the Atlantic to the Great Lakes. Both groups have limited membership. They are also alike in the tension that exists between them and their tribes. For many years the Midewiwin had to keep their practices underground because of the religious persecution by the U.S. government. Indian agents and tribal people at times worked alongside each other to oppress the Midewiwin."[16] In Burgess's reading of the novel, Stone Columbus plays the role of the midé healer as he tells a creation story of the Americas with Christopher Columbus as a main character. Stone's elaborations on this dominant narrative, such as the invention of Columbus's Mayan ancestry and the abduction of his spirit to the Mississippi headwaters by Samana, transform it from a story about death and domination to a story about self-determination and healing.

Vizenor augments this Anishinabe-specific religious framework, a structure the novel shares with the renaissance touchstone and "Red Power" novels by Momaday and Silko, with his incorporation into the narrative of the miigis shell and midé stones.[17] Vizenor begins *Summer in the Spring: Lyric Poems of the Ojibway*, his 1965 interpretation of Anishinabe songs, with the story of creation: "In the legendary history of the Ojibway, the magic megis shell arose from the sea and moved along the waters of the St. Lawrence guiding the Indians from the Atlantic Coast to Michilimackinac and Lake Superior where the megis shell appeared for the last time at *Moningwunakauning*. It is told that the Indian received his life color and wisdom from the sun reflecting on the megis shell during this migration."[18] Burgess, citing Lac Court Oreilles spiritual leader and author Edward Benton-Banai, explains that the Anishinabe creator blew into a miigis shell to make humans and then uses the miigis shell to guide the Anishinabe along the correct path. Stone and Felipa name their daughter after this shell; she represents the reappearance of this powerful sacred force. When the heirs step ashore at Point Assinika on October 12, 1992, Miigis "unfurled the royal banner" to claim, symbolically and parodically, their possession of the land.[19] The heirs, like their Anishinabe ancestors, follow the guidance of their creator to the west.

The midé stones so carefully guarded by the heirs play a role, like the miigis shell, in the midéwiwin ceremonies.[20] These midé stones are found, explains American Indian studies scholar and Anishinabe lan-guage teacher Meg Noori, on the south shore of Lake Superior.[21] "The first stones," Vizenor relates, "were tricksters at the wild creation of the tribe and the earth. The stones once told stories, trickster stories; now the stones listen at the mount. The stones heal and remember the blue radiance of creation and resurrections."[22] Stone Columbus takes his first name from the midé stones. The heirs also have a tavern at the headwa-ters apparently constructed from them, and they move the midé stone tavern, "one stone at a time," to their new tribal nation, Point Assinika or the Place of Stones.[23] As a narrative linked to the sacred powers of midé stones and the midéwiwin religion, *The Heirs of Columbus* is explicitly a healing ceremony, like Silko's much more widely celebrated *Ceremony* and Momaday's *House Made of Dawn*.

While the narrative is resolutely Anishinabe specific, the source of the healing power so vital to the heirs' practice of citizenship and sovereignty is Mayan. Columbus brings his Mayan genes to his union with Samana at the headwaters. These genes carry the Mayans' "bear signature of survivance, their stories in the blood."[24] The stories that activate the bear signature of survivance's healing power originate in a Mayan hieroglyphic book. Felipa discovers, with the help of a dream, the Mayan bear codex in a bookshop in London. "Felipa and the heirs to the stories were convinced," Vizenor observes, "that the bear codex was a translation of an original picture codex."[25] The bear codex is, like the collection of erotic trickster stories in the *Manabosho Bestiary Curiosa* published on Madeleine Island in 1563 as a "tribal antidote" to John Eliot's *Catechism in the Indian Language*, an elabo-ration of the dominant European narratives of New World encounters.[26] This Mayan text shapes the worldview of the heirs, who must remember the stories after they lose the last copy of the codex in the storm that sinks their ships and motivates their dedication to healing.

Vizenor indicates that the bear codex has the same Yucatán origin as the four extant Mayan codices identified contemporarily as Dresden, Paris, Madrid, and Grolier.[27] These texts, according to anthropologist Michael Coe, "are completely ritual, or ritual-astronomical, works com-piled in the Northern Area during the Post-Classic," or in Yucatán during the period from 925 to 1530 CE.[28] In Vizenor's novel, Augustus Le Plon-geon, an archaeologist who discovered the codex, travels to a town on the peninsula called Espíta in an attempt to trace its history.[29] The bear codex is, the heirs learn, "an incredible revelation from the ancient Maya House of Cocom" from this part of the Mayan world.[30] The House of Cocom (Kokom), explains Coe, was a dynasty from the Itza lineage that founded Mayapan in Yucatán. It rose to power in the late thirteenth century and survived by tribute before losing Mayapan in the mid-fifteenth century in a revolt by the Xiu lineage.[31] According to anthropologist and ethnohistorian Ruth Gubler, one son of the House of Cocom survived the revolt and founded Sotuta about fifty-five miles southeast of Merida. Of the other Itzas that survived the revolt, Coe explains, "They found themselves as outcasts in the deserted forests, this time wandering back to the Lake Peten Itza which they had seen in a previous K'atun 8 Ahaw. On an island in the midst of its waters they established a new capital, Tayasal (a Spanish corruption of *Tah Itza*), now covered in the city of Flores, chief town of northern Guatemala."[32] The descendants of the immigrants from Mayapan remained isolated and therefore protected from the Spaniards. They successfully resisted Franciscan missionary efforts until 1697, when the Spaniards sent their military to conquer them. "It seems almost beyond belief," observes Coe, "that Tayasal fell to the Spaniards only in 1697, and that while students at Harvard College had been scratching their heads over Cotton Mather's theology, Maya priests 2,000 miles away were still chanting rituals from hieroglyphic books."[33] Coe implies that these Itza refugees from Yucatán base their anticolonial resistance on their ancient religious texts.

When the Spaniards invaded, the Cocom family was still a political force in Yucatán. Gubler situates the Cocom in sixteenth-century Mayan history: "While several other Yucatec lineages had played important roles in pre-Conquest times—the Canul, Cheel, Couoh, Pech, etc.—two seemed to be preeminent and to dominate the political scene when the Spaniards arrived on the shores of Yucatan: the Xiu and the Cocom. Historically, they represent antithetical attitudes towards the invading Spaniards, cooperation on the part of the former, unabated hostility on the part of the latter."[34] In contrast to the Xiu, Gubler asserts, "the Cocom [. . .] continued to offer bitter resistance up to the last Great Maya Revolt of 1546–1547."[35] The Cocom fought, she observes, with a particular urgency: "According to the historical record, the combined forces fought with frenzy and cruelty, sparing none, neither women and children, Spaniards or even the Indians who had served them."[36] After the Spanish military victory over Nachi Cocom and his people, the House of Cocom did not recover its former position of power in Yucatán.

Despite the defeat of the House of Cocom first by the Xiu and then by the Spaniards and their indigenous allies, Mayans from the Cocomes region maintained a revolutionary presence in Yucatán. During the Caste War, Nelson Reed explains, the Cocomes were a formidable opponent. In the early years of the Mayan battle to regain control of their homeland, the Cocomes attacked "simultaneously at the many villages and ranchos in their area and [killed] all they captured, showing what could have been done in a simultaneous peninsula-wide revolt. At first it was pure anarchy, the Ladinos fighting and dying at their front doors and in the corral, hiding in the forest and uniting when they could."[37] Anticolonial resistance characterizes the history of the House of Cocom and the Cocomes region of Yucatán, while the migration by the Itza survivors of the Xiu revolt to a new homeland surrounded by water parallels the migration of the heirs to Point Assinika.

Stone Columbus and his family inherit Mayan intellectual and religious traditions in addition to this history of Mayan political strength and anticolonial resistance. The Mayans, Vizenor claims, "were the first to imagine the universe and to write about their stories in the blood. The shamans, the healers, and the hand talkers with their blue puppets presented a heliocentric cosmos over the geocentered notions at the time in the Old World. [...] the bear shamans and hand talkers touched an interior vision, and told the Old World how to use the arithmetic naught in measures of time."[38] Vizenor calls these healers *balams*, the Mayan word for jaguar; Memphis, "the black panther who was liberated by the heirs from a game park," therefore, suggests another Mayan presence in the novel.[39] A second balam appears at the new nation at Point Assinika. The manicurists at Point Assinika call the mute child with blue puppets Blue Ishi, after the Yahi man and multiple massacre survivor who emerged from the woods near Oroville, California, in 1911. The mute child takes his tribal name, Chilam Balam, "Jaguar Translator" or "Spokesman of the Jaguar," however, from the "alphabetic substitutes for hieroglyphic books" by Mayan writers in Yucatán and Guatemala.[40] There are fourteen *Books of Chilam Balam* composed of chronicles and prophecies, and they constitute a more recent literary tradition than the preinvasion codices.[41] Vizenor's reference to these later prophetic texts, though not developed, expands the Mesoamerican literary genealogy into which he has written *The Heirs of*

Columbus, from the earliest codex, the Grolier of approximately 1230 CE, to the latest Chilam Balam texts from the early nineteenth century.[42]

The most famous alphabetic translation of hieroglyphic books is the *Popul Vuh*, though it is not one of the Chilam Balam texts. It does, however, involve a long westward migration by indigenous people, the Quiché Mayans, that parallels the Anishinabe story of creation summarized by Vizenor in *anishinabe nagamon* (1970) and *The Heirs of Columbus*. While the Quiché Mayans occupy the western highlands of Guatemala, the *Popul Vuh*'s origins are in Yucatán. Dennis Tedlock explains that the evidence "indicate[s] that the east coast of Yucatán was the region where Quiché ancestors acquired the hieroglyphic Popul Vuh, or some part of it, on a pilgrimage."[43] In the final section of the *Popul Vuh*, the authors document the lineages from the first grandfathers to the present day: "Three Deer and Nine Dog, in the twelfth generation of lords. And they were ruling when Tonatiuh arrived. They were tortured by the Castilian people."[44] While Vizenor writes Columbus into an Anishinabe history, the authors of the *Popul Vuh* write the arrival of the Spaniards, specifically Tonatiuh or Pedro de Alvarado, into a Quiché Mayan sacred history.

These parallels and others between *The Heirs of Columbus* and the *Popul Vuh* suggest Vizenor is drawing from this Mayan literary work, though Vizenor does not include the *Popul Vuh* in his selected list of sources in the novel's epilogue. The heirs' midé stones have a sacred power like the stones containing the spirit familiars of the old Mayan gods Tohil, Auilix, and Hacauitz. After the gods turn to stone, the Quichés continued to treat them as gods by giving thanks and offerings. The stones spoke to them in return.[45] Stone's grandparents, who share the name Truman Columbus, together recall the singular figures of the Mayan mother-fathers.[46] Also, in their third attempt at creating humans, the Mayan gods in the *Popul Vuh* make wooden people.[47] Several of the characters in *Heirs* evoke these creations. Felipa loses both her hands while dreaming that she is in the land of the dead, the destination for two generations of Mayan gods in the *Popul Vuh*. After she awakens in a second dream, she recalls, "A shaman with a golden mask carved two new hands from a live cedar tree. The wood was cold, bloodless, but the hands moved."[48] One of the manicurists at Point Assinika, Harmonia Dewikwe, has a wooden head, and some of the wounded children who appear at the new tribal nation have wooden hearts.[49] Though "they became the first numerous people here on the face of the earth," they were a failed experiment.[50] The *Popul Vuh* describes their fate: "The manikins, woodcarvings were killed when the Heart of Sky devised a flood for them."[51] The flood is a violent rain followed by all the wooden people's belongings and animals attacking them and crushing their faces. Harmonia even arrives at Point Assinika after she capsizes in rough water and washes ashore.

The *Popul Vuh* is a story of origin and creation but also of extreme and divinely sanctioned violence, of human sacrifice and conquest, prior to the arrival of the conquistadors. If Harmonia is a survivor of the onslaught that destroys the wooden people, then Vizenor is elaborating, in the midéwiwin way described by Burgess, on this Mayan text as well as on the dominant stories of Columbus. Indeed, Vizenor's Chilam Balam embodies creative and healing forces. He is a hand talker with the blue light of creation in his hands; "the blue that traced his touch was the lambent animation of memories that healed."[52] "The heirs and the blues," Vizenor observes, "were masters of the energies that healed and regenerated lost limbs, the crushed, tormented, and those who were misconceived in wicked storms."[53] The heirs, in contrast to the Quiché Mayans of the *Popul Vuh*, do not follow their westward migration with a war against and eventual conquest of their enemies.

While interpreting *Heirs* as an explicit elaboration of the *Popul Vuh* requires some speculation, the healing in the novel definitively has a Mayan component. The source of the healing power is, Vizenor reminds readers near the end of the novel, "the genetic signature of survivance from ancient Mayan hand talkers" inherited from Columbus but activated by the stories in the bear codex.[54] Blue Ishi, like Miigis Flowers, represents a return of ancient sacred power. In contrast to Esteban in Downing's *The Cat Screams* but like Red Corn Woman in *Runner in the Sun*, he is a vital indigenous Mexican body and a source of community healing from indigenous Mexico.

Vizenor imagines, similarly to McNickle in *Runner in the Sun*, a Greater Indian Territory to assert a deep historical claim to sovereignty for and citizenship in an Anishinabe nation, while also implying that the claim can be made for all tribal communities and nations in North America. In the most explicitly political elaboration of the dominant narrative of the great discoverer Columbus, the heirs threaten to annex the United States if it does not give them five hundred years' worth of the 10 percent of the discovered precious metals and other commodities promised to their famous ancestor by the Spanish sovereigns. Though the heirs do not resist militarily, like the members of the Mayan House of Cocom to which Vizenor draws their political lineage, they imagine an indigenous nation founded on Anishinabe and Mayan sacred histories and ceremonies powerful enough to challenge U.S. hegemony. By the logic of Vizenor's Greater Indian Territory or Greater Indigenous Mexico, a United States annexed by the heirs would also belong to the Mayans. Like Downing in *The Mexican Earth* and Riggs in *The Year of Pilár*, Vizenor imagines a dramatic shift in power from settler-colonists to indigenous people. As in these two mid-twentieth-century works and McNickle's Runner, the dramatic shifts originate in Mexico. In contrast to Momaday in *House Made of Dawn* and Silko in *Ceremony*, Vizenor imagines a revolution—peaceful, intratribal—on tribal-national, U.S. settler-colonial national, continental, and indigenous-transnational scales.

Mayans at the Border

The indigenous peoples of Mexico and Central America, but primarily Mayans, play a central role in the emergent pan-North American indigenous, rather than tribal nation–specific, revolutionary movement in Silko's *Almanac of the Dead*. The turn in the last fifteen years to tribal-nation specificity and tribal nationalism in American Indian literary criticism has neither led to more fervent praise of Vizenor's fiction nor precipitated sustained challenges to Silko's status as one of the two most revered writers of the renaissance era. While *Heirs* is both tribal-nation specific and politically revolutionary, *Almanac*, with its pan-hemispheric emphasis on indigenous land reclamation, remains a more attractive novel than *Heirs* to most scholars. Vizenor specifically identifies the Mayans to whom the heirs trace their descent and integrates Mayan sacred history into an Anishinabe-specific narrative. Silko sacrifices that tribal-nation specificity, as in her conflation of Mayan with Mexican (Aztecan) codices, to a political vision that imagines a continent-wide coalition of the dispossessed and foregrounds Mayans as the preeminent indigenous revolutionaries.[55]

Indeed, *Almanac of the Dead* is one of only a few works by American Indian authors that are part of the transnational conversation in American studies and American literary studies. Shari Huhndorf asserts that the novel predicts a "transnational indigenous revolution" led by the Mayan military leader Angelita la Escapía and the Mayan twins and spiritual leaders Tacho and El Feo.[56] Eva Cherniavsky, Channette Romero,

John Muthyala, and Rachel Adams attend to the novel's various national, international, transnational, and transborder orientations in colonial, settler-colonial, and indigenous specific contexts. While this section of the chapter is in conversation with the work of these scholars, my primary goal is to place *Almanac* in an American Indian literary history that incorporates indigenous Mexico.

Though the nearly utopian vision of healing in Vizenor's *Heirs* contrasts with the imminent, violent indigenous-led revolution in *Almanac*, Silko's representations of Mayans, Mexicas, and Yaquis have numerous similarities to the representations of indigenous Mexico by her contemporary as well as her predecessors Downing, Riggs, and McNickle. The novel's kinship with Downing's *The Mexican Earth* and Riggs's *The Year of Pilár* and *A World Elsewhere* troubles generalizations about the quietist American Indian literary politics in the mid-twentieth century and the exceptional literary politics of the renaissance era. Silko even summarizes the thesis of Downing's history of Mexico in *Almanac*: "War had been declared the first day the Spaniards set foot on Native American soil, and the same war had been going on ever since: the war was for the continents called the Americas."[57] Silko's Greater Indigenous Mexico is on the verge of a revolution that, like the ones in *Runner* and *Heirs*, has a strong religious component but, like the ones in *The Mexican Earth* and Riggs's plays, carries the grave threat of armed uprising. *Almanac*'s narrative of land reclamation is not quite as anomalous in American Indian literary history as scholars tend to treat it.

Almanac has its origin, Silko asserts in a passage reminiscent of Stone Columbus, in her reading about "the great culture of the Maya people, who had invented the zero and who had performed sophisticated mathematical calculations so that they could predict the positions of the planets and the stars."[58] The extant Mayan codices particularly captured Silko's interest. The almanac of the novel's title refers, like Vizenor's bear codex, to a previously unknown preinvasion Mayan text, and the title identifies the novel as a contemporary almanac, an ancient text revised and expanded to account for the first five hundred years of European presence in the Americas. Though Silko apparently does not account for the Grolier text in her reckoning of the number of surviving codices, Penelope Myrtle Kelsey proposes it as a possible source for *Almanac*.[59] Photographs of the eleven surviving pages of the Grolier codex reveal that it is in the same degraded, fragmented condition as the almanac in Silko's novel.[60]

The almanac in the novel, owned in the narrative present by Lecha and Zeta Cazador, twin Yaqui, Mexican-born sisters, predicts the beginning and end of a five-hundred-year era called Death-Eye Dog, the era of European colonialism. When the Spaniards invade, the four children in possession of the almanac flee from southern Mexico to the north. Just as Salt in McNickle's novel journeys to the south to find ancient relatives and save his community, the four children hope to find sanctuary with family members in the north. "That had been the final argument," Silko explains. "Somewhere in the North there might be a few survivors of their tribe who had been given refuge by the strange people of the high, arid mountains."[61] Silko makes explicit near the end of the novel that by *north*, she means New Mexico and Arizona. The memory of their kinship with these previous migrants provides hope for the children. This kinship, as it is in Cherokee history and McNickle's novel, for example, binds indigenous people across tribal nations and communities as well as across settler-colonial borders. It is transtribal in the past and indigenous and settler-colonial transnational in the present. The almanac, with its Mayan origins, current Yaqui ownership, and pan-hemispheric prophecy, is transnational in both indigenous and settler-colonial contexts. It is a Greater Indigenous Mexican text.

Figure 5.1. The pages in the ancient almanac in Silko's novel resemble this selection from the Grolier codex. Copyright by Justin Kerr.

Yaquis figure most prominently in the sections set in the United States. Yaqui characters—Lecha, the psychic; her sister Zeta, the committed smuggler; and Calabazas, a drug smuggler—are in the vanguard of revolutionary border crossers. As members of a specific tribal world split by the U.S.–Mexican border, Yaquis have a precolonial claim to land in the southern part of the U.S. state of Arizona and the northern Mexican state of Sonora. They are also famous, as Downing explains in *The Mexican Earth*, for their determined resistance to the Spanish empire and the Mexican state: "The Yaquis of Sonora had been allowed to till their fields in peace for only eighty-five years during the centuries since they wiped out the first Spanish expedition that went against them, soon after the fall of Tenochtitlán. They had become a self-reliant Spartan group that Díaz failed to disrupt."[62] After he describes the Yaquis as a tribe rather than a racial minority and their worldview as "nationalistic," Downing adds with unconcealed pride, "Two Amerindian tribes are justified in boasting that they have fought every invader and have never been conquered: the Araucanians of Chile and Argentina and the Yaquis of Mexico."[63] Silko draws upon the same history of anticolonial resistance in her representation of Yaqui characters invested in revolution. Lecha and Zeta in particular are motivated by the stories their grandmother, "the wild old Yaqui woman" Yoeme, told them about the massacre and dispossession of their people.[64]

Mayan revolutionaries Angelita la Escapía, Tacho, and El Feo, however, remain the movement's leaders. They publicly assert their revolutionary aims, while Lecha and Zeta work covertly and indirectly to aid their allies. Tacho and El Feo are possible manifestations of the hero twins Slayer of Monsters and Child of Water of Navajo storytelling traditions.[65] They are also possibly incarnations of Hunahpu and Xbalanque, the "Hero Twins" of the *Popul Vuh*, though the *Popul Vuh* is not a preinvasion codex.[66] Hunahpu and Xbalanque are the twin sons of twin fathers, One Hunahpu and Seven Hunahpu, and Blood Moon. Like Hunahpu and Xbalanque, Tacho and El Feo are ballplayers: they use baseball to disguise their attempts to organize a revolutionary army.[67] Hunahpu and Xbalanque redeem their fathers by defeating their killers, the lords of Xibalba. "Such was the loss of their greatness and brilliance," the authors of the *Popul Vuh* explain, that "their domain did not return to greatness."[68] They then resurrect their father Seven Hunahpu and tell him, "We merely cleared the road of your death, your loss, the pain, the suffering that were inflicted upon you."[69] This section of the *Popul Vuh* ends with the twin brothers ascending into the sky as the sun and the moon. Silko's narrative of an anticolonial revolution against the destroyers—the colonialists and their allies—parallels this narrative of the defeat of the underworld, of the forces of death and destruction.

Silko embraces a textual, intellectual, and revolutionary Mesoamerica but, like McNickle, she disavows the inheritance of certain religious practices. Though they follow a south-north trade route, the children also walk in the direction that other indigenous Mexicans moved as fugitives from the cultures of human sacrifice. As Silko notes, "Long before Europeans ever appeared, the people had already disagreed over the blood and the killing. Those who went North refused to feed the spirits of blood anymore. Those tribes and people who had migrated North fled the Destroyers who delighted in blood."[70] Silko appears to acknowledge in these initial comments about the Destroyers that the Mayans, like the more notorious Mexicas, practiced human sacrifice. She suggests, too, like McNickle, that there must have been resistance to such ceremonies.

Almanac also shares with McNickle's *Runner* an unwillingness to trace a genealogy between indigenous peoples of the U.S. Southwest and the Mexicas of Tenochtitlan. This unwillingness is more explicit in *Almanac* and specific to the Laguna Pueblo world of Sterling, who after exile from his home pueblo becomes a handyman for Zeta:

> Aunt Marie had cautioned Sterling and the other children always
> to be careful around Mexicans and Mexican Indians because when
> the first Europeans had reached Mexico City they had found the
> sorcerers in power. Montezuma had been the biggest sorcerer of all.
> Each of Montezuma's advisors had been sorcerers too, descendants
> of the very sorcerers who had caused the old-time people to flee to
> Pueblo country in Arizona and New Mexico, thousands of years
> before. [. . .] The appearance of Europeans had been no accident; the
> Gunadeeyahs had called for their white brethren to join them. [. . .]
> No wonder Cortés and Montezuma had hit it off together when they
> met; both had been members of the same secret clan.[71]

Sterling's Aunt Marie perpetuates a familiar representation of the Aztecan world as brutally violent. To her, this Aztecan past also casts into suspicion all Mexicans, indigenous or otherwise. This characterization of Aunt Marie is consistent with Silko's depiction of some citizens of the Laguna Pueblo, in *Ceremony* as well as in *Almanac*, as conservative and xenophobic. Silko's

brief reference to Mayan human sacrifice and Aunt Marie's refusal to claim
kinship with the most familiar Mesoamerican practitioners of it helps
Silko to avoid totalizing the cultures and politics of indigenous Mexicans
and American Indians.

Yet Quetzalcoatl, the plumed serpent of Mesoamerica, is the defining
sacred figure of the revolution, and Silko uses the more familiar Mexican
or Nahuatl name for him rather than the Yucatec Mayan name, K'uk'ulcan,
for the same deity. In the Mexican creation story, Quetzalcoatl travels
to the underworld, gathers bones, and sprinkles them with his blood
to create humankind. Anthropologist Richard Townsend provides the
following description of Quetzalcoatl: "Ancient wind and storm deity.
His name also a title of rulers; historically associated with a celebrated
ruler of Toltec Tula. At time of Spanish Conquest, the cult was seated in
Cholula."[72] According to Townsend, the stories of the historical figure,
Topiltzin Quetzalcoatl, identify him "as the ruler of the powerful Toltec
people, venerated predecessors of the Aztecs." Townsend continues,
"Although revered and respected, the hero-king fell victim to drunkenness
and, in a quarrel with a rival faction led by the sorcerer Tezcatlipoca, was
tricked into committing incest with his sister. The humiliated Quetzalcoatl
was forced to depart with his retinue in a year 1 reed, and made his way to
the Gulf Coast, where he embarked on a seagoing raft towards the Yucatan Peninsula in the east."[73] The story continues in the Yucatecan Mayan
world, where Topiltzin Quetzalcoatl arrives in the late tenth-century CE
as a brutal conqueror.[74] Silko elides this history of Toltec imperialism
and emphasizes the divine Quetzalcoatl to make the pan-Mesoamerican
god a more appropriate spiritual force behind the novel's anticolonial,
pan-hemispheric indigenous revolution.

Clinton, an African American and Cherokee veteran and talk-radio
host, first mentions Quetzalcoatl on one of his "Liberation Radio Broad-
casts." He associates the god with Damballah, a father god of Africa
depicted as a serpent: "The spirits of Africa and the Americas are joined
together in history, and on both continents by the sacred gourd rattle.
Erzulie joins the Mother Earth. Damballah, great serpent of the sky and
keeper of all spiritual knowledge, joins the giant plumed serpent, Quetzalcoatl."[75] The macaw spirits inform Tacho that "the great serpent was
in charge of electricity" and, in an act of supernatural anticolonialism,
Quetzalcoatl disrupts its flow to cause machines to malfunction and
crash.[76] Angelita, the militant revolutionary, has a different view: "She

Figure 5.2. Quetzalcoatl is an important figure of indigenous revolution in Downing's The Mexican Earth *and Silko's* Almanac of the Dead. *This image of Quetzalcoatl at Teotihuacan is on a postcard sent on June 12, 1940, from John Joseph Mathews to his future stepson, John Hunt, in Pawhuska. Courtesy of the Western History Collections, University of Oklahoma Libraries, John Joseph Mathews Collection, box 1, folder 18.*

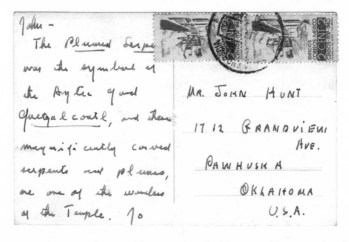

Figure 5.3. Mathews was also moved by Quetzalcoatl. The reverse of the postcard reads "John, The Plumed Serpent was the symbol of the Aztec god Quetzalcoatl, and these magnificently carved serpents and plumes, are one of the wonders of the Temple. Jo." Courtesy of the Western History Collections, University of Oklahoma Libraries, John Joseph Mathews Collection, box 1, folder 18.

knew the old nuns had got the story of benevolent, gentle Quetzalcoatl all wrong too. The nuns had taught the children that the Morning Star, Quetzalcoatl, was really Lucifer, the Devil God had thrown out of heaven. The nuns had terrified children with the story of the snake in the Garden of Eden to end devotion to Quetzalcoatl."[77] These contradictory beliefs underscore the tension in the novel between competing visions of peaceful and violent revolutions. Tacho's and Angelita's contradictory beliefs about Quetzalcoatl also make explicit the challenges Aztecan and Mayan history presents for contemporary American Indian authors. Despite the history of human sacrifice, Silko, like Downing, McNickle, and Vizenor, celebrates Mesoamerica civilization against prevailing notions of its unmitigated brutality.

In *Almanac*, as in Downing's *The Mexican Earth*, Quetzalcoatl did not return as Hernán Cortés in 1519, as he does in postconquest myths. Instead, the almanac reads: "Error in translation of the Chumayel manuscript: 11 AHU was the year of the return of fair Quetzalcoatl. But the mention of the artificial white circle in the sky could only have meant the return of Death Dog and his eight brothers: plague, earthquake, drought, famine, incest, insanity, war, and betrayal."[78] The Chumayel manuscript is one of the Mayan books of Chilam Balam, rather than a codex, that Vizenor incorporates into *Heirs*. Silko conflates Aztec and Mayan texts and histories in the novel's almanac. While the interpretive "error" that perpetuates the myth that Quetzalcoatl returned as Cortés to Tenochtitlan refers to events in 1519, the authors of the Chumayel manuscript recorded the arrival of the Spaniards at Heaven Born Merida in the year 11 Ahau of the Mayan calendar, or 1540 in the Julian. "For this indeed was the beginning of misery / For us," assert the authors of the Chumayel book of Chilam Balam.[79] A long catalog of the misery and oppression brought by the Spaniards follows this passage. The Cortés-as-Quetzalcoatl myth was not an error. According to Townsend, "anthropologist Susan Gillespie has argued convincingly that the whole story of Cortés as Quetzalcoatl was created after the Conquest by Aztec historians in an attempt to make sense of the Spaniards' arrival and victory, interpreting it as the outcome of a pattern of events established long ago, in the remote Toltec past."[80] Silko obscures these distinct histories and intellectual acts.

This almanac fragment cited also refers to Death Dog, or Xolotol, another Aztec deity; he is an aspect of Quetzalcoatl or his twin, the "bringer of lightning" and the "god of deformities."[81] Elizabeth Hill Boone, a specialist in Latin American art, spells the name Xolotl and translates it as "monster" or "Dog/Monster."[82] Xolotl plays a role in several stories about the creation of the sun and a trip to the underworld that leads to the creation of humans.[83] Silko cites Xolotl's journey in the second fragment of the almanac: "Death Dog traveled to the land of the dead where the God of death gave him the bone the human race was created with."[84] A passage in the same fragment refers to the unlucky days without names in both the Aztec and Mayan calendars, and Silko uses the day names (Day 4, *Lizard*; Day 5, *Serpent*; Day 6, *Death*; etc.) of both calendars throughout this section.[85] She thus emphasizes Mesoamerican unity and shared culture over political and military conflict.

As if promising to return to end the rule of Xolotol, Quetzalcoatl appears on a page of the prophetic almanac: "The outline of the giant plumed serpent could be made out in pale blue on the largest fragment."[86] Lecha and Zeta's Yaqui grandmother also tells them that the giant snake will return, and Lecha and Zeta interpret the appearance of a great stone serpent in New Mexico as a sign that Quetzalcoatl's arrival is imminent.[87] The Barefoot Hopi, one of the indigenous revolutionaries based in the United States, also reports on the Aztec god's return: "In Africa and in the Americas too, the giant snakes, Damballah and Quetzalcoatl, have returned to the people. [. . .] The snakes say this: From out of the south the people are coming, like a great river flowing restless with the spirits of the dead who have been reborn again and again all over Africa and the Americas, reborn each generation more fierce and more numerous. Millions will move instinctively; unarmed and unguarded, they begin walking steadily north, following the twin brothers."[88] Fifty years after Downing writes in *The Mexican Earth* that Quetzalcoatl is still on his way home, Silko imagines his arrival as prophesized in a Mayan codex. Her novel ends with an image that encapsulates indigenous Mexico in the American Indian literary imagination: the stone serpent looks south in apparent anticipation of welcoming the revolution that approaches from that direction.

Mayans in Contemporary American Indian Literary Criticism

Vizenor and Silko, the latter with her essays as well as her novel, both anticipate a literary critical turn to indigenous Mexico, especially Mayans, in the 1990s and 2000s. It is *Almanac* rather than *Heirs*, however, that contemporary scholars have embraced as the quintessential novel of indigenous revolution with origins in Mexico. In her survey of late twentieth-century American Indian fiction, Elizabeth Cook-Lynn comments, "The unfortunate truth is that there are few significant works being produced today by the currently popular American Indian fiction writers which examine the meaningfulness of indigenous or tribal sovereignty in the twenty-first century."[89] Silko's novel, however, disrupts this trend: "Perhaps the most ambitious novel yet published by an American Indian fiction writer which fearlessly asserts a collective indigenous retrieval of the lands stolen through colonization is Leslie Marmon Silko's *Almanac of the Dead*. [...] Silko's new novel seems to stand alone in creating a fictionalized pantribal nationalism, an event which provides an interesting, antagonistic, rebellious moment in contemporary literary development."[90] Similar interesting, antagonistic, and rebellious moments, several of them surprisingly explicit, occurred in American Indian literature in the middle of the twentieth century.

Womack provides an explanation for the tepid and often hostile response to *Almanac* from nonacademic reviewers that Cook-Lynn laments. He observes that novels about cultural revitalization, such as Silko's *Ceremony*, are more popular than books about Native politics, such as *Almanac*: "America loves Indian culture; America is much less enthusiastic about Indian land title."[91] Womack then considers the political implications of Silko's strategy in *Almanac*: "Leslie Silko's prophetic work *Almanac of the Dead* predicts broad alliances between indigenous people, especially the tribal people of Latin America. The political reality is that U.S. Native numbers are around .5 percent of the total population, and though this is probably undercounted, it would seem that any real political clout that Indian country will be able to muster in the future might depend on looking to South America, Canada, and pressure from indigenous people worldwide, some type of 'rising up,' to borrow Silko's phrase from her astounding novel."[92] The novel's "broad alliances between indigenous people," like its ostensibly anomalous rebellious literary moment, are also visible in the novels, plays, and histories by Downing, Riggs, and McNickle. Vizenor's novel emphasizes the necessity of alliances, too, among all the people damaged by New World colonial enterprises and from within the political context of specific tribal-nation jurisdiction.

The discourse of Mexican indigeneity in contemporary American Indian literary criticism is both political and literary historical. In the same essay in which she praises *Almanac*, Cook-Lynn traces the history of indigenous American resistance to the Mayans: "The interest in decolonization goes back to the Mayan resistance narratives of the 1500s and has always played an important role in political and social life."[93] Jace Weaver situates the origins of indigenous American literature in Mexico and Central America in his influential study *That the People Might Live*: "The earliest books in the Americas were produced not by European immigrants but by the Maya. [...] The most famous of these volumes was the Council Book or *Popul Vuh*."[94] In his equally influential *Red on Red*, Womack roots his study in the same literary history: "Indian people have authored a lot of books, a history that reaches back to the 1770s in terms of writing in English, and hundreds of years before contact in terms of Mayan and Aztec pictoglyphic alphabets in which were written the vast libraries of Mesoamerica."[95] Thus in two of the most widely read and cited works of American Indian literary criticism, Mexico figures as one of the key origins of American Indian literatures.

While contemporary American Indian writers share this literary history, they also inherit the same history of violence against indigenous literary expression. Silko comments, "Books have been the focus of the struggle for the control of the Americas from the start. The great libraries of Americas were destroyed in 1540 because the Spaniards feared the political and spiritual power of books authored by the indigenous people."[96] Womack considers the same act of destruction in *Red on Red*: "If we take the Spanish book burnings of the Mayan codices in the 1540s as an example, we might describe this act of cultural genocide as one culture finding itself threatened by the profundity of the Other's literacy. These were illiteracy campaigns, sponsored by the group claiming to be the most literate."[97] Womack also emphasizes that the codices are written complements to oral traditions and examples of a Mayan national literature. His assessment of the literary and political work of the codices establishes a key part of the critical foundation of his study of Creek writers.

The Mayan codices also provide the origin for American Indian writing in the Northeast in *The Common Pot: The Recovery of Native Space in the Northeast* (2008) by Lisa Brooks. Brooks begins her study by relating a conversation in which she participated about the destruction of the codices: "We talked about the burning of those libraries, the destruction of their systems of learning, the knowledge lost. We deliberated about the meaning of those cycles of history and considered what they might mean for us here, now. We talked about how these codices need to come home."[98] During the conversation, the interlocutors notice a corn plant and wonder—like Downing in *The Mexican Earth* and McNickle in *They Came Here*

First—about the distance that it traveled from Mesoamerica. In the subsequent passages, Brooks establishes a literary genealogy that begins with the codices and extends to Ojibwe birchbark scrolls and *Almanac of the Dead*. Following Erdrich's comments on the nearly identical Ojibwe words for book and rock painting, Brooks introduces the Abenaki root word *awigha* (to write, draw, or map): "An Ojibwe scroll is an *awikhigan*. The road map that Natalie and I used to navigate our trip is an *awikhigan*. Erdrich's account of her travels among the islands of the Ojibwe country is *awikhigan*. *Almanac of the Dead* and the codices on which it is modeled are all *awikhiganak*. You are reading one now."[99] In the identification of these shared indigenous spaces and shared indigenous text-making practices, Brooks imagines a Greater Indian Territory.

Two contributors to the collection of essays *Reasoning Together* (2008) also draw these connections between the Mayans and contemporary American Indian life, literature, and politics. Daniel Justice mentions the destruction of the Mayan codices as an example of the repression of "the very *memory* of an unbroken Native presence."[100] Chris Teuton considers the *Popul Vuh* "as one of the earliest and continuously influential works of critical writing produced in the Americas." In the spirit of Silko's and Vizenor's novels and Womack's own reading of the codices, he observes: "The *Popul Vuh* is also a postcolonial text that calls attention to itself as both a record of a colonized people and a source of their resistance."[101] The Mayans are thus exempla of both an extraordinary intellectual world nearly destroyed by colonialism and anticolonial resistance.

American Indian community activists also turn south for transnational political solidarity. In March 2006, approximately twenty-five citizens of the Hopi Nation ran two thousand miles from Hopi to Anáhuac, the Valley of Mexico, for the 4th World Water Forum in Mexico City.[102] The run was organized by the Black Mesa Trust, which was founded in 1999 to educate people about the devastating environmental impact of the Peabody Coal Company's daily pumping of millions of gallons of water from the Navajo Aquifer.[103] The runners, who ranged in age from twelve to seventy-five years and who followed a route similar to Salt's in McNickle's novel, arrived at the Otomi Ceremonial Center in Temoaya and then completed their journey at Teotihuacan, a two-thousand-year-old urban center of Mesoamerica prior to the rise of Mexico-Tenochtitlan in 1325 CE. Roberto Rodriguez reports in the April 6, 2006, edition of *Indian Country Today* on the welcome that the Hopis received from their relatives throughout the journey and in Anáhuac: "Everywhere they go, the runners are treated with utmost respect and great reverence, particularly the elders. Many of those they meet with acknowledge that they/ we are related and that the Hopi represent memory. The people do not need linguists, archaeologists or anthropologists to affirm this. The stories, the common languages, the water and the maize communicate this same message: *San ce tojuan. Ti masehualme, okichike ka centeotzintli*: We are one. We are *macehual*, made from sacred maize."[104] This meeting of relatives separated by colonial borders within a Greater Indigenous Mexico illustrates at least two ways that indigenous sovereignty is practiced transnationally: by a local movement deeply rooted in an indigenous nation's land and worldview as it travels between other Native nations and communities—Zuni, Isleta, Otomi—to a global conference on water policy and by the recognition of indigenous nationhood by other indigenous nations and communities.

In *The Mexican Earth*, Downing, who as a tour guide more than seventy years earlier repeatedly traveled a similar route to Mexico City as the Hopi runners, models the same concern for the distinct histories of indigenous nations and communities while acknowledging shared indigenous North American experiences. Lynn Riggs and Jace Weaver, Lisa Brooks and Craig Womack, D'Arcy McNickle and Elizabeth Cook-Lynn, Leslie Marmon Silko and Gerald Vizenor, and other American Indian writers make similar literary, intellectual, and political gestures to indigenous Mexico. The literary history made legible through American Indian perspectives on indigenous Mexico establishes a new trajectory in the literary, intellectual, and political histories of Native writing. These histories challenge the dominance of the Native American renaissance in American Indian literary studies. They encourage us to look more attentively to other eras and to elaborate new literary genealogies. The talented, prolific, and often quite popular American Indian writers in the middle decades of the twentieth century produced a rich and dynamic body of work. *The Red Land to the South* represents what I hope will be only one of many critical turns to the era.

Revolutions before the Renaissance

WHILE PROMINENT SCHOLARS SUCH AS Robert Warrior, Jace Weaver, and Craig Womack have challenged the exceptionalism of the post-1968 era within the long history of American Indian writing, the renaissance continues to stand as a formidable creative and intellectual border between 1968 and the mid-twentieth century. In his foreword to *The Singing Bird*, Weaver observes, "Native authors who toiled prior to 1968 have been swamped and submerged in the wake of the dreadnaught Momaday and the many fine authors (Silko, Welch, Vizenor, Ortiz, Harjo, and others) who saw print after him. The problem with the so-called Native American Literary Renaissance, as the post-1968 period was labeled, was that it confused critical awareness with literal presence."[1] The concurrent rise of American Indian studies programs and Red Power activism helped to produce this critical awareness. The directly confrontational politics consolidate the creative and intellectual border, however, as these new institutional and activist forces worked together to establish a Red Power hermeneutic that takes Momaday's *House Made of Dawn* and Leslie Marmon Silko's *Ceremony* as literary, cultural, and political touchstones and draws critical attention away from the many American Indian writers in the mid-twentieth century.

The Red Land to the South identifies, defines, and contextualizes a mid-twentieth-century transnational American Indian literary politics that coheres with the renaissance and Red Power and repudiates the invented border between the two eras. The revolutions depicted by Todd Downing, Lynn Riggs, and D'Arcy McNickle are, indeed, more explicit and emphatic expressions of indigenous political strength than readers find in the three novels that Sean Teuton uses in *Red Land, Red Power* to represent Red Power literature. The indigenous revolution to which Downing only hints in *The Cat Screams* is in *The Mexican Earth* a centuries-long process of cultural and military resistance to Spanish colonialism and Mexican settler colonialism. Riggs stages in *The Year of Pilár* the opening

battles in an armed revolution to reclaim a homeland, while the revolution in McNickle's *Runner in the Sun* involves an indigenous community
using its oral history to reimagine its relationship to the land and completely rebuild itself. In comparison to armed indigenous revolution and
the social transformation of an entire community, Teuton's three Red
Power novels that end with Abel running after evil, Tayo telling his story
to the elders in a kiva, and Welch's unnamed narrator in *Winter in the Blood*
throwing his grandmother's tobacco pouch into her grave, appear politically tentative or ambiguous.

The emphasis on the enduring social and political value of distinct
American Indian cultural expressions in *House Made of Dawn* and *Ceremony* distinguishes these Red Power novels from most of Downing's
detective fiction and Riggs's plays. Yet even in the generally pessimistic
works of the interwar and early contemporary period, such as Riggs's *The
Cherokee Night*, McNickle's *The Surrounded*, and Mathews's *Sundown*, the
authors make clear that their characters need these cultural expressions
and that their absence exacerbates individual, familial, and community
crises. As I argue in chapter 1, McNickle and Mathews also portray young
people other than the protagonists participating in ceremonial life. In
addition, *The Cat Screams* depicts the maintenance of distinct indigenous
cultural beliefs and practices in the middle of the twentieth century, and
Downing's *The Mexican Earth* and McNickle's *Runner in the Sun* are forceful assertions of indigenous cultural continuity across many centuries.
American Indian literary history of the mid-twentieth century is far more
nuanced culturally and politically than we generally acknowledge.

The renaissance is also ostensibly exceptional as a movement of writers, academics, and activists working together. Cherokee-Quapaw/
Chickasaw scholar Geary Hobson conveys the excitement about this
collective effort in his introduction to *The Remembered Earth* (1979), an
anthology of renaissance writing that is also an influential renaissance
text: "We must begin to view this activity [. . .] as a renascence and not
just simply as a 'boom'—both of these things contemporary Native
American literature certainly is. It is indeed much more than a 'boom,'
or a 'fad'—to echo what certain literary scholars have said. It is renewal,
it is continuance—and it is remembering."[2] Almost thirty years later,
Teuton asserts in *Red Land, Red Power* that the Red Power novel "represents the political and moral transformation of Native people responding
to various forms of repression. Red Power provided the social vision for

this kind of novel to emerge. This was a time when American Indian activists, scholars, and artists, across myriad differences, joined hands and raised their voices to claim a forgotten history and a stolen land. So began a political awakening that made available alternative narratives of tribal lives: new knowledge for a new Indian future."[3] Teuton's much more recent testimony demonstrates the enduring literary critical influence of a political era that, as Warrior and Smith emphasize, had its defining moments during a brief three-and-a-half year period between the occupations of Alcatraz and Wounded Knee.

While the collective political and artistic efforts in the mid-twentieth century achieved neither the scale nor the influence of Red Power and the renaissance, writers, intellectuals, and activists in this earlier era worked tirelessly together and with less media attention. They also joined hands, raised voices, and created powerful social visions of American Indian futures. Tuscarora Chief Clinton Rickard formed the Indian Defense League of America (IDLA) on December 1, 1926, in protest of two pieces of legislation: the Indian Citizenship Act of 1924 and the Immigration Act of 1924, also called the Johnson-Reed or National Origins Act. "Rickard's foremost message," explains political scientist Kevin Bruyneel, "was that the Iroquois people did not want U.S. citizenship in any form, whether it was dual-citizenship or citizen-ward status. [. . .] Rickard saw political integration, even if it involved an ambivalent form of American citizenship, as leading to cultural assimilation within America society and the loss of the Iroquois nations' government-to-government relationship with the United States."[4] The Johnson-Reed Act prevented indigenous peoples from other nations in the hemisphere from entering the United States. The U.S.-Canadian border passes through the territory of the Iroquois Confederacy, and the act, therefore, restricted the movement of the confederacy's citizens within its own borders. The IDLA successfully lobbied for an amendment to exclude Native people from the act's jurisdiction; Rickard's indigenous nationalist political orientation, which he shared with his supporters and other Native leaders, such as Wyandotte activist Jane Zane Gordon, produced immediate results.[5] The celebratory parade on July 14, 1928, across the bridge at Niagara Falls, has become an annual IDLA tradition as well as an expression of protest against settler colonialism.[6]

On a broader U.S. national scale, McNickle, Bronson, and many others spent years planning the NCAI before its official inception in 1944. Young

American Indian activists began attending the Southwest Regional Indian Youth Council in 1955, and they participated in the Workshops on American Indian Affairs conceived during a conversation between McNickle and Bronson and held at the University of Colorado at Boulder beginning in 1956.[7] American Indians from at least ninety Native communities attended the June 1961 American Indian Chicago Conference (AICC), including McNickle, Menominee activist and eventual Assistant Secretary of Indian Affairs Ada Deer, Powhatan-Renápe / Delaware-Lenápe scholar of Native American studies Jack Forbes, and Cherokee anthropologist Robert Thomas.[8] Laurence Hauptman and Jack Campisi argue that the Chicago conference "contributed significantly to increased efforts by the Abenaki, Gay Head Wampanoag, Haliwa, Houma, Lumbee, Mashpee Wampanoag and Narragansett to seek federal recognition over the past quarter-century."[9] The National Indian Youth Council was founded in August 1961 by young American Indian activists, such as Clyde Warrior (Ponca), Mel Thom (Walker River Paiute), and Clinton Rickard's daughter Karen Rickard (Tuscarora), disillusioned by more conservative leaders.[10] Warrior participated in the 1961 and 1962 Boulder workshops and returned later as a guest lecturer, and Thom attended in 1964.[11] Despite their often conflicting positions on important social and political issues, Thom consistently looked to D'Arcy McNickle and Robert Thomas for guidance.[12]

Writers also did not work in isolation in the mid-twentieth century, and Indian Territory writers in particular had both personal and professional connections. As Daniel Justice explains in *Our Fire Survives the Storm*, Riggs, Will Rogers, and John Oskison, as well as Cherokee historian Emmet Starr, "all lived at various times in the Cooweescoowee District in or around what is now Claremore and Vinita, Oklahoma, and all likely knew one another directly through family connections."[13] Riggs was born near Claremore, and Oskison was born in a double log house, he records in his unpublished autobiography, "not far from Tahlequah."[14] Rogers's birthplace was about fourteen miles northwest of Claremore and two miles east of Oologah at a home his father called "The White House on the Verdigris." Mathews and Downing were citizens of other tribal nations but still close neighbors. Mathews was born in the Osage Nation at Pawhuska about 60 miles northwest of Claremore, while Downing was born in the Choctaw Nation at Atoka about 160 miles south of Claremore.

The most well-known members of this generation—Downing, Mathews, Oskison, Riggs, and Rogers—crossed paths with each other throughout their lives. Oskison and Rogers knew each other as young men: Oskison went to school with Rogers at Willie Halsell College in Vinita, and they attended the Chicago World's Fair together in 1893.[15] Riggs was much younger than Oskison and Rogers, though he was acquainted with the Rogers family. The families were close enough that Riggs recalled riding Rogers's uncle Billy's horse.[16] As a young man, he attended the University of Oklahoma from 1920 to 1923 at the same time as Downing (1920–24) and before he followed the poet Witter Bynner to New Mexico, and he was in the Blue Pencil literary fraternity at the university with Mathews during the Osage writer's senior year. As Professor Hoople, Downing was writing a column for the *Daily Oklahoman* during these years.[17]

These authors also followed the careers of the other members of their cohort, and they often expressed admiration for each other. In their introduction to *The Singing Bird*, Powell and Smith note that "throughout his life [Oskison] maintained close ties with Will Rogers."[18] Oskison puts his friend's familiar opening to his weekly newspaper columns— "all I know is what I read in the paper"—in the mouth of a prostitute in his novel *Black Jack Davy* (1926) and refers to Rogers in his novel *Brothers Three* (1935) as "that calf-riding, wise-cracking rope juggler and word twister."[19] He sent Rogers a copy of the book, too, with the following inscription: "For Will Rogers—in memory of our school days together at Willie Halsell, and of a period in the old Indian Territory that we both knew and, I hope, loved. Cordially—as one Cherokee to another—Yours, John Oskison."[20] In a telegram to Earl Walker, another student who attended Halsell, Rogers recollects: "Now that I find that they are celebrating the passing out of Willie Halsell Institute well there were guys went there that would have put even Harvard or Yale out of business I believe John Oskison was the only one we really got educated but they taught a lot of em to go out and lead fine useful lives to their communities."[21] Riggs claimed to have been in a Rogers's film and to have met with him in New York.[22] He planned to honor Rogers in *Green Grow the Lilacs* but later revised the play to disguise what he decided was a distracting reference to one of the world's most famous celebrities.[23] Mathews was involved with trying to get either the Ponca Singers or Osage dancers for a celebration of *Green Grow the Lilacs* on "Claremore Night" in April of 1947. Though these associations were enduring, others were brief and tangential: Todd Downing's sister, Ruth, interviewed

Rogers some time during the summer of 1930, and Todd and Ruth's grandmother expresses in a letter to Ruth a desire to see Rogers when he came through Norman, Oklahoma, on a tour in 1931.[24]

The Red Land to the South tells only one story about Downing, Riggs, and McNickle. Scholars could look at Riggs's *Toward the Western Sky* (1951), a historical drama about the founding of Case Western Reserve, and Downing's "Journey's End" (1972), a historical drama that ends at Oklahoma statehood in 1907 with the cast singing "Oklahoma," and reach substantially different conclusions about their politics. Downing's other detective novels are also a serious consideration of U.S.-Mexican relations and, especially in the later novels, of what we now call the borderlands. Riggs's plays such as *Dark Encounter* and *The Cream in the Well* offer scathing commentary on the consequences of warfare on the home front, while McNickle's nonfiction, including *They Came Here First* (1949), *Indians and Other Americans* (1959), *Indian Man: A Life of Oliver LaFarge* (1971), *Native American Tribalism* (1973), and contributions to periodicals and conferences, such as the "Declaration of Indian Purpose" for the American Indian Chicago Conference, awaits the same attention we have accorded his fiction. A careful study of these works will bring new historical and political perspectives to our interpretations of his fiction.

This study also tells only one story about American Indian writers and indigenous Mexico. The representation of indigenous Mexico by Cherokee authors Rogers and Oskison challenges the coherent focus in the preceding chapters. Neither Rogers nor Oskison sees Mexico as an indigenous nation and a political resource for American Indians, although, for Rogers, Mexico has a remarkable similarity to the Cherokee Nation and Indian Territory. Rogers frets constantly in his newspaper columns about U.S. intervention in the affairs of its southern, settler-colonial neighbor. His Mexico is a landscape populated by kind, friendly people; full of desirable resources like oil; and under siege by a much stronger, intrusive neighbor. Rogers's affection for what he represents as a simpler, premodern life in the Mexico of the 1920s and 1930s correlates directly to his nostalgia for Indian Territory. Oskison, who turns to Mexico only sporadically during his career, produces a conventional representation of Mexico as premodern, politically inept, and prone to brutality. For Oskison, Mexico is a desolate landscape of social and political disorder that threatens the slow but steady social change about which he wrote throughout his career. Oskison appears to embrace this social change, with some ambivalence, as progress. Oskison's more familiar depiction of a turbulent, uncivilized Mexico correlates to his cautiously optimistic view of the transformation of Indian Territory by Oklahoma statehood. We can thus situate Oskison within a long history of Cherokee authors who, at least publicly in their writing, emphasize Cherokee social order and civilization as the dominant features of Cherokee life. While these representations by Rogers and Oskison diverge from those imagined by Riggs, they are still embedded in Cherokee Nation and Indian Territory contexts. The overlapping and conflicting narratives of revolution, diplomacy, and indigenous or Anglo superiority in the work of Downing, Riggs, Oskison, Rogers, and McNickle reveal in extraordinary detail a richly diverse literary, intellectual, and political context in the interwar and early contemporary era of American Indian writing.

We cannot reduce this era to a few novels, plays, and histories or to a few male members of a privileged educated and socioeconomic class. The narratives of revolutionary indigenous Mexico by Downing and Riggs are a small and selective but nevertheless a compelling part of the literary, political, and intellectual history of mid-twentieth-century American Indian writing. That they imagined indigenous revolution during this "arid," "hesitant," "uncertain," or "dormant" era demands that we adjust our understanding of the relationship they have with authors of the next, renaissance era. However, recognizing that the imagined Mexico of this period is not essentially revolutionary but multidimensional politically is as important as acknowledging the same about the American Indian civil rights and early renaissance era. *The Red Land to the South* demonstrates, still, that this era is far more literarily and politically robust than conventional American Indian literary history tells us. This era also coheres in its turn to Mexico and in many other ways yet to be considered. Future studies of Downing, Riggs, and McNickle's many contemporaries, including Kirby Brown's work with Oskison, Riggs, and fellow Cherokee authors Ruth Muskrat Bronson and Rachel Caroline Eaton, will reveal more surprises and much greater nuance to this still neglected era.[25] When we recontextualize McNickle, as well as authors such as Luther Standing Bear and Ella Deloria, in broader American Indian literary and political histories and recognize this era as the one into which Erdrich, Harjo, Momaday, Ortiz, Silko, Vizenor, and Welch were born, we will have a much greater understanding of its role in producing the renaissance.

We will also see with greater clarity and precision this era's own literary, historical, and political value. Downing's detective novels and McNickle's *Runner in the Sun* contain critical American Indian perspectives on past and present life in the borderlands. Their work, including Riggs's Mexican plays, rejects the anti-Mexican hysteria that motivated the raid at La Placita in Los Angeles on February 16, 1931, and the decision on December 11, 1935, by federal judge John Knight of the First Federal Circuit Court in Buffalo, New York, to deny "Timoteo Andrade's application for citizenship on the grounds that he was a 'Mexican Indian.'"[26] Both authors also produce narratives of migration and immigration that could inform incisive condemnations of SB 1070 and HB 2281, the infamous pieces of anti-immigrant and antiethnic studies legislation passed in Arizona in 2010, or help to explain the murder of Sergio Adrian Hernandez Guereca, the fifteen-year-old boy shot in the head by border patrol agent Jesus Mesa Jr. on June 7, 2010. Their literary and intellectual inquiries into American Indian and indigenous Mexican life in the mid-twentieth century affirms local, tribal national, transnational, and continental modes of indigenous belonging in the Americas and asserts the urgency and desirability of indigenous self-determination in all these contexts.

Notes

Introduction

1. Parker, *Singing an Indian Song*, 83.

2. The Western History Collection at the University of Oklahoma has eighteen postcards and seventy-two letters that Mathews wrote from October 13, 1939, to August 21, 1940, while he was in Mexico. He also continued to keep his diary during this period.

3. "Assimilation, Apocalypticism, and Reform (1900–1967)" is the title of the third chapter of Weaver's *That the People Might Live* (1997). Weaver follows Warrior, who titles a section of the first chapter of *Tribal Secrets* (1995) "1890–1916: Assimilationism and Apocalypticism." See also Justice, *Our Fire Survives the Storm*, 16.

4. Warrior, *Tribal Secrets*, 3. When he assesses the presence or absence of "associative cohesion" in a particular era of Native writing, Warrior's primary interests include the general interactions among Native writers and, more specifically, their political commitments. Warrior asserts, for example, that "[John Joseph] Mathews and his writing contemporaries did little of the political associating with one another of the previous generation." He sees 1973 to the present, or in hindsight 1973 to 1995, as a period also marked by this absence of association among Native writers. Warrior notes, however, that "unifying categories [. . .] obscure crucial differences in a discourse much in need of recognizing the variety of contemporary American Indian experiences. Cohesion, on this reading, is neither beneficial, possible, or necessary." Warrior, *Tribal Secrets*, 25 and 43.

5. Ibid., 14. "Without the presence of a national organization or a coherent political project," Warrior explains, "the work of these intellectuals has no common theme except in the few years during which the movement toward John Collier's Indian Reorganization Act under President Franklin Roosevelt provided something of a focal point."

6. Teuton, *Red Land, Red Power*, 20.

7. Womack, *Red on Red*, 6.

8. Lyons, *X-Marks*, 132.

9. Drewey Wayne Gunn's catalog of U.S. writers that visited and wrote

about Mexico during this period includes, for example, Conrad Aiken, Sherwood Anderson, Carleton Beals, Saul Bellow, Elizabeth Bishop, Paul Bowles, William S. Burroughs, Anita Brenner, Witter Bynner, Gregory Corso, Hart Crane, John Dos Passos, Lawrence Ferlinghetti, Allen Ginsberg, Robert Hayden, Ernest Hemingway, Langston Hughes, Jack Kerouac, Archibald MacLeish, Wright Morris, Charles Olson, Katherine Anne Porter, Kenneth Rexroth, Muriel Rukeyser, John Steinbeck, Tennessee Williams, and William Carlos Williams.

10. Robinson, "The Extended Presence," 3.

11. Warrior, *Tribal Secrets*, 10.

12. Garroutte, *Real Indians*, 25.

13. Shoemaker, *American Indian Population Recovery in the Twentieth Century*, 4.

14. Ibid., 5.

15. See Schmal, "Indigenous Identity in the Mexican Census."

16. Gutiérrez, *Nationalist Myths and Ethnic Identities*, 6.

17. Ibid., 33.

18. See Schmal.

19. Shoemaker, 4.

20. Gutiérrez, 40.

21. Ibid., 51.

22. Ibid., 52.

23. Garroutte, 15. Throughout *The Red Land to the South*, bracketed ellipses indicate deleted material.

24. Ibid., 19.

25. Ibid., 24–25. See also 52–53 for additional consideration of the inaccuracy and unreliability of the rolls.

26. Sturm, *Blood Politics*, 86.

27. Ibid., 87.

28. Ibid., 88.

29. Ibid., 108.

30. Ibid., 110.

31. Stephen, *Transborder Lives*, xv. Both communities in Stephen's study had residents who participated in the first bracero program from 1942 to 1964.

32. Warrior and Teuton orient their studies of American Indian writing, *Tribal Secrets* and *Red Land, Red Power*, respectively, to the implications of that writing for American Indian futures. See Warrior, *Tribal Secrets*, xvi, and Teuton, *Red Land, Red Power*, xvi–xvii.

33. See, for example, Rudolfo Corky Gonzales, *Yo Soy Joaquin/I Am Joaquin* (1967), a bilingual epic poem; the poem "El Plan Espiritual de Aztlán" (1969) by Alurista; and "El Plan de Espiritual de Aztlán" (1969), the coauthored manifesto of Chicano nationalism adopted at the First National Chicano Youth Liberation

Conference in Denver, Colorado. Sheila Marie Contreras provides a concise summary of Aztlán as a feature of Chicana/o indigenism in *Blood Lines: Myth, Indigenism, and Chicana/o Literature.*

34. Contreras, 32. See also pages 72–78 for her review of the various interpretations of Aztlán in Chicana/o literary critical discourse.

35. See Riley, *Becoming Aztlán*, 5, and note 2 of chapter 2 on 205.

36. Aztlán, Riley asserts, "is [. . .] generally bounded by the southern Great Plains and the northern Mexican plateaus to the east, and the southern flank of the Rocky Mountains to the north. Its western boundary is the lower Colorado River and Gulf of California. To the south a fuzzy line of demarcation runs from the major Sonoran river basins eastward across the Sierra Madre Occidental through the high plateaus and interior basins of Chihuahua and Coahuila. In modern terms the region includes the U.S. states of Arizona and New Mexico, as well as parts of Utah, Nevada, Colorado, California, and Texas. In Mexico it encompasses much of Sonora and Chihuahua, with influences that reach into portions of Sinaloa, Durango, and Baja California Norte" (6).

37. Menchaca, *Recovering History, Constructing Race*, 21.

38. Meyer and Sherman, *The Course of Mexican History*, 56.

39. See Menchaca, 19–26. Emilio Rodriquez Flores says, for example, that Aztlán is north of the Gila River and west of the Colorado River in California. See Menchaca, 8.

40. Downing, *The Mexican Earth*, 36.

41. See chapter 2, "Early Invasions," of Conley, *The Cherokee Nation*, 17–23. Conley indicates that De Soto likely encountered Cherokees during his 1539–42 expedition, while the Cherokees did not encounter the English, Conley explains, until 1654. Dianna Everett is more specific: "Their first encounter with Europeans came in 1540 when members of a Spanish expedition led by Hernando de Soto camped along the Keowee River in present-day South Carolina." Everett, *The Texas Cherokees*, 5.

42. Starr, *History of the Cherokee Indians*, 22.

43. Conley, *The Cherokee Nation*, 6.

44. Ibid.

45. Power, *Early Art of the Southeastern Indians*, 157.

46. Power, 158. Power provides additional details to explain what leads her to this conclusion: "Specific evidence of contacts between these two areas includes the Osages' apparent awareness of the Mesoamerican date Thirteen Reed and its association with the birth of the sun, the strong parallel between the Iowa/Winnebago myth of Red Horn and the experiences of the character One Hunter in the Quiché Mayan *Popul Vuh*, the similarity of origin myths of the Choctaws and Aztecs, and the use in the greater Cahokia area of blood autosacrifice in a form and function like that found in Mexico. Consequently, a comparable cultural background may have contributed to a similar worldview and a resulting slow,

informal (e.g. person-to-person) exchange of ideas over time. However, the depictions of exact features in iconography, such as the regalia and accessories of the Winged Beings, suggest a more direct artistic relationship" (158).

47. Riley, 7. For earlier scholarship that shaped Riley's ideas, see *The Meso-american Southwest* (1974). Riley coedited the collection with Basil C. Hedrick and J. Charles Kelley.

48. Mooney, *Myths of the Cherokees*, 391.

49. Everett, 11, 13. Everett notes that the Cherokees shared a common history as members of the Mississippian culture with "the Choctaws, the Chickasaws, the Creeks, the Natchez, such other southeastern groups as the Kadohadachos, and other tribes of eastern Texas" (4). Their move to Texas, therefore, could be understood as an opportunity to reestablish historical, cultural, and political ties.

50. Ibid., 23.

51. See Everett, 25–29, for the description of Fields as a "red" or war leader for the Texas Cherokees and his diplomatic journey to Mexico City.

52. See Everett, 75 and 88.

53. Littlefield explains, "When removal appeared inevitable, John Ross wrote to Señor de Costello y Lanza, charge d'affaires of Mexico, on March 22, 1835, informing him that Ross's people would move out of the limits of the United States if they could make arrangements with the Mexican Government to secure for the Cherokees land 'sufficient for their accommodation—and also the enjoyments of equal rights and privileges of citizenship.'" The plan did not come to fruition. Littlefield, "Utopian Dreams," 408.

54. See Conley, *The Cherokee Nation*, 162. Mooney reports in *Myths of the Cherokees* that while some of Chief Bowl's Texas Cherokees escaped to Indian Territory, others went to Mexico. See Mooney, 146. Perhaps Sequoyah was hoping to find some of these Cherokee relatives. In "Historical Sketches of the Cherokees," 71–89, Lucy Lowrey Hoyt Keys also reports on Sequoyah's trip.

55. See Littlefield, 409–10.

56. See Ibid., 411–19. Littlefield provides details of these plans and the various intrigues in which opponents and proponents of them engaged.

57. Conley, *The Cherokee Nation*, 196. The Snake faction of the Creek Nation also contemplated moving to Mexico. See Littlefield's edition of Alexander Posey's *The Fus Fixico Letters*, especially letters four and five. In his description of the anti-allotment Snakes led by Chitto Harjo, Littlefield explains: "In addition to refusing to participate in allotment, many Snakes reconsidered an old plan: emigration to Mexico. Shortly after removal in the 1830s, some Creeks and members of other tribes had gone to Mexico and remained there. Thus Mexico was considered a political haven by many conservatives of the Creek and other Indian nations." Posey, *The Fus Fixico Letters*, 57. In her analysis of Posey's shift from opposition to support of Creek immigration to Mexico, Tereza Szeghi argues, "For some full-blood traditionalists, Mexico represented a safe haven from the United States; for

many mixed-blood progressives, it was an answer to their own 'Indian problem,' which they believed jeopardized their social standing in the United States." See Szeghi, "'The Injun Is Civilized,'" 14.

58. Conley, *The Cherokee Nation*, 174.

59. Ibid., 203.

60. Littlefield relates, "For almost a century after 1838 different factions of the Cherokee tribe entertained and fostered various utopian dreams of escaping life as they found it within their nation and within the United States." He then elaborates, "The utopian schemes of the fullblood Cherokees took two main forms. The most persistent and longest lasting, and one that was popular among the fullbloods of many other tribes, was emigration to Mexico, the purchase of land, and the establishment of a colony there. Generally, the idea of emigration became popular in the 1890s when the fullbloods realized that allotment and the dissolution of tribal government were inevitable and remained popular until Oklahoma statehood in 1907. It was then revived periodically for two more decades." Littlefield, "Utopian Dreams," 404, 407.

61. See Mould, *Choctaw Tales*, 64–66, for versions of this story, including one that indicates the Cherokees also emerged from Nanih Waiya.

62. In May of 1539, Hernándo de Soto landed on the western coast of Florida at what is now the town of Bradenton. De Soto's journey through the Southeast, until his death on May 21, 1542, parallels Cortés's journey into Anáhuac in many of the most brutal ways, including his meeting with Muskogean people under the leadership of Tuscaloosa at Mabila. See Duncan, *Hernando de Soto*, 374–84. Duncan calls Tuscaloosa's community *Atahachi*, while other commentators identify him as Alibamu or Alabama, Mobile, or Choctaw. Valerie Lambert explains that the French, however, "initiated the first European relationship with the Choctaws in 1699." See Lambert, *Choctaw Nation*, 32. Lambert adds that this alliance with the French led to warfare with the Chickasaws and Muscogee Creeks throughout the 1700s.

63. See Everett, 22, and for more information about Choctaws in Texas, see 16 and 25. By 1834, an official of the Mexican government estimated that there were five hundred Cherokees and five hundred Choctaws in Texas. See Everett, 67.

64. See the back matter of the reprint of *The Cat Screams* by Popular Library.

65. Parker, *Singing an Indian Song*, 1–6.

66. See Schroeder, "Introduction: The Genre of Conquest Studies," 14. She explains, "The Tlaxcalteca, of course, are the best known of the indios conquistadores, for theirs was the first major polity to ally with Cortés in significant numbers."

67. Here I am thinking of Ortiz's influential essay "Towards a National Indian Literature: Cultural Authenticity in Nationalism."

68. Jace Weaver and others have made similar observations. See, for example,

Weaver's comments on the renaissance in his foreword to the posthumously published novel *The Singing Bird* (2007) by Oskison.

69. Teuton, *Red Land, Red Power*, 2.

70. Cook-Lynn, "The American Indian Fiction Writers," 94.

71. The Oklahoma Indian Welfare or Thomas-Rogers Act extended the Indian Reorganization Act to the tribal nations of the old Indian Territory.

72. Anzaldúa, *Borderlands/La Frontera*, 25; Truett, *Fugitive Landscapes*, 9.

73. Paredes, *A Texas-Mexican Cancionero: Folksongs of the Lower Border*, xiv. Ramón Saldívar explains that Paredes used Greater Mexico "to indicate the Mexican labor diasporas north from the border, as well as the social, economic, political, and symbolic overlap between those contiguous worlds." More specifically, "With the making of Greater Mexico as an analytical concept, Paredes would bypass the apparent necessity of the binary situation, of being either Mexican or American exclusively, in an attempt to imagine a social formation between nation-states where cultural citizen-subjects could claim and exercise rights in the civic, public sphere of open debate and exchange, and in the ideational domain of the subject." See Saldívar, *The Borderlands of Culture*, 5 and 235.

74. Adams, *Continental Divides*, 18.

75. Ibid.

76. Ibid., 35.

77. Huhndorf, *Mapping the Americas*, 19.

78. Ibid., 2.

79. See the special issue of *American Quarterly*, 62.3, titled "Alternative Contact: Indigeneity, Globalism, and American Studies," coedited by Lai and Smith.

80. Stephen, 6.

81. Warrior, *The People and the Word*, 107.

82. Ibid.

83. This evaluation of Lawrence is based on my own reading of *The Plumed Serpent*. On Crane and Greene, see Gunn, *American and British Writers in Mexico, 1556-1973*, 156–57 and 185. These summaries of Crane's and Greene's views of Mexico come from the documents that Gunn cites.

84. See Rodríguez, "The Fiction of Solidarity."

85. Kerouac, *On the Road*, 253. Italics are in the original.

86. Womack, *Red on Red*, 13.

87. The term "early contemporary" is Chadwick Allen's from his *Blood Narrative* (2002).

88. There are some retellings of oral stories published and/or written by American Indian intellectuals in this period as well, such as Bertrand Walker, *Tales of the Bark Lodges* (1920); Arthur C. Parker, *Seneca Myths and Folktales* (1923); Joseph Griffis, *Indian Circle Stories* (1928); Ella Deloria, *Dakota Texts* (1932); Mourning Dove, *Coyote Stories* (1933); Luther Standing Bear, *Stories of the Sioux* (1934); Jesse

Cornplanter, *Legends of the Longhouse* (1935); and Edmund Nequatewa, *Truth of a Hopi: Stories Relating to the Origins, Myths, and Clan Histories of the Hopi* (1936).

89. Warrior, *Tribal Secrets*, 22.

90. Braunlich, *Haunted by Home*, 103 and 140.

91. See Ware, "The Cherokee Kid," for a critical assessment of Rogers's star power and its roots in the Cherokee Nation.

92. *Black Elk Speaks* (1932) is an as-told-to autobiography based on interviews Black Elk gave to the poet John Neihardt. Neihardt constructed a conventional narrative of American Indian loss from these interviews. In 1985, Raymond DeMallie published *The Sixth Grandfather: Black Elk's Teachings to John Neihardt*.

93. Deloria Jr., Preface to *Black Elk Speaks*, xi, and Krupat, *For Those Who Come After*, 126. In his preface to *Black Elk Speaks*, Deloria Jr. also discusses the book's substantial influence on Native people: for "the contemporary generation of young Indians who have been aggressively searching for roots of their own in the structure of universal reality, the book has become a North American bible of all tribes" (xii). In his assessment of *Black Elk Speaks*, Krupat considers Black Elk's view of his story in contrast to Neihardt's presentation of it. He also questions Deloria Jr.'s apparent willingness to disregard the significance of the narrative's source.

94. In fact, Charles Curtis (Kaw) served as the vice president under Hoover during this period from 1929 to 1933.

95. Warrior, *Tribal Secrets*, 25.

1. Dreadful Armies

1. The United States and Mexico are postcolonial in the most orthodox use of the term by first generation postcolonial theorists such as Ashcroft, Griffiths, and Tiffin, the authors of *The Empire Writes Back*. See Allen, *Blood Narrative*, 28–36, for a critique of orthodox postcolonial theory's failure to account for indigenous people and their writing.

2. For example, see Collier's essays "Mexico: A Challenge" and "Mexico's Rural Schools and Our Indian Schools." Responses by Native Americans to Collier's reform program were mixed. The Indian Reorganization Act, also known as the Wheeler-Howard Act, ended the official federal policy of allotment but also provided for only a limited form of tribal nation self-governance. On the Indian Reorganization Act, see Deloria Jr., *Custer Died for Your Sins*.

3. The legislation established the guidelines for terminating the Choctaw Nation's federal trust status as a sovereign though domestic dependent nation. See Lambert's *Choctaw Nation* for a specific history of the Choctaw Nation of Oklahoma's fight against the termination of its federal trust status. The Choctaw leadership was prepared to accept termination until a coalition of young adult Choctaws and off-reservation citizens quickly organized an ultimately successful

effort to stop it. For broader and more general histories of the termination era, see Deloria Jr., "The Disastrous Policy of Termination" in *Custer Died for Your Sins*, and Fixico, *Termination and Relocation: Federal Indian Policy, 1945–1960*.

4. Downing's parents married on August 1, 1899.

5. See Downing, "A Choctaw's Autobiography," 49; Tindall, "George Downing Family"; and Parman, "Downing, George Todd (1902–1974)." Samuel Downing's Dawes Roll number is 14068. His son Todd's Dawes Roll number is 14069.

6. Downing, "A Choctaw's Autobiography," 49. Samuel Downing served in Troop M of the Rough Riders with many other American Indians from Indian Territory.

7. Lambert, 60.

8. Downing, "A Choctaw's Autobiography," 49.

9. Ibid. "Not" is a troubling word in the context of what Downing is saying. "Now" is more consistent with the message of this passage and the entire text.

10. Downing, *Cultural Traits*, 1.

11. Ibid., 2.

12. Cook-Lynn was born in 1930; Ortiz was born in 1941. I am thinking of Cook-Lynn's "The American Indian Fiction Writers" and Ortiz's "Towards a National Indian Literature."

13. *The American Indian* also had a predominantly American Indian staff. For a biography of Harkins, whose family history and life story parallel Downing's, see Wright, "Lee F. Harkins, Choctaw."

14. By continental, I mean North American but with the understanding, following Adams in *Continental Divides*, that North America is an invention with a multiplicity of geographical, political, and economic meanings. Downing's interest was Mexico, but his vision of a transnational indigenous world is applicable to Canada. Adams explains, "During the post-World War II period the idea of North America as a continent unto itself thus came to replace the prevailing conception of America as a single metageographic unit. In the 1950s the division of the Americas into North and South became the dominant convention for maps produced in the Western world" (13). Downing's indigenous North America constitutes what Adams would call an "alternative version of continentalism" (17).

15. Rzepka makes a distinction between detective fiction, "any story that contains a major character undertaking the investigation of a mysterious crime or similar transgression," and a story of detection, "in which the puzzle element directly engages the reader's attention and powers of inference." Downing's novels are both classical, rather than hard-boiled, detective novels and novels of detection. "The perfect fit between the Golden Age plot formula and a relatively affluent and conservative middle-class readership," Rzepka explains, "led

to classical detection's dominance of the interwar best-seller lists." See Rzepka, *Detective Fiction*, 12 and 154.

16. Woolsey, "The Shooting of Two Mexican Students," 514. Guess shot the fugitive Elbert Hart twice in the back and once in the head as Hart fled from authorities in Esteline, Texas, on January 29, 1931. Six days earlier, Hart had murdered Guess's former partner, Detective Elmer "Buddy" Moorehead of the Ardmore Police Department. See Owens, *Oklahoma Heroes*, 146–47. Guess was also part of the posse looking for Haney Horace Liddell and the men that he led in a locally famous robbery of the Love County National Bank in Marietta, Oklahoma, on January 25, 1928. The bandits took $9,321. See Leonard, *Bah, Bah, Black Sheep*.

17. Following the murders, President Herbert Hoover sent a brief message to Mexican President Pascual Ortiz Rubio, and Secretary of State Henry L. Stimson requested that Congress authorize payments of $15,000 each to the families of the dead men. For documents from the Hoover administration related to the case, see Woolley and Peters, *The American Presidency Project*.

18. Rzepka owns a collection of Downing family letters, though only a few are from Todd. Downing wrote this letter on *Books Abroad* letterhead and sent it from Norman. The letter begins "Dear Sis." It does not have a date.

19. After his stint at N. W. Ayer and Son, Inc., Downing took a position in 1947 on the copy staff of the advertising firm Gray and Rogers. The *New York Times* reported in 1949 that Downing then secured an appointment as a "special consultant on Latin American advertising" at Weightman Advertising in Philadelphia. He was, simultaneously, the editor of *Panamericanismo*, which was published by the Pan American Association in the same city. See "Advertising News and Notes" in the *New York Times* from 1947 and 1949, respectively.

20. The *New York Times* mentions that Downing was Choctaw at least three times. See "Books-Authors," "Napoleon's Letters," and "Book Notes" from 1934. The Popular Library reprint of *The Cat Screams* also identifies him as Choctaw on the back cover, which reads: "He is especially qualified to write about Mexico, an Indian country, since he is one quarter Choctaw, his paternal grandmother having been one of the survivors of the Trail of Tears, when the Choctaws were forced to migrate from Mississippi to Indian territory in 1832." See Figure 1.2.

21. The *New York Times* announced in 1935, for example, that Downing "has resigned from the faculty of the University of Oklahoma to devote all his time to writing." See "Book Notes," 1935.

22. The translations of Downing's work include Italian editions of *The Cat Screams, La Pensione di Madame Fournier* (1938), and *Murder on the Tropic, La Luce Gialla* (1939). The Spanish, Italian, and Finnish translations of *Vultures in the Sky* are titled, respectively, *Buitres en el Cielo* (1952), *Il Terribile Viaggio: Romanzo* (1940; 1977); and *Kuoleman Linnut: Salapoliisiromaani* (1942). There are eight

Dutch editions of his work: *Het Mysterie Van de Zijden Kousen, Een Kat Huilt, De Gele Dood, Sprekende Kogels, Het Uur Zonder Schaduw, Het Mysterie Van de Gebroken Naald, Met Bloed Gekocht,* and *De Dood Slaat Toe.* I have not seen copies of these editions with the exception of *Een Kat Huilt, The Cat Screams.* The British publisher Methuen published editions of *The Cat Screams* (1935), *Murder on the Tropic* (1936), *Vultures in the Sky* (1936), *The Case of the Unconquered Sisters* (1937), *The Last Trumpet: Murder in a Mexican Bull Ring* (1938), and *Night Over Mexico* (1938).

23. Marion E. Gridley, in the 1936 edition of *Indians of Today,* and Wolfgang Hochbruck indicate that *The Cat Screams* was also translated into Swedish and German. I have not been able to find these editions of the novel.

24. Arthur Pierson was the director, and Broadway veterans Mildred Dunnock, Lloyd Gough, Lea Penman, Martin Wolfson, and Herbert Yost starred. Dunnock, Gough, and Penman acted in more than twenty Broadway shows each, and Wolfson and Yost acted in more than thirty. I have not discovered any evidence that Downing was involved in the production. For a review of *The Cat Screams,* see Bordman, 215.

25. See "Murder in May," *Time,* June 9, 1941. Accessed May 24, 2007, http://www.time.com/time/magazine/article/0,9171,795384,00.html.

26. Wright includes Downing in a list of "Choctaw[s] prominent in the history of the Indian Territory and Oklahoma since 1898." Wright, *A Guide to the Indian Tribes of Oklahoma,* 114.

27. Pronzini authors the entry on Downing. He calls *Vultures* "an expertly crafted whodunit." Of Downing's other novels, Pronzini comments that "all are well worth investigating." Pronzini and Muller, *1001 Midnights,* 217.

28. Krupat, *The Voice in the Margin,* 66. In the canonical hierarchy outlined by Krupat, WASP, eastern, male writers appear first and are followed by feminist, African American, and then gay and lesbian authors, respectively.

29. Owens, *Other Destinies,* 20.

30. For examples of brief scholarly discussions of Downing's work, see A. LaVonne Brown Ruoff's contribution to *The Cambridge Companion to Native American Literature,* edited by Joy Porter and Kenneth Roemer; Luis Leal's review of the reprint of *The Mexican Earth;* and Jace Weaver's *That the People Might Live.* Downing's status as a nearly forgotten writer has to this point contributed to a lack of reliable information about his work.

31. Hochbruck, "Mystery Novels to Choctaw Pageant," 217. He begins his essay by asserting that "Native American literature did not exist before N. Scott Momaday's *House Made of Dawn.*" Rather than considering Downing's work in detail after a discussion of various methods of identifying what constitutes Native American literature, he proceeds to "approach the problem of defining Native American Literature on the basis of the individual text." He outlines seven

categories of texts that rigidly circumscribe the borders of Native literatures. See Hochbruck, 205 and 208.

32. Powell, "Blood and Scholarship," 6. Powell discusses Arnold Krupat's work, including *New Voices in Native American Literary Criticism* (1993). Hochbruck's essay appears in this collection.

33. "Books and Authors," 95.

34. Gridley, *Indians of Today* (1936), 43. Gridley revised the entry on Downing in the 1947 edition of *Indians of Today*: "An instructor in Spanish at Oklahoma University, he also conducted student tours to Mexico. The murder of two Mexican youths disrupted one of these tours, but the details of the murder were the inspiration for his first book, 'Murder on Tour.'" See Gridley, *Indians of Today* (1947), 33.

35. See Allen, 7–10, for a discussion of the distinctions among kinds of indigeneity and colonial practice.

36. I am indebted to Lucy Maddox in *Citizen Indians* for this argument about Downing claiming a public space from which to speak. Maddox cites Ross Posnock on W. E. B. Du Bois and Edward Said on intellectuals broadly speaking. She explains: "My understanding of the role that Native intellectuals envisioned for themselves around the turn of the century is consistent with (and indebted to) the ways in which Said and Posnock describe the impulse and the method of the intellectual. The challenge for Native intellectuals, a dauntingly difficult challenge, was to define and represent the particularities of Native experience in ways that made them congenial with contemporary assumptions about universal values—that is, to articulate a specifically Native perspective on a set of universal principles to which Native people themselves could subscribe." See Maddox, *Citizen Indians*, 13.

37. Vaughan and Lewis, *The Eagle and the Virgin*, 1.

38. Deloria, *Indians in Unexpected Places*, 6.

39. Vaughan and Lewis, 8. As Konkle demonstrates in *Writing Indian Nations*, nineteenth century American Indian leaders were already challenging the exile of their people from history by writing American Indians into it.

40. López, "The Noche Mexicana and the Exhibition of Popular Arts," 36.

41. See Huhndorf, *Mapping the Americas*, 46–70.

42. López, 23–24.

43. Stocking Jr., *The Shaping of American Anthropology*, 4.

44. Ibid., 18–19.

45. See Hoefel, "'Different by Degree,'" 181–202. For Boas's influence on Parker, see Hertzberg, *The Search for an American Indian Identity*, 52–53 and 61.

46. Lewis, "The Nation, Education, and the 'Indian Problem' in Mexico, 1920–1940," 177.

47. See Stocking Jr., for an overview of the changes that Boas helped to bring

to U.S. anthropology. Stocking Jr. argues that challenges to Boasian anthropology emerged in the 1930s and 1940s and became much more forceful in the 1950s and 1960s.

48. Hertzberg, 305. Hertzberg notes here that Boas was opposed to Collier's appointment as Commissioner of Indian Affairs.

49. See Lewis, 189–90.

50. See Knight, "Racism, Revolution, and Indigenismo: Mexico, 1910–1940," 87–98 for his assessment of various racist features of indigenismo.

51. See Sanjinés, "Indigenismo and Mestizaje," for a brief discussion of the links between indigenismo and mestizaje.

52. Pérez-Torres, *Mestizaje*, 6.

53. Hedrick, *Mestizo Modernism*, 4.

54. Bonfil Batalla, *México Profundo*, 24.

55. Knight, 77. Ashcroft, Griffiths, and Tiffin discuss the appropriation of indigeneity by settler colonists in *The Empire Writes Back*. Though indigenismo is a similar postcolonial appropriation of indigeneity, Mexican leaders and intellectuals also incorporated actual indigenous Mexican history and culture and, on occasion, people, into their imagined national identity.

56. López, 38.

57. Ibid., 41.

58. Lewis, 190. Later, the archaeologist Alfonso Caso pondered but rejected a reservation system for Mexico. See Knight, 84.

59. See Latorre and Latorre, *The Mexican Kickapoo Indians*, 122–32. In the 1950s, many Mexican Kickapoos returned to the United States as migrant laborers.

60. Lewis, 192. Just as John Collier encouraged the U.S. federal government to use Mexico's Indian policy as a guide, Mexican officials, such as Manuel Puig Casauranc, the director of the Secretario de Educacion Publica (SEP) in the mid-1920s, looked to U.S. federal Indian policy. Puig visited Native communities and boarding schools in New Mexico and returned to Mexico unimpressed by the U.S. attempt to incorporate American Indians into the nation. See Lewis, 191.

61. Rus, "The 'Comunidad Revolucionaria Institucional,'" 266–67. However, Rus argues: "Although the myth of the 'time of Cárdenas' is that it empowered the Indians and brought them new rights, a closer look reveals that in the long run it actually led to a more intimate form of domination." Rus, 267. See also Rus, 270–72, for a description of some of the cultural revitalization efforts and for specific examples of Maya resistance to interference by outsiders.

62. Knight describes the 1930s as "years of radical *indigenismo*," during which many indigenistas made their belief in Indian superiority to mestizos and Europeans part of the public discourse. See Knight, 85 and 92.

63. See Balderrama and Rodríguez, *Decade of Betrayal*, for a detailed account of the hysteria and the attendant deportations. González explains that the peon

was for U.S. authors "synonymous for Indian," and the peon as "an obstacle to modernization" became "conventional wisdom" by 1930. See González, *Culture of Empire*, 80–81. Michael Hilger identifies imminent Indian attacks as a distinctive feature of many of the early sound films in the 1930s that featured Native Americans.

64. The death of a "poet of the United States" named Helen Carstairs recalls Hart Crane's suicide after he wrote his last finished poem, "The Broken Tower," in Taxco in early 1932. While on his way from Mexico to the United States, Crane jumped to his death from the deck of the steamship *Orizaba* in April of 1932. Downing, *The Cat Screams*, 2. See Gunn, *American and British Writers in Mexico, 1556–1973*, 155–60, for a description of the poem's origins in one of Crane's visits to Taxco.

65. French, British, and Spanish troops invaded Mexico in 1862, and Ferdinand Maximilian, a member of the Austrian Habsburg royal family, was proclaimed Emperor of Mexico in 1863. He was executed by firing squad in 1867, after which Benito Juárez returned to the presidency. See Meyer and Sherman, 387–401.

66. Downing, *The Cat Screams*, 12. A casa de huésped ("guest house") consists of a room in a private home. It is usually an inexpensive option for travelers.

67. Ibid.

68. See Meyer and Sherman, *The Course of Mexican History*, 374–410, for a history of Juárez's career.

69. Downing, *The Cat Screams*, 1 and 3.

70. See, for example, *Murder*, 73, and *Vultures* 66–67.

71. Downing was familiar with Brinton's work. He owned *Rig Veda Americanus: Sacred Songs of the Ancient Mexicans, with a Gloss in Nahuatl* (1890). For the references in Herrera and Sahagún, see Brinton, *Nagualism*, 4–5 and 5–6, respectively.

72. Brinton, 5.

73. Downing, *The Cat Screams*, 20.

74. Other academics include Professor Horace Starns Bymaster in *Murder on Tour*; Professor Garnett Voice, Professor Fogarty, and the archaeological students Karl Weikel and John Clay Biggerstaff in *The Case of the Unconquered Sisters*; and Professor Gulliver Damson in *Night Over Mexico*.

75. Downing, *The Cat Screams*, 209–10.

76. See Rzepka's cultural history of detective fiction, specifically page 15, for an assessment of the detective genre's debt to the modern sciences.

77. Van Dine, "Twenty Rules for Writing Detective Stories," 198.

78. Downing, "Murder Is a Rather Serious Business," 182.

79. Rzepka, 15.

80. Downing, *The Cat Screams*, 250–51 (italics in original).

81. Ibid., 252.

82. John R. Reed argues that "Collins' detective novel, apparently concerned with little more than a love story and a theft, is actually a broad indictment of an entire way of life" and then proposes that "imperial depredation is the true crime of *The Moonstone*." John R. Reed, "English Imperialism and the Unacknowledged Crime of *The Moonstone*," 288–89.

83. Rzepka, 107.

84. Ibid., 109.

85. Thank you to Nantinee Nualnim of the Thai Student Association at the University of Texas at Austin for confirming the accuracy of this translation. In private correspondence with Chadwick Allen, he noted the significance of the "noon" and "moon" rhyme and suggested that "Noon," as in Gwendolyn Noon's name, could be considered an inversion of "moon," as in the moonstone of Collins's novel.

86. Downing, *The Cat Screams*, 206.

87. Ibid., 207.

88. Ibid., 293–94.

89. Brinton, 35–36.

90. Hedrick, *Mestizo Modernism*, 22.

91. Bonfil Batalla, 138.

92. Ibid., 139.

93. See chapter 5 for a detailed discussion of *Runner*. The most well-known work of American Indian spirituality in this era is *Black Elk Speaks*. Neihardt's version of Black Elk's teachings forecloses on the possibility that distinctly indigenous religious practices can coexist with modernity. Other nonfiction works of this era such as Ella Deloria's *Speaking of Indians* (1944) and Ruth Muskrat Bronson's *Indians Are People, Too* (1944) advocate for American Indian human rights and economic and political self-determination but reject the continuation or revitalization of indigenous languages and religious traditions as a meaningful part of twentieth-century American Indian life. Both authors assure their audiences that Native people want to be both Christians and U.S. citizens participating fully in American democratic institutions.

94. These observations about Oskison's novels originated in lengthy conversations with Kirby Brown and should be understood properly as the product of a collaborative intellectual practice.

95. See Purdy's detailed reconstruction of the history of *Wind* in chapter 4 of *Word Ways*.

96. Weaver, "Foreword," *The Singing Bird*, xii–xiii.

97. Justice, *Our Fire Survives the Storm*, 114.

98. Oskison, *The Singing Bird*, 22.

99. Ibid., 38.

100. Ibid., 78.

101. Ibid., 110.

102. Powell and Smith explain the history of these religious items in the introduction: "Three of the noted early historians of Cherokee culture—James Adair, Cephas Washburn, and James Mooney—all confirm the existence of the sacred 'Ark.' Its contents, however, remain unknown to Western historians; although stories are still told in the Smoky Mountains about ancient forms of writing that predate the invention of Sequoyah's syllabary." *The Singing Bird*, xxxvii.

103. Ibid., 149.

104. Ibid., 156.

105. Ibid., 168.

106. McNickle, *Wind from an Enemy Sky*, 9.

107. Bull calls it "our old Indian power"; Henry Jim calls the Feather Boy their "strongest" bundle; Iron Child, also of Henry Jim's generation, calls it "our Indian flag, our Indian Lord Jesus." McNickle, *Wind from an Enemy Sky*, 24, 18, 85. Feather Boy "visited the people and showed them how to live." *Wind from an Enemy Sky*, 135.

108. Ibid., 208.

109. Ibid., 148. McNickle might have based the character Carlos, the indigenous Peruvian who leads this revolution, on the Peruvian writer and activist José Carlos Maríategui.

110. Ibid., 11 and 12. Bull thinks, "The boy would grow up to be a leader"; Two Sleeps says, "This boy [. . .] will have power."

111. Ibid., 256. The italics are in the original.

112. Ruppert reads *Wind from an Enemy Sky* as an act of mediation: "McNickle aimed to re-educate both Native and non-Native readers so that they could better understand each other's cultural codes." His final comments on *Wind from an Enemy Sky* capture the tenuousness of the hope in the novel: "The identity of the Little Elk Indians as a specific historical formulation, or as McNickle might say, the fit of an individual to the world, is forever broken when the Feather Boy bundle is lost. The elements of identity posited in Bull, Henry Jim, and Two Sleeps must be united and reconfigured in Antoine, for out of him will emerge a renewed Indian identity." See Ruppert, *Mediation in Contemporary Native American Fiction*, 110 and 130.

113. See Bernardin, "Mixed Messages," and Brown, "Mourning Dove's Voice in *Cogewea*," for discussions of the role that Lucullus V. McWhorter had in editing the novel. Brown describes the novel, which Mourning Dove began in 1912, as "quintessentially a spiritual autobiography" (6). Like McNickle, Mourning Dove's family had Canadian roots. Her father, Joseph Quintasket, was born in British Columbia at Lake Okanagan. His mother was Nicola and Okanagan (spelled with an "a" rather than an "o" in Canada), and his father was a Scot. Her mother,

Lucy Stui-kin, was, Quintasket says, a full-blood born at Kettle Falls, Washington. Quintasket explains, "Her father was Stui-kin (Beaver Head) of the Trout Lake (Sin-na-aich-kis-tu) band of the Arrow Lakes people, with a strain of Kootenay ancestry. Her mother was Soma-how-atqhu (She Got Her Power From Water), youngest daughter of Head Chief See-whelh-ken of the People of the Falls (Swhy-ayl-puh), the true Colvile tribe." See Mourning Dove, *A Salishan Autobiography*, 6.

114. See Mourning Dove, *Cogewea*, 131. Brown argues, "It is Stemteema who most completely embodies the Indian beliefs and way of life in the novel" (11).

115. Mourning Dove, *Cogewea*, 40–41.

116. Ibid., 41.

117. Ibid., 59–60.

118. Ibid., 129 and 160.

119. Cogewea, for example, rejects the lesson of "The Story of Green-Blanket Feet" that Stemteema tells to warn her to avoid Densmore. Later, she recalls the story as impressing her. Eventually, she understands its lesson, only to continue to desire to marry Densmore. See Mourning Dove, *Cogewea*, 176, 192, 231, and 248. At the end of the novel, Cogewea and Jim LaGrinder, the ranch hand she plans to marry, affirm their belief in the practice of reading hot stones in a sweathouse. See page 284.

120. Warrior, *Tribal Secrets*, 46.

121. Ibid., 47, 54.

122. See chapter 13 of Matthews, *Sundown*, for the summer dances and chapter 14 for the peyote ceremony. Like Warrior, Schedler also recuperates *Sundown* but by reading it as a compelling interrogation of modernist literary practice: "Although Mathews's novel bears no formal resemblance to the intricate textual experiments of metropolitan modernism, by creating his protagonist, Chal Windzer, in the mold of the isolated and deracinated metropolitan modernist subject, Mathews shows this form of identity to be untenable for the modern American Indian." See Schedler, *Border Modernism*, 43.

123. McNickle, *The Surrounded*, 297.

124. Purdy, 77–78.

125. Ibid., 81.

126. Oskison, *Black Jack Davy*, 272.

127. This statement also applies to *Black Elk Speaks*. Krupat asserts that "even in 1931, Black Elk was engaged in traditional ritual means to influence the fate of the Lakota." *For Those Who Come After*, 129.

128. For Deloria Jr., see especially *Custer Died for Your Sins: An Indian Manifesto* (1969); *We Talk, You Listen: New Tribes, New Turf* (1970); and *Behind the Trail of Broken Treaties: An Indian Declaration of Independence* (1974). For Alfred, see *Peace, Power, Righteousness: An Indigenous Manifesto* (1999).

129. Allen, 42.

130. Downing, *The Mexican Earth*, 319–20. See the laudatory review of Downing's book from the archaeologist and historian Philip Ainsworth Means in the *New York Times* in March of 1940.

131. McNickle published *Native American Tribalism: Indian Survivals and Renewals* in 1973. It is a revision of *The Indian Tribes of the United States: Ethnic and Cultural Survival* (1962).

132. "Oklahoma Deputy Kills 2 Mexican Students," 1.

133. "Two Held for Trial in Mexican Deaths," 16.

134. The reconstruction of the crime by the detective is a convention of classical detective fiction of the 1920s and 1930s. Rzepka explains, "It is easy to see the vital role that analepsis plays at the end of the classical detective story, when the detective (or sometimes the criminal himself) provides a summary narrative that connects and puts in proper order both the array of events leading up to the crime and the array of events by which the detective himself arrived at the correct sequence of the first array." Rzepka, 19.

135. For a description of the four types of migrants, see Lambert, 137–38.

136. Downing, *Murder on the Tropic*, 191.

137. Ibid., 192 (italics in original).

138. Momaday, *House Made of Dawn*, 58.

139. Thank you to Maria Rose Hynson, executive secretary to the provost and dean of the college, for finding Todd Downing in the 1950–51 *Washington College Catalog* and the 1951 Washington College yearbook, *Pegasus*.

140. Hochbruck explains that Downing returned to Atoka to take care of his mother and father. See Hochbruck, 212.

141. The quoted passage is from a pamphlet titled "Choctaw Bilingual Education Program." My gratitude again belongs to Charles Rzepka for sharing these materials.

142. Ibid.

143. See Lambert, 3.

2. ¡Indian Territory!

1. Braunlich discusses the Pulitzer rumors for *Green Grow the Lilacs* and *Russet Mantle*. See *Haunted by Home*, 103 and 140.

2. Riggs, *Green Grow the Lilacs*, 161.

3. Riggs designates his characters "citizens without a state" in a brief description of the play titled "The Cherokee Night." This document is in the Lynn Riggs Collection at the University of Tulsa's McFarlin Library.

4. Chapman, *The Best Plays of 1951–1952*, 345.

5. Teuton, *Red Land, Red Power*. Teuton discusses Silko's *Ceremony*, Momaday's *House Made of Dawn*, and James Welch's *Winter in the Blood*.

6. Information on the order in which Riggs wrote the plays comes from Braunlich's biography.

7. For recent inquiries into how experience might function as a literary critical category, see Warrior, *The People and the Word*, especially xxiii–xxx and the chapter on Apess; Womack, "Theorizing American Indian Experience" in *Reasoning Together: The Native Critics Collective*; and Teuton, *Red Land, Red Power*.

8. Quoted in Braunlich, *Haunted by Home*, 80. Braunlich quotes the letter at the beginning of her own literary analysis of the play, "*The Cherokee Night* of R. Lynn Riggs."

9. Quoted in Braunlich, *Haunted by Home*, 80.

10. Weaver, *That the People Might Live*, xiii.

11. Ibid., 103.

12. Womack, *Art as Performance*, 116.

13. Womack, *Red on Red*, 273, 276.

14. Ibid., 277.

15. See Lee, "Scholars Say Chronicler of Black Life Passed for White," 1.

16. Womack, *Red on Red*, 288, 289, 290.

17. Ibid., 295.

18. Ibid., 300.

19. Justice, *Our Fire Survives the Storm*, 92.

20. Ibid, 93.

21. Ibid., 98.

22. Ibid., 101.

23. Darby, "Broadway (Un)Bound," 9.

24. Sturm, *Blood Politics*, 98.

25. Ibid., 140.

26. Riggs, *Russet Mantle and The Cherokee Night*, 259.

27. Ibid., 260.

28. Riggs, "The Cherokee Night."

29. Riggs, *Russet Mantle and The Cherokee Night*, 223.

30. The incomplete and unfinished manuscript of the novel is at the Beinecke. Parts of the manuscript are dated as late as April 1954, just two months before his death in June.

31. Riggs, *Russet Mantle and The Cherokee Night*, 132.

32. The unpublished play *Verdigris Primitive*, retitled *All the Way Home* and produced in 1948, is set in Indian Territory, while *Out of Dust*, written in 1948 and produced in 1949 but not published until 2003, is also set in Indian Territory during the 1880s on the Shawnee Cattle Trail. Though the cattle drive in *Out of Dust* begins in Indian Territory, passes near Pryor Creek, and crosses the Verdigris River, Riggs does not provide any more indications of the precise setting of the play's action. The Grant family is driving its cattle towards Baxter Springs, Kansas, which is in the far southeast corner of Kansas just north of the Cherokee Nation.

They are seventy-five miles and about a week's ride with the herd from Baxter Springs but only a day-and-a-half horse ride for one person. See Riggs, *The Cherokee Night and Other Plays*, 260 and 293.

33. Said, *Culture and Imperialism*, xii–xiii.

34. Teuton, *Red Land, Red Power*, 45.

35. Allen describes the complex in *Blood Narrative*: "What I call the blood/land/memory complex is an expansion of Momaday's controversial trope blood memory that makes explicit the central role that land plays both in the specific project of defining indigenous minority personal, familial, and communal identities (blood) and in the larger project of reclaiming and reimagining indigenous minority histories (memory). Like Momaday's trope, the blood/land/memory complex articulates acts of indigenous minority recuperation that attempt to seize control of the symbolic and metaphorical meanings of indigenous 'blood,' 'land,' and 'memory' and that seek to liberate indigenous minority identities from definitions of authenticity imposed by dominant settler cultures, including those definitions imposed by well-meaning academics" (16).

36. Womack, *Red on Red*, 20.

37. Mathews, *Wah'Kon-Tah*, 349.

38. Eaton, "The Legend of the Battle of Claremore Mound," 376.

39. Anderson, "An Osage Niobe," 49.

40. Ibid., 50.

41. Braunlich, *Haunted by Home*, 22.

42. Burton, *Indian Territory and the United States*, 3–4.

43. Green, "Indian Territory, 1866–1889," 98.

44. Denson describes the decision to make these leasing arrangements: "Cherokee leaders were capable of making deals with American companies when it suited their purposes. The most famous example was the Cherokee government's leasing of a vast stretch of territory to the Cherokee Strip Live Stock Association. It was hoped that such leasing arrangements would help the tribe increase the national treasury and keep control of its underused land, thus turning the corporation from a threat into an ally." Denson, *Demanding the Cherokee Nation*, 193–94.

45. I am indebted to Amy Ware and her dissertation on Will Rogers for important biographical and historical details such as this one. See Ware, "The Cherokee Kid," 62.

46. Mathews, *Life and Death of an Oilman*, 72.

47. Weaver, *That the People Might Live*, 99.

48. Ibid. Albert Borowitz, in contrast, identifies the person on which Riggs based Jeeter Fry, Curly's antagonist, as a Cherokee. He argues, "the character of Jeeter Fry, and his dark color, reflect the Cherokee in Lynn Riggs and the dramatist's painful sense of the devaluation of Cherokees in American life." See Borowitz, "'Pore Jud is Daid,'" 21.

49. Weaver writes similarly of *Green Grow the Lilacs* in the "Clowns and Villains: American Natives and the American Musical" chapter of *Other Words*: "Both the play and the musical take place in Indian Territory—not Oklahoma Territory. Claremore is in the heart of the Cherokee Nation. What I am driving at is the suggestion that *Green Grow the Lilacs* is not devoid of Indian characters at all but is in some sense a play *about* them. It is entirely possible that the hero, Curly McClain, is an Indian." See Weaver, *Other Words*, 105.

50. Riggs, *Green Grow the Lilacs*, 6.

51. Ibid., 24.

52. Ibid., 75.

53. See Weaver, *That the People Might Live*, 100; and Riggs, *Green Grow the Lilacs*, 97–99.

54. Denson, 238.

55. Riggs, *Green Grow the Lilacs*, 156.

56. Ibid., 161.

57. Samuel French included the program between the copyright page and the foreword of the published play.

58. Borowitz, 172. The U.S. Secretary of the Interior reported on the contested status of Big Lake district in 1916: "There are contained in the Cherokee Nation a total of 4,420,068 acres, of which 22,880 were reserved for town sites, railroad rights of way, and other purposes; 4,346,203 acres were allotted to 40,193 citizens and freedmen; and the remainder, consisting of 50,905 acres, was sold except an 80-acre tract, which is involved in litigation, and a 226-acre tract included in what is known as Big Lake, the title to which has not yet been definitely determined." See the *Annual Report of the Secretary of Interior for the Fiscal Year Ended June 30, 1915*, vol. 2, *Indian Affairs, Territories* (Washington: Government Printing Office, 1916), 35.

59. See Borowitz, 172.

60. Ibid., 173.

61. Riggs, *Big Lake*, 15.

62. Riggs, *Big Lake*, 3. In the directions for scene 2, Riggs describes Elly as "a tall, dark woman of thirty-five" with "thick black hair" (13). While Elly is from Kansas City and is the character who says that she has not seen two Indians since she arrived in Indian Territory, her regional origins or this statement do not preclude a reading of her as Cherokee. As Weaver notes in his reading of Riggs in *That the People Might Live*, Cherokees have a history of distinguishing themselves from Indian nations that adapted differently to the European presence: "It should be remembered [. . .] that the Cherokee were one of the Five Civilized Tribes. They often had scant respect for those other nations that my mother used to dismiss as 'blanket Indians' or Elias Boudinot called 'American Arabs.'" See Weaver, *That the People Might Live*, 100. John Rollin Ridge's depiction of indigenous

Californians in his novel *The Life and Adventures of Joaquin Murieta, the Celebrated California Bandit* (1854) has been cited often as an example of this Cherokee sense of superiority.

63. Justice, *Our Fire Survives the Storm*, 105.

64. Ibid., 105–6. The italics are in the original.

65. Riggs, *Big Lake*, 13.

66. Ibid., 4.

67. Ibid., 66–67.

68. Again, Samuel French includes the program for the first performance between the foreword and act I in this edition of the play.

69. Riggs, *Roadside*, 5.

70. Ibid.

71. Ibid., 21–22.

72. Riggs, *Green Grow the Lilacs*, 75.

73. Ibid., 157.

74. Riggs, *Roadside*, 12. Texas and Hannie also make multiple comments about scalping that an audience might have a predisposition to understand as references to American Indians.

75. Ibid., 148.

76. Riggs, *Roadside*, 80: The Ikes chant, "Fight, fight, nigger and a white! Fight, fight!"

77. Riggs to Johnson, June 28, 1950. Quinn became a naturalized U.S. citizen in 1947.

78. Braunlich, *Haunted by Home*, 190, also mentions Quinn's portrayal of Texas.

79. See Rogers, *Will Rogers' Weekly Articles*, vol. 6, 139.

80. Weaver notes in "A Lantern To See By," 326, that Grant is the middle name of Riggs's father.

81. Riggs, *The Cherokee Night and Other Plays*, 234.

82. Ibid., 298.

83. Ibid., 339.

84. Braunlich, *Haunted by Home*, 6. See the first chapter of Braunlich's biography for a description of this time in Riggs's life. Bynner's biographer James Kraft lingers only a moment on the affair between Riggs and Bynner: "[Bynner's] lecture tour took him through the Southwest, and on his way there he went to the University of Oklahoma where he met and advised Lynn Riggs, a young student who later followed Bynner to New Mexico, became his lover, and served briefly as his secretary. Riggs was the future writer of the play *Green Grow the Lilacs*, from which Oscar Hammerstein II and Richard Rodgers adapted *Oklahoma*." See Kraft, *Who Is Witter Bynner?*, 50.

85. Riggs, *Russet Mantle and the Cherokee Night*, 83.

86. Ibid., 13.

87. The simultaneous analysis of these two indigenous places also illuminates an effort, in the words of Eric Gary Anderson, "to repossess and redefine" a South that includes Mexico as Native ground. Anderson asserts, "'The Native American South' is ironically being radically repossessed as well as redefined by Indian writers such as [LeAnne] Howe, in ways that pressure and even expunge the received term 'southern' as well as the interestingly loaded 'before' and 'after' formulations applied to historical concepts of the 'South.'" See Anderson, "On Native Ground."

88. Braunlich, *Haunted by Home*, 107, 147–49.

89. Bonfil Batalla, *México Profundo*, 49.

90. Ibid., 51 and 49.

91. Ibid., 52. The original is all in italics.

92. Ibid.

93. Riggs, *4 Plays*, 74.

94. Ibid., 75.

95. Ibid., 84.

96. Ibid., 90.

97. Ibid., 95.

98. Ibid., 102.

99. Ibid., 107.

100. Ibid.

101. Ibid., 115–16.

102. Ibid., 117.

103. Ibid., 135.

104. Ibid., 132.

105. Rosaldo defines imperialist nostalgia in *Culture and Truth*: "Curiously enough, agents of colonialism—officials, constabulary officers, missionaries, and other figures from whom anthropologists ritually dissociate themselves—often display nostalgia for the colonized culture as it was 'traditionally' (that is when they first encountered it). The peculiarity of their yearning, of course, is that agents of colonialism long for the very forms of life they intentionally altered or destroyed. Therefore, my concern resides with a particular kind of nostalgia, often found under imperialism, where people mourn the passing of what they themselves have transformed" (69).

106. Riggs, *4 Plays*, 152.

107. Reed, *The Caste War of Yucatán*, 51.

108. See Reed, *The Caste War of Yucatán*, chapter 1.

109. Ibid., 97–98.

110. Ibid., 125.

111. Ibid., 186.

112. Ibid., 255, 265.

113. Ibid., 281.

114. Ibid., 282.

115. Ibid., 283.

116. Meyer and Sherman, *The Course of Mexican History*, 462.

117. Fallaw, *Cárdenas Compromised*, 15.

118. Ibid., 16.

119. Ibid., 2.

120. Ibid., 2. Fallaw's choice of the TVA as analogous to Cárdenas land reform is ironic in the context of this study. See Matthiessen. "Lost Eloheh Land," for a description of the Tennessee Valley Authority's Tellico Dam project and the destruction of Cherokee land it caused.

121. Ibid.

122. Riggs calls it a hemp plantation. Henequen appears to be identified inaccurately as hemp or sisal with some frequency.

123. Riggs, *4 Plays*, 8.

124. See Meyer and Sherman, 439–51 and 457–64, respectively, for a discussion of the modernization of Mexico under Díaz and the cost of this modernization to indigenous Mexicans.

125. Ben Fallaw calls Pedro Crespo "a hero of the armed phase of the Revolution in Temax." See Fallaw, 50. Temax is a town in Yucatán about fifty miles east of Merida. The revolutionary leader shares the essence of his first name with Pilár as well: Pedro is the Spanish variant of Peter and has as its root the Latin petra (stone). Gilbert Michael Joseph describes the events that made Crespo a hero: "On March 4, 1911, Crespo rode into the *cabecera* just before dawn, rousted the corrupt *jefe político*, Colonel Antonio Herrera, and treasury agent Nazario Aguilar Brito from their beds, and hauled them, clad only in their skivvies, to the central plaza. [. . .] Crespo strapped Herrera and Aguilar to chairs and riddled them with bullets. [. . .] The bodies were piled into a meat wagon and then dumped at the gates of the town cemetery." See Joseph, "Rethinking Mexican Revolutionary Mobilization," 156–57.

126. Gutiérrez, *Nationalist Myths and Ethnic Identities*, 38.

127. Ibid., 151.

128. Chicle became a valuable commodity in Yucatán in the early twentieth century, particularly in the new federal territory of Quintana Roo. Quintana Roo was formed in 1902 from the eastern part of Yucatán dominated by the Cruzob. See Reed, *The Caste War of Yucatán*, 305 and 308–10.

129. Riggs, *4 Plays*, 17.

130. Ibid., 30–31.

131. Ibid., 13.

132. Fallaw, 13.

133. Ibid.

134. Riggs, *Russet Mantle and The Cherokee Night,* 259 and 262. Emphasis in original.

135. Womack, *Red on Red,* 299.

136. Riggs, *4 Plays,* 60.

137. Ibid., 60.

138. See Reed, 237.

139. Riggs, *4 Plays,* 31.

140. Ibid., 64.

141. Ibid., 65.

142. Ibid., 70.

143. Ibid., 72.

144. Cook-Lynn, "The American Indian Fiction Writers," 85.

145. Ibid., 90.

146. Womack, *Red on Red,* 11.

147. The draft of "Encounter in Guerrero," a third play set in Mexico, is not dated in the Lynn Riggs Papers at the Beinecke Rare Book and Manuscript Library. The wartime setting of the play suggests that he wrote it, like *Dark Encounter,* during or after World War II. Indigenous Mexicans have an even more prominent role in the play than they do in *The Year of Pilár* and *A World Elsewhere,* but the incomplete narrative is difficult to assess. However, in the manuscript, the island seat of an ancient indigenous Mexican community serves as a primitive paradise isolated from an ominous, violent modernity represented by the war planes in the skies above the jungle.

148. Riggs, *4 Plays,* 163.

149. Ibid., 164.

150. Ibid., 172.

151. Ibid., 159 and 204.

152. I am thinking here of Spokane author Gloria Bird's essay "Writing as Witness" in *Speaking for the Generations.* Bird demonstrates in poignant detail the emotional, psychological, and spiritual legacies of colonialism and conversion within her own family.

153. Riggs, *4 Plays,* 184.

154. Womack, *Red on Red,* 295.

155. Riggs, *4 Plays,* 206.

156. Ibid., 208.

157. See Teuton, *Red Land, Red Power,* 125–27 for his story of this visit to the hospital.

158. Ibid., 81.

159. Riggs, *4 Plays,* 219.

160. Ibid., 222.

3. "Mexico Is an Indian Country"

1. Peyer, *American Indian Nonfiction*, 293.

2. Of the Indian Hospital in Claremore, Oklahoma, Amy Ware notes, "the building of the facility itself was due to Rogers's celebrity lobbying efforts; he mentioned the hospital several times in print and on the air and likely spoke privately to influential senators about the idea." Ware, "Will Rogers's Radio," 62. Cowger explains that the organization, ARROW (Americans for the Restitution and Rightings of Old Wrongs), had a vexed relationship with the NCAI but still "served an invaluable role in financially sustaining the NCAI through its early troubled times." Cowger, *The National Congress of American Indians*, 71.

3. Cowger, 38.

4. Ibid., 53.

5. Cobb, *Native Activism in Cold War America*, 154.

6. Ibid., 183–84.

7. Ibid, 185. Cobb mentions the Mexican Embassy as one of many destinations for groups of marchers.

8. See Anderson for a discussion of three waves of nationalism: creole and vernacular, state or official, and colonial. Anderson uses the term colonial nationalism for anticolonial nationalist movements by native populations in colonized regions. He notes an absence of "that dubious entity known as 'reverse racism' [. . .] in the anticolonial movements." Anderson, *Imagined Communities*, 157.

9. Warrior, *The People and the Word*, xvi–xvii.

10. Ibid., xx.

11. Nonfiction is well represented in *Native American Writing in the Southeast*, edited by Littlefield and Parins. The editors note that nonfiction "dominated the literature of the reform era." Warrior sees this dominance of non-fiction throughout the history of American Indian writing. See Littlefield and Parins, *Native American Writing in the Southeast*, xxiii.

12. See Cobb, passim, but especially 58–79.

13. See Cobb, passim, but especially 23–27; and Smith and Warrior, *Like a Hurricane*.

14. See, for example, Weaver, *That the People Might Live*, 35–36, and Womack, "A Single Decade," 85, and "Theorizing American Indian Experience," 370.

15. Ruppert, *Mediation in Contemporary Native American Fiction*, 3.

16. Ibid., 7.

17. Ibid., 10.

18. Rogers was also later identified by P. J. O'Brien as "The Ambassador of Good Will" in the title of a biography published in 1935.

19. Denson, *Demanding the Cherokee Nation*, 11.

20. Ibid.

21. See Denson, 12.

22. Rogers had already published two books, *Rogers-isms: The Cowboy Philosopher on the Peace Conference* (1919) and *Rogers-isms: The Cowboy Philosopher on Prohibition* (1919). Both books are collections of jokes or what Rogers called his "gags." One of the gags is about U.S. diplomacy: "One thing we got to be thankful for our Soldiers can win wars faster than our Diplomats can talk us into them." See *Rogers-isms: The Cowboy Philosopher on the Peace Conference*, 29.

23. Rogers, *Letters*, 26.

24. Ibid., 27.

25. There are two references to Claremore, one to the Verdigris bottoms, and one to Oklahoma in *There's Not a Bathing Suit in Russia*. These references emphasize that we should see Rogers as a visitor from Claremore—his home—rather than as a visitor from a homogenous United States.

26. Rogers, *Letters*, 129. He makes the comparison of the Tiber to the Grand and Verdigris Rivers, as well as to the Arkansas and South Canadian, on 170; he suggests that Coolidge vacation in Claremore on 233–35.

27. Ibid., 20.

28. Ibid., 209.

29. This oppositional space resembles but is not precisely what Bruyneel calls a third space of sovereignty. Rogers is an indigenous political actor, like those under consideration in Bruyneel's study, but it is difficult to isolate specific claims to and defenses of Cherokee or American Indian sovereignty in his diverse writings.

30. See Meyer and Sherman, *The Course of Mexican History*, 585–87.

31. Rogers, *The Autobiography of Will Rogers*, 165.

32. Ibid., 166.

33. Ibid., 167.

34. Ibid., 169.

35. Ibid., 171.

36. Ibid., 172.

37. Ibid., 172–73.

38. See the first chapter of Vizenor's *Manifest Manners*, "Postindian Warriors of Survivance." "The postindian warriors," Vizenor explains, "encounter their enemies with the same courage in literature as their ancestors once evinced on horses, and they create their stories with a new sense of survivance. The warriors bear the simulations of their time and counter the manifest manners of domination." Vizenor, *Manifest Manners*, 4. Vizenor uses Standing Bear's life and writing as a refrain throughout the book.

39. Standing Bear, *My People the Sioux*, 59.

40. Ibid., 91.

41. Ibid., 163.

42. Ibid., 178.

43. Ibid., 220.

44. Ibid., 276.

45. Ibid., 278.

46. Ibid., 287.

47. Standing Bear, *My Indian Boyhood*, between the dedication and table of contents.

48. Maddox, *Citizen Indians*, 161.

49. Standing Bear, *Land of the Spotted Eagle*, 44.

50. Ibid., 73.

51. Ibid., 74.

52. Ibid., 91.

53. Ibid., 109.

54. Ibid., 179.

55. Ibid., 67–68. The text reads "they" rather than "there."

56. Ibid., 184.

57. Ibid., 190.

58. Ibid., 235.

59. Ibid., 236.

60. Ibid., 144.

61. Ibid., 145.

62. Maddox, 165.

63. See Wilson, "John Joseph Mathews," 246.

64. "Osages before Oil," 1.

65. "Osage Lore Left by Hoover's Uncle," 19.

66. See, for example, Hunt, "John Joseph Mathews," 364; and Wilson, 246.

67. *Wah'Kon-Tah* has, Kalter explains, some of the general characteristics of history, biography, and fiction. After an overview of the debate about the book, she asserts, "the general questioning of the factuality of history itself ought to allow us to acknowledge the faithfulness of *Wah'Kon-Tah* as history while also recognizing its compositional formation as novel." Kalter, "John Joseph Mathews' Reverse Ethnography," 44.

68. Kalter, 32 and 27.

69. Ibid., 27.

70. Mathews, *Wah'Kon-Tah*, 11.

71. Ibid., 12.

72. Ibid., 26.

73. Ibid., 30.

74. Ibid., 32.

75. Ibid., 34.

76. Ibid., 35.

77. Ibid., 37.
78. Ibid., 38.
79. Ibid., 39.
80. Ibid., 62.
81. Ibid., 90.
82. Ibid., 93.
83. Ibid., 170.
84. Ibid., 205.
85. For these scenes, see Mathews, *Wah'Kon-Tah*, 201–6 and 212–16.
86. Ibid., 239.
87. Ibid., 287.
88. Ibid., 302.
89. Ibid., 305.
90. Ibid., 321.
91. Warrior, *Tribal Secrets*, 58.
92. Ibid.
93. See Bone, "Osage Oil."
94. Allen, *Blood Narrative*, 91–92.
95. Mathews, *Talking to the Moon*, 126.
96. Ibid., 84.
97. Ibid., 212.
98. Ibid.
99. Ibid., 213.
100. Mathews, Letter to Oliver La Farge.
101. Warrior, *Tribal Secrets*, 68.
102. I owe a debt of gratitude to Susan Kalter for sharing with me the specific dates of Mathews's residence in Mexico and confirming his attendance at the conference. At the time of this writing in July 2009, Kalter was working on Mathews's writings—diaries and letters—about and from Mexico. In her biography of McNickle, Parker mentions his attendance at the conference. Parker, *Singing an Indian Song*, 83. Frederick W. Boling and Lou Brock of the Osage Tribal Museum were also generous with their time and effort as I attempted to confirm that Mathews was at the conference.
103. Hunt, 363. He asserts, however, that Africa most reminded Mathews of home: "It was during his European years, in the course of a hunting trip in North Africa, that Mathews rediscovered deep within himself a profound attachment to his people. This reconnection with his own cultural tradition occurred after an encounter with a group of Kabyle tribesmen who were racing across the desert firing their Winchesters in a display of joy that recalled for Mathews the vision of Osage warriors, with only their breechcloths and their guns, riding across the prairie and firing shots out of sheer exuberance" (364).

104. Rus explains, "With the end of Cárdenas's term in 1940, the pace of change in Mexico and Chiapas slowed drastically. After 1940, agrarian reform essentially stopped." However, more land was expropriated and returned to indigenous people in the 1970s. See Rus, "The 'Comunidad Revolucionaria Institucional,'" 280.

105. See the laudatory review of Downing's book from the archaeologist and historian Philip Ainsworth Means in the *New York Times* in March 1940.

106. McNickle published *Native American Tribalism: Indian Survivals and Renewals* in 1973. *Native American Tribalism* was a revised and expanded version of *Indian Tribes of the United States: Ethnic and Cultural Survival* (1962).

107. Downing, *The Mexican Earth*, 2–3.

108. Ibid., 15; Momaday, *House Made of Dawn*, 57.

109. Downing, *The Mexican Earth*, 14.

110. Ibid., 15.

111. Ibid., 16.

112. Ibid.

113. Ibid., 9.

114. Ibid.

115. Ibid., 10.

116. Ibid., 17.

117. Ibid.

118. The red pieces of cloth might have been the paliacates that are referenced by a speaker quoted by Downing earlier in the chapter. See Downing, *The Mexican Earth*, 3. Fallaw reports one instance in Yucatán in which "peasants waved small red pennants emblazoned with the phrase *Agrario* (land reform) and a scythe (a symbolic reference to the peasants taken from Communist iconography—a tool completely unknown as wheat was not grown in the state)." See Fallaw, *Cárdenas Compromised*, 89. The PSS party, the Partido Socialista del Sureste or Socialist Party of the Southeast, also had as a symbol a "red triangular banner." Fallaw, 101.

119. McNickle's position is that the "generalized picture today is of a people that has survived in numbers, in social organization, in custom and outlook, in retention of physical resources, and in its position before the law. The situation might be described as a survival of fragments, of incomplete entities—but there we would miss the mark. Any people at any time is a survival of fragments out of the past. The function of culture is always to reconstitute the fragments into an operational system. The Indians, for all that has been lost or rendered useless out of their ancient experience, remain a continuing ethnic and cultural enclave with a stake in the future." See McNickle, *Native American Tribalism*, 15.

120. León-Portilla explains that the "x" in Nahuatl, the language of the Mexicas, is pronounced as "sh." Mexica refers throughout this chapter to those people commonly called the Aztecs. León-Portilla, *The Broken Spears*, xlvii.

121. For a discussion of the Mexicas' origins, see Brundage, *The Fifth Sun*, 135–37.

122. Downing, *The Mexican Earth*, 15.

123. Ibid., 5.

124. Ibid., 42.

125. Hudson, *The Southeastern Indians*, 23.

126. See Duncan, *Hernando de Soto*, 374–84. Duncan calls Tuscaloosa's community Atahachi, while other commentators identify him as Alibamu or Alabama, Mobile, or Choctaw.

127. Downing, *The Mexican Earth*, 84.

128. Ibid., 87. The Mexica Empire was dominated by the Mexica from Tenochtitlan, but the Acolhuans of Texcoco and the Tepanecs of Tlacopan had joined the Mexicas in the Triple Alliance.

129. Ibid., 91.

130. Florescano, *National Narratives of Mexico*, 314–15.

131. Downing, *The Mexican Earth*, 111.

132. This translation of the Mexican Constitution of 1917 can be found at http://www. latinamericanstudies.org/mexico/1917-Constitution.htm.

133. Fallaw, 23.

134. Ibid. By forcing indigenous Mexican farmers to compete against U.S. farmers and agricultural conglomerates that produce inexpensive and subsidized corn, the North American Free Trade Agreement (NAFTA) has also seriously undermined the ejido system. Chahta Enterprise, a firm owned by the Mississippi Band of Choctaws, has also benefited from NAFTA. The corporation owns a factory in Sonora, Mexico, where employees, including Yaquis, earn six dollars a day assembling wire harnesses for Ford vehicles. See "Choctaw Chief Leads His Mississippi Tribe into the Global Market."

135. Downing, *The Mexican Earth*, 108.

136. Ibid., 53.

137. Meyer and Sherman, 60.

138. Downing, *The Mexican Earth*, 224.

139. Ibid., 108–9.

140. Ibid., 43.

141. Downing's discussion of indigenous empire in Central Mexico anticipates Robert Warrior's suggestion in *Tribal Secrets* that readings of indigenous traditions "can be more honest and less celebratory." Warrior, *Tribal Secrets*, 10.

142. For a detailed discussion of the political battles between the Juáristas and Porfiristas, see Falcone, "Benito Juárez versus the Díaz Brothers." Díaz overthrew President Sebastián Lerdo de Tejada in 1876 and ruled until 1911 as a dictator whose policies favored wealthy landowners and corporations.

143. Downing, *The Mexican Earth*, 223.

144. Ortiz, "Towards a National Indian Literature," 7–8.

145. Downing, *The Mexican Earth*, 125.

146. Tonantzin is also called Dios Ynantzin or Dios Inninantzin, the mother of God. Sahagún says Tonantzin is another aspect of Cihuacoatl, while other commentators describe her as a manifestation of Coatlicue and Tlazolteotl. See Sahagún 26–27, and for a discussion of the Nahuatl goddesses to which Tonantzin has some connection, see Rebolledo, *Women Singing in the Snow*, 49–53.

147. For Downing's discussion of the competing Virgins, see *The Mexican Earth*, 146–47.

148. Downing considers the miracles on pages 128–31 of *The Mexican Earth*.

149. Downing, *The Mexican Earth*, 131.

150. Ibid., 133.

151. Ibid., 319–20. Downing cites population statistics from 1910, when the white population stood at 7.5 percent, the mestizo population at 53 percent, and the indigenous population at 39 percent. Downing says, "Comparing these figures with those of 1805, it appears that there had been little change in the number of whites, although in relation to the total population it had diminished fifty per cent. Indians had more than doubled in numbers, while keeping close to their percentage. *Mestizos* had quadrupled in numbers, while increasing their percentage *at the expense of whites.*" Ibid., 223.

152. Anishinabe scholar Basil Johnston discusses a similar story about Nana'b'oozoo: "Nana'b'oozoo left his home, his family, and his village, accompanied only by his grandmother aboard his canoe. No one was on shore to bid him farewell. Some say that he left his village and the people in disappointment, heartbroken by their rejection of him and by their turning away from him to accept the pale-faced latecomer and his new ways. They say that he also left word that he would return some day when his people were ready to welcome him into their lives once again." Johnston, *The Manitous*, 95. Contreras observes, "Chicanos who would insist on a filial relationship to [the Aztec] empire recuperate the image of Quetzalcoatl as a symbol of resistance rather than acquiescence." Contreras, *Blood Lines*, 79. Downing adopts the same strategy.

153. Power, *Early Art of the Southeastern Indians*, 156–57. LeAnne Howe (Choctaw Nation of Oklahoma) mentions a feathered serpent in her novel *Shell Shaker*, 80 and 99.

154. Power, 157–58.

155. Ibid., 158.

156. Downing, *The Mexican Earth*, 326.

157. Some influential Chicana/o indigenistas, argues Contreras, value indigenous Mexican mythology over history and contemporary indigenous Mexican people. The main argument of *Blood Lines* is "that the characteristic form of Chicana/o indigenism is myth." Contreras, 40.

158. See the essays by Ortiz and Cook-Lynn for examples of their American Indian literary critical practice.

159. Weaver, Womack, and Warrior, *American Indian Literary Nationalism*, 6.

160. Weaver, Womack, and Warrior, *American Indian Literary Nationalism*, 216.

161. Oskison, *Tecumseh and His Times*, dedication page.

162. Ibid. 7.

163. Ibid., 4.

164. Ibid., 75.

165. Ibid., 114.

166. See Birchfield on Choctaw leader Pushmataha's refusal to join Tecumseh's confederacy in *How Choctaws Invented Civilization and Why Choctaws Will Conquer the World*.

167. Oskison, *Tecumseh and His Times*, 145.

168. Ibid., 236.

169. Ibid.

170. Ibid., 236–37.

4. The Red Land of the South

1. Parker, *Singing an Indian Song*, 134. See 132–36 for a discussion of the founding of AID and its first workshops.

2. Ibid., 40, 55–56.

3. Ibid., 68.

4. Ibid., 65.

5. Ibid., 66.

6. Braunlich, *Haunted by Home*, 199.

7. Fixico, *Termination and Relocation*, 101.

8. Cobb, *Native Activism in Cold War America*, 9.

9. Ibid. Also see Parker, *Singing an Indian Song*, 40–52, for the specific details of *The Surrounded* that she identifies as autobiographical.

10. See Parker, *Singing an Indian Song*, 25–27.

11. Ibid., 83. The planning for the Congress began in 1938 at the Eighth International Conference of American States in Lima, Peru, which Collier attended.

12. Collier, "Notes on the First Inter-American Congress on Indian Life," 4.

13. The staff at the Newberry Library has been unable to locate its copy of this text.

14. These works are available in the Edward E. Ayer collection at the Newberry Library's D'Arcy McNickle Center for American Indian and Indigenous Studies.

15. Mathews, "John Joseph Mathews' Mexico Diary."

16. Gutiérrez, *Nationalist Myths and Ethnic Identities*, 96.

17. Ibid., 97.

18. Collier, "Editorial," 1.

19. Kirk, "A Meeting on Indians," 139.

20. Ibid.

21. Parker, *Singing an Indian Song*, 83. In his contributor's biography in the "Colaboradores" section at the beginning of at least one issue of *América Indígena*, Collier identifies himself as an indigenista. See *América Indígena* 13 (October 1953).

22. Parker, *Singing an Indian Song*, 83.

23. See ibid., 83–85, for a description of the NII's troubled history and McNickle's involvement in it.

24. Ibid., 84.

25. Cowger, *The National Congress of American Indians*, 25–26.

26. In his foundational study of McNickle's writing, Purdy observes that by the time he wrote *Runner in the Sun*, "the Native peoples and landscape of the Southwest had captured his interest." Purdy's archival research also reveals that "McNickle's papers contain book after book of notes that he painstakingly collected over years of involvement with the peoples of the Southwest." Purdy, *Word Ways*, 84.

27. Dorothy Parker compares Salt's village to Mesa Verde and Canyon de Chelly. However, she reads the map by the novel's illustrator, Allan Houser, as placing the village at Chaco Canyon, "which in fact has no cliff dwellings that resemble Salt's home." Lori Burlingame draws a stronger connection between Salt's village and Mesa Verde, while John Purdy and Jay Hansford C. Vest agree that Salt's village has features of both Chaco Canyon and Canyon de Chelly. See Parker, "D'Arcy McNickle's *Runner in the Sun*," 120; Burlingame, "Cultural Survival in *Runner in the Sun*"; Purdy, 87; and Vest, "A Legend of Culture," 159.

28. McNickle, *Runner in the Sun*, 164.

29. The Holy One's assertion of his village's kinship with indigenous Mexicans participates in the frequently contentious discussions about tribal enrollment in the United States. Tribal enrollment is often tied to a kinship defined by blood quantum or biological inheritance. Tribally enrolled indigenous people in the United States have a tribal enrollment and CDIB (Certificate of Degree of Indian Blood) card.

30. McNickle, *Runner in the Sun*, 198.

31. Ibid.

32. Warrior, *The People and the Word*, 107.

33. McNickle, *Runner in the Sun*, 144.

34. Ibid., 165.

35. Parker, "D'Arcy McNickle: An Annotated Bibliography," 4.

36. Ortiz, "Afterword," 237; Burlingame, 136 and 143; Vest, 155.

37. McNickle, *Runner in the Sun*, 169.

38. Ibid., 171.

39. John Purdy discusses right or appropriate action in the Native Southwest in the chapter on *Runner in the Sun* in *Word Ways*.

40. McNickle, *Runner in the Sun*, 172.

41. Ibid., 173.

42. Ibid., 175.

43. Ibid.

44. George Tinker's *Missionary Conquest* (1993) is a case study of four missionaries and the way that they actively promoted colonialism and the destruction of Native American worlds.

45. McNickle, *Runner in the Sun*, 178.

46. Álvar Núñez Cabeza de Vaca and Estevanico also passed through Culiacán. They arrived in Culiacán or Sant Miguel in early April 1536 near the end of the long journey that he recounts in *Adventures in the Unknown Interior of America* (1542). He stayed there until May 15, 1536, when he began the journey to Tenochtitlan or Mexico City, where he arrived July 24, 1536, one day before the fiesta for Santiago or Saint James. Estevanico was a Moroccan slave who also survived the Panfilo de Narvaez expedition. Coronado left Culiacán on April 22, 1540. Gilbert M. Joseph and Timothy J. Henderson explain that Culiacán is in the early twenty-first century the "holy city" of drug smuggling: "souvenir shops sell items glorifying smugglers and drug lords as romantic outlaws, and its own patron saint, Jesús Malverde, [is] a bandit who, according to lore, stole from the rich and gave to the poor, and was hanged in 1909." They continue, "Ordinary folks come to pay homage at his shrine in Culiacán, while drug smugglers offer him thanks for successful shipments." Joseph and Henderson, *The Mexico Reader*, 747.

47. McNickle, *Runner in the Sun*, 182.

48. Ibid., 183.

49. Downing, *The Mexican Earth*, 28.

50. McNickle, *Runner in the Sun*, 190.

51. Ibid., 188.

52. Ibid., 193.

53. Ibid., 197.

54. Ibid., 231–32.

55. Meyer and Sherman, *The Course of Mexican History*, 37.

56. Ibid., 54.

57. Ibid., 54–55.

58. Ibid., 55.

59. McNickle, *Runner in the Sun*, 190.

60. Ibid., 205.

61. Ibid., 202.

62. Meyer and Sherman, 38.

63. Ibid.

64. Ibid., 41.

65. McNickle, *Runner in the Sun*, 203.

66. Ibid., 204.

67. Ibid., 205.

68. Meyer and Sherman, 38–39.

69. Ibid., 59.

70. Meyer and Sherman define this period, from 900 to 1521 CE, as having the following characteristics: "Societies increasingly yield to rule by warriors; emergence of conquest states; appearance of metallurgy; origin of authentic historical sources; an excess of human sacrifice; final destruction of the Indian states by Spanish Conquest" (4). Downing challenges the assertion that the Spanish conquest led to the "final destruction" of the Indian states.

71. Parker, "D'Arcy McNickle's *Runner in the Sun*," 236–37, note 9.

72. For readings of the map in *Almanac*, see Bell, "Counter-Chronicling," and Huhndorf, *Mapping the Americas*, 140–42 and 155–57. For the photographic documentary on Houser, see Houser, *Allan Houser: A Life in Art*.

73. McNickle, *Runner in the Sun*, 54.

74. Thomas King observes, "'All my relations' is the English equivalent of a phrase familiar to most Native peoples in North America. [. . .] 'All my relations' is at first a reminder of who we are and of our relationship with both our family and our relatives. It also reminds us of the extended relationship we share with all human beings. But the relationships that Native people see go further, the web of kinship extended to the animals, to the birds, to the fish, to the plants, to all the animate and inanimate forms that can be seen or imagined. More than that, 'all my relations' is an encouragement for us to accept the responsibilities we have within this universal family by living our lives in a harmonious and moral manner." King, "Introduction," ix.

75. Perlman, *Allan Houser (Ha-o-Zous)*, 61–62.

76. Ibid., 64–65.

77. Ibid., 66.

78. Ibid., 79.

79. McNickle, *Runner in the Sun*, 176.

5. The Return to Mexico

1. Other American Indian novels published in the early 1990s, such as Michael Dorris and Louise Erdrich's *The Crown of Columbus* (1991) and Thomas King's *Green Grass, Running Water* (1993), share with *Heirs* and *Almanac* an interest in the historical connections among American Indians and indigenous

Caribbeans. Neither Dorris and Erdrich nor King, however, foreground these connections either as explicitly or extensively as Vizenor and Silko.

2. Womack connects *The Year of Pilár* to *Almanac of the Dead* in *Art as Performance, Story as Criticism*. He notes, "Unlike *The Cream in the Well*, *The Year of Pilár* takes up a singular subject unparalleled in twentieth-century Indian literature at the time of its writing: it focuses on the return of Indian land. An author would not broach this theme again until decades later, when Leslie Marmon Silko, in *Almanac of the Dead* (1991), would represent land redress as future prophecy rather than as a historical reality in a particular geography in southern Mexico the way Riggs does." Womack, *Art as Performance, Story as Criticism*, 139–40.

3. Parker comments, "I will note that there is a great deal more criticism on *Ceremony* than I cite here. I have done my best to read it all (probably missing some more recent work), but given the quantity of material and the availability of bibliographies (William Dinome, Connie C. Thorson), there is not the same need for extensive citation that I try to live up to in discussing other works. Moreover, so much criticism has come out so quickly, often produced by critics who do not read each other's work, that redundancy is the norm." Parker, *The Invention of Native American Literature*, 210. In the first thirty years of *Studies in American Indian Literatures*, the journal devoted the most articles to Silko and Louise Erdrich.

4. See Bird, "The Exaggeration of Despair in Sherman Alexie's *Reservation Blues*," and for the Alexie quote, Silko, *Ceremony*, thirtieth anniversary edition, back cover.

5. See Vizenor's autobiography, *Interior Landscapes*.

6. See, for example, the eight chapters of the section "The American Indian Movement," especially "Urban Militants on Reservations," in *Tribal Scenes and Ceremonies*. These editorials were published originally in the *Minneapolis Tribune* in March 1973 and February and March 1974. Also see the chapter "Radical Durance" in Vizenor's *Manifest Manners*.

7. Vizenor situates White Hawk's crime in the settler-colonial contexts that shaped his life. I have not been able to find a copy of Vizenor's work on White Hawk collected in *Thomas James White Hawk*, published in 1968 by Four Winds Press. Two reports on the case, titled "Murder on Good Friday" and "Commutation of Death" and originally published in the *Twin Citian* in June 1968 and January 1970, appear in *Tribal Scenes and Ceremonies* (1976) and *Crossbloods: Bone Courts, Bingo, and Other Reports* (1990). Vizenor also discusses White Hawk in *Wordarrows* (1978) and *Interior Landscapes* (1990). See Rodriguez, "Gerald Vizenor's Shadow Plays," as well as Blaeser, *Gerald Vizenor*, 44–48, for an analysis of these writings.

8. See Ripley, "Death Sentence against Indian Commuted by Dakota Governor."

9. Adkins, "White Earth Delegates Ratify New Constitution."

10. See Coe, *The Maya*, 34–38, for a description of the thirty-one contemporary Mayan languages and the regions in which these languages are spoken.

11. See Vizenor, *The Heirs of Columbus*, 9, for Stone's initial assertion that Columbus was Mayan. See *The Heirs of Columbus*, 19–20, for an explanation of how Columbus landed at the headwaters of the Mississippi. "Samana was a hand talker from the stone tavern and the headwaters of the great river," Vizenor explains, though she appears in a canoe in the Caribbean on the night that Columbus arrives (38). The next summer, her daughter, also named Samana, is born at the headwaters as the first of the heirs of Columbus.

12. Lyons, *X-Marks*, 171.

13. Blaeser's chapter "Trickster Signatures" and Vizenor's own "Trickster Discourse" in *Narrative Chance* are excellent introductions to Vizenor's use of Naanabozho.

14. Johnston, *The Manitous*, 243.

15. Burgess, "Elaboration Therapy in the Midewiwin and Gerald Vizenor's *The Heirs of Columbus*," 24.

16. Ibid., 29.

17. Teuton identifies and analyzes *House Made of Dawn* and *Ceremony* as Red Power novels in *Red Land, Red Power*.

18. Vizenor, *Summer in the Spring*, 9. The poems in *anishinabe nagamon* (1970), the reprint and revision of *Summer in the Spring*, are accompanied by photographic reproductions of Anishinabe pictomyths. Here is the same passage from the reprint: "The sacred *migis* shell of the *anishinabe* spirit rose from the eastern sea and moved along the inland waters guiding *the people* through the sleeping sun of the woodland to *bawitig*—the long rapids in the river. The *anishinabe*— the *original people* of the woodland—believe they were given wisdom and life color from the sun reflecting on the sacred shell during this long migration. Five hundred years ago the *migis* shell appeared in the sun for the last time at *moningwanekaning* in *anishinabe kitchigami*—the great sea of the *anishinabe*" (9).

19. Vizenor, *The Heirs of Columbus*, 119. The miigis shell also plays an important role in midéwiwin ceremonies. See Burgess, 23, and Blaeser, 178.

20. Burgess notes, for example, that the miigis shell identifies initiates to the midéwiwin society.

21. I am indebted to Meg Noori for her explanation of the stones in personal correspondence.

22. Vizenor, *The Heirs of Columbus*, 13.

23. Ibid., 121.

24. Ibid., 25.

25. Ibid.

26. Ibid., 113.

27. Scholars have debated the authenticity of the Grolier Codex, but Coe argues the radiocarbon dating places its creation in the thirteenth century. See Coe, 200.

28. Coe, 200. The lowlands of the Yucatán peninsula comprise the northern area, while the highlands of Guatemala and the Mexican state of Chiapas form the main part of the southern area. There is a central area between Yucatán and Guatemala. See Coe, 12, for a map of the three areas and Coe, 10, for his list of Mayan historical eras.

29. Vizenor, *The Heirs of Columbus*, 25. Le Plongeon was an archaeologist known for what many other scholars considered poor translations of part of the Madrid Codex and outlandish theories of Mayan global migrations. He spent many years in Yucatán.

30. Ibid., 25.

31. See Coe, 181–85, for a brief narrative of the reign of the House of Cocom.

32. Ibid., 182.

33. Ibid., 185.

34. Gubler, "*Primus inter pares:* The Ruling House of Cocom," 241.

35. Ibid.

36. Ibid., 246.

37. Reed, *The Caste War of Yucatán*, 80.

38. Vizenor, *The Heirs of Columbus*, 26.

39. Ibid., 16.

40. Tedlock, *Popul Vuh*, 25. The former translation of "Chilam Balam" is Tedlock's, and the latter is Edmonson's.

41. See Edmonson, *Heaven Born Merida and Its Destiny*, 1.

42. Ibid., 2. Edmonson argues that Mayans wrote the Chumayel book between 1824 and 1837 and the Mani book in 1837.

43. Tedlock, 16.

44. Ibid., 195.

45. See, for example, Tedlock, 161–65.

46. See Tedlock, 44, for his explanation of the mother-fathers.

47. Ibid., 32 and 70–71. The Lords of Xibalba, the Mayan underworld, also place what Tedlock translates as "manikins" at the entrance to fool visitors, and the Quiché place manikins at the walls of their fortress to fool their enemies.

48. Vizenor, *The Heirs of Columbus*, 24.

49. Nichols and Nyholm, *A Concise Dictionary of Minnesota Ojibwe*, 44, translate *dewikwe* as "have a headache."

50. Tedlock, 71.

51. Ibid.

52. Vizenor, *The Heirs of Columbus*, 140.

53. Ibid., 143–44.

54. Ibid., 170.

55. Kelsey, however, insists that *Almanac of the Dead* awaits a rich tribally specific reading: "By reflecting upon the specific tradition of Mayan bookmaking and epistemic record and situating *Almanac* within that tribal literary inheritance, an understanding of Silko's novel is achieved that is only possible with such tribally grounded criticism. In fact, by closely considering Mayan hieroglypics and codices and their creators and surrounding culture vis-à-vis *Almanac of the Dead*, a novel whose very existence is predicated upon these Mesoamerican written traditions, we as readers are practicing tribal theory by allowing the tribal foundation of the text to emerge and motivate our theoretical praxis." Kelsey, *Tribal Theory in Native American Literature*, 2.

56. Huhndorf, *Mapping the Americas*, 141.

57. Silko, *Almanac of the Dead*, 133. This passage is part of a section of free indirect speech from Zeta's point of view.

58. Silko, "Notes on *Almanac of the Dead*," 135.

59. See Kelsey, 2. Silko counts three extant codices: "Of course, those two old Yaqui women in my novel *Almanac of the Dead* possess large portions of a fourth Maya book, which survived the five-hundred-year war for the Americas." See Silko, "Notes on *Almanac of the Dead*," 158.

60. See Justin Kerr, "A Precolumbian Portfolio," for photographs of all eleven pages from the Grolier Codex.

61. Silko, *Almanac of the Dead*, 246.

62. Downing, *The Mexican Earth*, 215.

63. Ibid., 215 and 216.

64. Silko, *Almanac of the Dead*, 125.

65. See the stories of Sandoval, Hastin Tlo'tsi hee or Old Man Buffalo Grass, as told in Navajo over the course of seventeen days to Aileen O'Bryan in 1928 and published in 1956. The twins have several other names, including Slayer of Alien Gods and He Who Cuts Around. See O'Bryan, *The Dîné*, 84.

66. Though she is writing about the Mexican codices, Boone compares a journey to the underworld by Quetzalcoatl and Xolotl to the same journey made by Hunahpu and Xbalanque or, in her words, the "Hero Twins." See Boone, *Cycles of Time and Meaning in the Mexican Books of Fate*, 192. Coe also calls Hunahpu and Xbalanque "Hero Twins," 207.

67. See Silko, *Almanac of the Dead*, 474.

68. Tedlock, 139.

69. Ibid., 141.

70. Silko, *Almanac of the Dead*, 336.

71. Ibid., 760.

72. Townsend, *The Aztecs*, 111.

73. Ibid., 18.

74. Coe, 168.

75. Silko, *Almanac of the Dead*, 429.

76. Ibid., 512.

77. Ibid., 519.

78. Ibid., 572.

79. Edmonson, 110. The "Heaven Born" preceding Merida indicates the city's status as a "seat of the cycle" during the historical period recounted in the text. Edmonson explains, "The city that had this honor was held to be sacred: born of heaven, *ziyan caan.*" Chumayel is the name of the town in Yucatán where the book was kept. Edmonson believes the Chumayel book of Chilam Balam "mustt [. . .] have been written between 1824 and 1837." See Edmonson, 5 and 2.

80. Townsend, 18. See also Restall, *Seven Myths of the Spanish Conquest,* for a discussion of the Cortés-as-Quetzalcoatl myth.

81. Boone, 194 and 269.

82. Ibid., 41 and 51.

83. Ibid., 189 and 192.

84. Silko, *Almanac of the Dead*, 571.

85. See Boone, 16, for a chart of the day names.

86. Silko, *Almanac of the Dead*, 569.

87. See Silko, "Notes on *Almanac of the Dead*," 138–39, for Silko's report on the stone snake near the uranium mine at the Laguna Pueblo.

88. Silko, *Almanac of the Dead*, 735.

89. Cook-Lynn, "The American Indian Fiction Writers," 85.

90. Ibid., 89–90. Cook-Lynn adds that Silko's approach still fails, "since it does not take into account the specific kind of tribal/nation status of the original occupants of this continent." The novel represents, nevertheless, a "gallant effort." Ibid., 93.

91. Womack, *Red on Red*, 11.

92. Ibid., 226.

93. Cook-Lynn, "The American Indian Fiction Writers," 96.

94. Weaver, *That the People Might Live*, 47.

95. Womack, *Red on Red*, 2.

96. Silko, "Books," 165.

97. Womack, *Red on Red*, 13.

98. Brooks, *The Common Pot*, xix–xx.

99. Ibid., xxi.

100. Justice, "'Go Away, Water!,'" 155.

101. Teuton, "Theorizing American Indian Literatures," 200. Kimberly Roppolo also quotes William S. Penn on the structural affinities of Mayan texts with narrative essays by contemporary academics though not exclusively American Indian scholars. See Roppolo, "Samson Occom as Writing Instructor," 315.

102. *Anáhuac* means "near the water" or "the land between the waters" in Nahuatl, which, like Hopi, is an Uto-Aztecan language.

103. For more information about Black Mesa Trust, see its website: http://www.blackmesatrust.org.

104. Rodriguez, "The H2opi Run into the Land of Quetzalcoatl," 1 (italics in the original).

Conclusion

1. Weaver, Foreword to *The Singing Bird*, ix. See also the introductions to Warrior's *The People and the Word* and Womack's *Red on Red*.

2. Hobson, *The Remembered Earth*, 1–2. Hobson mentions in his introduction Oskison, McNickle, Rogers, and Riggs, four of the five main authors under my consideration.

3. Teuton, *Red Land, Red Power*, xvii.

4. Bruyneel, *The Third Space of Sovereignty*, 113.

5. Ibid., 120, where he identifies Rickard and Gordon as indigenous nationalists. Thank you to Sallie Andrews of the Wyandotte Nation for sharing all her materials on Gordon.

6. Ibid., 119.

7. See Smith and Warrior, *Like a Hurricane*, 40–41, and D. Parker, *Singing an Indian Song*, 181–82. Paul McKenzie-Jones explained to me in private correspondence that the workshops ran from 1956 to 1972.

8. See Hauptman and Campisi, "The Voice of Eastern Indians," 316. The numbers vary widely for the number of American Indian tribal nations or communities represented at the conference. Hauptman and Campisi say ninety.

9. Ibid., 317.

10. McKenzie-Jones, "'We Are among the Poor, the Powerless, the Inexperienced and the Inarticulate,'" 227. See Hauptman and Campisi, 324, for the identification of Karen Rickard as one of the founders of the NIYC.

11. McKenzie-Jones, 227 and 249.

12. McKenzie-Jones indicated in private correspondence that Warrior often sought McNickle's advice. See McKenzie-Jones, 225, for the observation that Thomas was also Warrior's mentor.

13. Justice, *Our Fire Survives the Storm*, 92.

14. Oskison, "A Tale of the Old I.T.," 4.

15. Oskison refers to the visit to Chicago with Rogers in "A Tale of the Old I.T.," 104.

16. Braunlich, *Haunted by Home*, 29.

17. See Hochbruck, "Mystery Novels to Choctaw Pageant," 209.

18. Powell and Smith, Introduction to *The Singing Bird*, xx. In private

conversation, Amy Ware said that Rogers had Oskison's books in the library at his ranch outside Beverly Hills.

19. Oskison, *Black Jack Davy*, 179, and *Brothers Three*, 324.

20. Quoted in Ware, "Unexpected Cowboy, Unexpected Indian," 28.

21. Wertheim and Bair, ed., *The Papers of Will Rogers*, vol. 1, 109.

22. Braunlich, *Haunted by Home*, 122.

23. In the conversation with Jeeter in the smokehouse, Curly refers to a roper named Will Parker. In an early draft of the play, Riggs calls the roper Will Rogers. Riggs writes of the revision: "I've cut out 'Will Rogers'—in favor of 'Will Parker.' Although completely naturalistic and possible, it seemed self-concious." See "A Note on the Principal Revisions Done on Green Grow the Lilacs" at the University of Tulsa Library.

24. The letter is part of Charles Rzepka's private collection. It is from Todd's grandmother, Nanna, to his sister, Ruth. She writes, "The family were thrilled to hear of your interview with the famous Will Rodgers [*sic*]. Am sure you enjoyed it, and so would he." Rzepka dates this letter July 1930. In a letter dated January 1, 1931, Nanna writes, "Will Rodgers' Tour will bring in a large amount of money. If we were only in Norman this winter we might be able to squeeze into the fieldhouse."

25. See Brown's dissertation, "Stoking the Fire: Nationhood in Early Twentieth Century Cherokee Writing."

26. Rodriguez, "Shades of Mexican," September 3, 2007. Accessed March 13, 2012, http:// www.latimes.com/news/opinion/la-oe-rodriguez3sep03,0,3733464. column. See Rodriguez, *Mongrels, Bastards, Orphans, and Vagabonds*, 164–72, for the full story of Andrade's legal battle.

Bibliography

Adams, Rachel. *Continental Divides: Remapping the Cultures of North America.* Chicago: University of Chicago Press, 2009.

Adkins, Jason. "White Earth Delegates Ratify New Constitution." Accessed March 14, 2012, http://indiancountrytodaymedianetwork.com/ictarchives/ 2009/04/22/white-earth-delegates-ratify-new-constitution-82233.

"Advertising News and Notes." *New York Times*, March 28, 1947: 39.

"Advertising News and Notes." *New York Times*, June 8, 1949: 44.

Allen, Chadwick. *Blood Narrative: Indigenous Identity in American Indian and Maori Literary and Activist Texts.* Durham: Duke University Press, 2002.

Anderson, Benedict. *Imagined Communities.* New York: Verso, 2006.

Anderson, Eric Gary. "On Native Ground: Indigenous Presences and Countercolonial Strategies in Southern Narratives of Captivity, Removal, and Repossession." *Southern Spaces*, August 9, 2007. Accessed March 14, 2012, http://southernspaces.org/2007/native-ground-indigenous-presences-and-countercolonial-strategies-southern-narratives-captivity.

Anderson, Mabel Washbourne. "An Osage Niobe." In *Native American Writing in the Southeast: An Anthology, 1875–1935,* edited by Daniel F. Littlefield Jr. and James Parins, 49–52. Jackson: University Press of Mississippi, 1995.

Annual Report of the Secretary of Interior for the Fiscal Year Ended June 30, 1915. Vol. 2, *Indian Affairs, Territories.* Washington, D.C.: Government Printing Office, 1916.

Anzaldúa, Gloria. *Borderlands/La Frontera: The New Mestiza.* San Francisco: Aunt Lute, 1987.

Ashcroft, Bill, Gareth Griffiths, and Helen Tiffin. *The Empire Writes Back: Theory and Practice in Post-Colonial Literatures.* New York: Routledge, 1989.

Balderrama, Francisco E., and Raymond Rodríguez. *Decade of Betrayal: Mexican Repatriation in the 1930s.* Albuquerque: University of New Mexico Press, 1995.

Bell, Virginia E. "Counter-Chronicling and Alternative Mapping in *Memoria del fuego* and *Almanac of the Dead.*" *MELUS* 25.3/4 (Fall/Winter 2000): 5–30.

Bernardin, Susan K. "Mixed Messages: Authority and Authorship in Mourning

Dove's *Cogewea, the Half-Blood: A Depiction of the Great Montana Cattle Range*." *American Literature* 67 (1995): 487–509.

Birchfield, D. L. *How Choctaws Invented Civilization and Why Choctaws Will Conquer the World*. Albuquerque: University of New Mexico Press, 2007.

Bird, Gloria. "The Exaggeration of Despair in Sherman Alexie's *Reservation Blues*." *Wicazo Sa Review* (Fall 1995): 47–52.

Blaeser, Kimberly M. *Gerald Vizenor: Writing in the Oral Tradition*. Norman: University of Oklahoma Press, 1996.

Bone, Corey. "Osage Oil." Accessed October 11, 2009, http://digital.library.okstate.edu/encyclopedia/entries/O/OS006.html.

Bonfil Batalla, Guillermo. *México Profundo: Reclaiming a Civilization*. Translated by Philip A. Dennis. Austin: University of Texas Press, 1996.

"Books and Authors." *New York Times*, March 17, 1940: 95.

"Books-Authors." *New York Times*, March 5, 1940: 26.

"Book Notes." *New York Times*, August 18, 1934: 7.

"Book Notes." *New York Times*, May 4, 1935: 11.

Boone, Elizabeth Hill. *Cycles of Time and Meaning in the Mexican Books of Fate*. Austin: University of Texas Press, 2007.

Bordman, Gerald. *American Theatre: A Chronicle of Comedy and Drama, 1930–1969*. New York: Oxford University Press, 1996.

Borowitz, Albert. "'Pore Jud is Daid': Violence and Lawlessness in the Plays of Lynn Riggs." *Legal Studies Forum* 27.1 (2003): 157–84.

Braunlich, Phyllis Cole. *Haunted by Home: The Life and Letters of Lynn Riggs*. Norman: University of Oklahoma Press, 1988.

———. "*The Cherokee Night* of R. Lynn Riggs." *Midwest Quarterly* 30.1 (Autumn 1988): 45–59.

Brinton, Daniel G. *Nagualism: A Study in Native American Folk-Lore and History*. Philadelphia: MacCalla & Company, 1894.

Brooks, Lisa. *The Common Pot: The Recovery of Native Space in the Northeast*. Minneapolis: University of Minnesota Press, 2008.

Brown, Alanna Kathleen. "Mourning Dove's Voice in *Cogewea*." *Wicazo Sa Review* 4.2 (Fall 1988): 2–15.

Brown, Kirby. "Indigenous Communities, Indigenous Nations: Interrogating Contemporary Indigenous Intellectualisms." In *Sovereignty, Separatism, and Survivance: Ideological Encounters in the Literature of Native North America*, edited by Benjamin D. Carson, 82–109. Newcastle, U.K.: Cambridge Scholars, 2009.

Brundage, Burr Cartwright. *The Fifth Sun: Aztec Gods, Aztec World*. Austin: University of Texas Press, 1979.

Bruyneel, Kevin. *The Third Space of Sovereignty: The Postcolonial Politics of U.S.-Indigenous Relations*. Minneapolis: University of Minnesota Press, 2007.

Burgess, Benjamin. "Elaboration Therapy in the Midewiwin and Gerald Vizenor's *The Heirs of Columbus*." *Studies in American Indian Literatures* 18.1 (Spring 2006): 22–36.

Burlingame, Lori. "Cultural Survival in *Runner in the Sun*." In *The Legacy of D'Arcy McNickle: Writer, Historian, Activist*, edited by John Purdy, 136–51. Norman: University of Oklahoma Press, 1996.

Burton, Jeffrey. *Indian Territory and the United States, 1866–1906: Courts, Government, and the Movement for Oklahoma Statehood*. Norman: University of Oklahoma Press, 1995.

Cabeza de Vaca, Álvar Núñez. *Adventures in the Unknown Interior of America*. 1542. Translated by Cyclone Covey. Albuquerque: University of New Mexico Press, 1997.

Chapman, John, ed. *The Best Plays of 1951–1952*. New York: Dodd, Mead, and Company, 1952.

Cherniavsky, Eva. "Tribalism, Globalism, and Eskimo Television in Leslie Marmon Silko's *Almanac of the Dead*." *Angelaki: Journal of the Theoretical Humanities* 6.1 (April 2001): 111–26.

"Choctaw Bilingual Education Program." Southeastern State College. Durant, Oklahoma.

"Choctaw Chief Leads His Mississippi Tribe into the Global Market." *Wall Street Journal*, July 23, 1999. Accessed March 14, 2012, http://www.mexica.net/immigrat/choctaw.php.

Cobb, Daniel M. *Native Activism in Cold War America: The Struggle for Sovereignty*. Lawrence: University Press of Kansas, 2008.

Coe, Michael D. *The Maya*. 6th ed. 1966. New York: Thames & Hudson, 1999.

Collier, John. "Editorial." *Indians at Work* 8 (August 1941): 1–9.

———. "Mexico: A Challenge." *Progressive Education* 9 (February 1932): 95–98.

———. "Mexico's Rural Schools and Our Indian Schools." *Indians at Work* 1 (December 1933): 10–15.

———. "Notes on the First Inter-American Congress on Indian Life." *Indians at Work* 7 (June 1940): 1–4.

Colonnese, Tom, and Louis Owens. *American Indian Novelists: An Annotated Critical Bibliography*. New York: Garland, 1985.

Conley, Robert J. *A Cherokee Encyclopedia*. Albuquerque: University of New Mexico Press, 2007.

———. *The Cherokee Nation: A History*. Albuquerque: University of New Mexico Press, 2005.

Contreras, Sheila Marie. *Blood Lines: Myth, Indigenism, and Chicana/o Literature.* Austin: University of Texas Press, 2008.

Cook-Lynn, Elizabeth. "American Indian Intellectualism and the New Indian Story." In *Natives and Academics: Researching and Writing about American Indians,* edited by Devon A. Mihesuah, 111–38. Lincoln: University of Nebraska Press, 1998.

———. "The American Indian Fiction Writers: Cosmopolitanism, Nationalism, the Third World, and First Nation Sovereignty." In *Why I Can't Read Wallace Stegner and Other Essays: A Tribal Voice.* Madison: University of Wisconsin Press, 1996. 78–96.

Cowger, Thomas W. *The National Congress of American Indians: The Founding Years.* Lincoln: University of Nebraska Press, 1999.

Darby, Jaye. "Broadway (Un)Bound: Lynn Riggs's *The Cherokee Night.*" *Baylor Journal of Theater and Performance* 4.1 (Spring 2007): 7–23.

Deloria, Ella Cara. *Waterlily.* Lincoln: University of Nebraska Press, 1988.

Deloria, Philip J. *Indians in Unexpected Places.* Lawrence: University Press of Kansas, 2004.

———. *Playing Indian.* New Haven: Yale University Press, 1998.

Deloria, Vine, Jr. *Custer Died for Your Sins: An Indian Manifesto.* 1969. Norman: University of Oklahoma Press, 1988.

———. Preface to *Black Elk Speaks: Being the Life Story of a Holy Man of the Oglala Sioux,* by John G. Neihardt, xv–xix. Lincoln: University of Nebraska Press, 1961.

Denson, Andrew. *Demanding the Cherokee Nation: Indian Autonomy and American Culture, 1830–1900.* Lincoln: University of Nebraska Press, 2004.

Downing, Todd. *The Case of the Unconquered Sisters.* Garden City, N.Y.: Doubleday, 1936.

———. *The Cat Screams.* Garden City, N.Y.: Doubleday, 1934. New York: Popular Library, 1945.

———. *Chahta Anompa: An Introduction to the Choctaw Language.* Durant, Okla.: Choctaw Bilingual Education Program, Southeastern State College, 1971.

———. "A Choctaw's Autobiography." In *The American Indian, 1926–1931,* edited by J. M. Carroll and Lee F. Harkins, 49. New York: Liveright, 1970.

———. *Cultural Traits of the Choctaws.* Durant, Okla.: Choctaw Bilingual Education Program, Southeastern State College, 1973.

———. *The Last Trumpet: Murder in a Mexican Bull Ring.* Garden City, N.Y.: Doubleday, 1937.

———. Letter to Ruth Downing, ca. 1932. Charles Rzepka private collection.

———. "The Life and Works of Florencio Sanchez." Thesis, University of Oklahoma, 1928.

———. *The Mexican Earth*. New York: Doubleday, 1940.

———. "Murder Is a Rather Serious Business." In *Writing Detective and Mystery Fiction*, edited by A. S. Burack, 180–85. Boston: The Writer, 1945.

———. *Murder on Tour*. New York: Putnam's, 1933.

———. *Murder on the Tropic*. Garden City, N.Y.: Doubleday, 1935.

———. *Night over Mexico*. Garden City, N.Y.: Doubleday, 1937.

———. "The Shadowless Hour." *Mystery Book Magazine*, November 1945: 86–130.

———. *Vultures in the Sky*. Garden City, N.Y.: Doubleday, 1935.

Driskill, Qwo-Li. "Ha'nts: The Booger Dance Rhetorics of Lynn Riggs's *The Cherokee Night*." In *American Indian Performing Arts: Critical Directions*, edited by Hanay Geiogamah and Jaye Darby, 179–96. Los Angeles: UCLA American Indian Studies Center, 2009.

Duncan, David Ewing. *Hernando de Soto: A Savage Quest in the Americas*. New York: Crown, 1995.

Eaton, Rachel Caroline. "The Legend of the Battle of Claremore Mound." *Chronicles of Oklahoma* 8.4 (December 1930): 369–76.

Edmonson, Munro S., trans. *Heaven Born Merida and Its Destiny: The Book of Chilam Balam of Chumayel*. Austin: University of Texas Press, 1986.

Everett, Dianna. *The Texas Cherokees: A People Between Two Fires, 1819–1840*. Norman: University of Oklahoma Press, 1990.

Falcone, Frank S. "Benito Juárez versus the Díaz Brothers: Politics in Oaxaca, 1867–1871." *The Americas* 33 (1977): 630–51.

Fallaw, Ben. *Cárdenas Compromised: The Failure of Reform in Postrevolutionary Yucatán*. Durham: Duke University Press, 2001.

Fixico, Donald L. *Termination and Relocation: Federal Indian Policy, 1945–1960*. Albuquerque: University of New Mexico Press, 1986.

Florescano, Enrique. *National Narratives in Mexico: A History*. Translated by Nancy Hancock. Norman: University of Oklahoma Press, 2006.

Garroutte, Eva Marie. *Real Indians: Identity and the Survival of Native America*. Berkeley: University of California Press, 2003.

González, Gilbert G. *Culture of Empire: American Writers, Mexico, and Mexican Immigrants, 1880–1930*. Austin: University of Texas Press, 2004.

Green, Michael D. "Indian Territory, 1866–1889." In *Historical Atlas of Oklahoma*, edited by Charles Robert Goins and Danney Goble, 98–99. Norman: University of Oklahoma Press, 2006.

Gridley, Marion E., ed. *Indians of Today*. Chicago: Donnelley and Sons, 1936.

Gubler, Ruth. "*Primus inter pares:* The Ruling House of Cocom." Accessed June 20, 2011, http://www.iai.spk-berlin.de/fileadmin/dokumentenbibliothek/Indiana/Indiana_17_18/11gubler.pdf.

Gunn, Drewey Wayne. *American and British Writers in Mexico, 1556–1973*. Austin: University of Texas Press, 1969.

Gutiérrez, Natividad. *Nationalist Myths and Ethnic Identities: Indigenous Intellectuals and the Mexican State*. Lincoln: University of Nebraska Press, 1999.

Hauptman, Laurence M., and Jack Campisi. "The Voice of Eastern Indians: The American Indian Chicago Conference of 1961 and the Movement for Federal Recognition." *Proceedings of the American Philosophical Society* 132.4 (December 1988): 316–29.

Hedrick, Basil C., J. Charles Kelley, and Carroll L. Riley, ed. *The Mesoamerican Southwest: Readings in Archaeology, Ethnohistory, and Ethnology*. Carbondale: Southern Illinois University Press, 1974.

Hedrick, Tace. *Mestizo Modernism: Race, Nation, and Identity in Latin American Culture, 1900–1940*. New Brunswick, N.J.: Rutgers University Press, 2003.

Hertzberg, Hazel. *The Search for an American Indian Identity: Modern Pan-Indian Movements*. Syracuse: Syracuse University Press, 1971.

Hilger, Michael. *From Savage to Nobleman: Images of Native Americans in Film*. Lanham, Md.: Scarecrow, 1995.

Hobson, Geary, ed. *The Remembered Earth: An Anthology of Contemporary Native American Literature*. Albuquerque: University of New Mexico Press, 1980.

Hochbruck, Wolfgang. "Mystery Novels to Choctaw Pageant: Todd Downing and Native American Literature(s)." In *New Voices in Native American Literary Criticism*, edited by Arnold Krupat, 205–21. Washington, D.C.: Smithsonian Institution, 1993.

Hoefel, Roseanne. "'Different by Degree': Ella Cara Deloria, Zora Neale Hurston, and Franz Boas Contend with Race and Ethnicity." *American Indian Quarterly* 25.2 (Spring 2001): 181–202.

Houser, Allan. *Allan Houser: A Life in Art*. Santa Fe: Museum of New Mexico, 1991.

Howe, LeAnne. *Shell Shaker*. San Francisco: Aunt Lute, 2001.

Hudson, Charles. *The Southeastern Indians*. Knoxville: University of Tennessee Press, 1976.

Huhndorf, Shari M. *Mapping the Americas: The Transnational Politics of Contemporary Native Culture*. Ithaca, N.Y.: Cornell University Press, 2009.

Hunt, John. "John Joseph Mathews." In *Encyclopedia of North American Indians*, edited by Frederick E. Hoxie, 363–65. Boston: Houghton Mifflin, 1996.

Johnston, Basil. *The Manitous: The Spiritual World of the Ojibway*. New York: HarperCollins, 1995.

Joseph, Gilbert M. "Rethinking Mexican Revolutionary Mobilization: Yucatán's Seasons of Upheaval, 1909–1915." In *Everyday Forms of State Formation: Revolution and the Negotiation of Rule in Modern Mexico*, edited by Gilbert M. Joseph and Daniel Nugent, 135–69. Durham: Duke University Press, 1994.

Joseph, Gilbert M., and Timothy J. Henderson, eds. *The Mexico Reader: History, Culture, Politics*. Durham: Duke University Press, 2002.

Justice, Daniel Heath. "'Go Away, Water!': Kinship Criticism and the Decolonization Imperative." In *Reasoning Together: The Native Critics Collective*, edited by Craig S. Womack, Daniel Heath Justice, and Christopher B. Teuton, 147–68. Norman: University of Oklahoma Press, 2008.

———. *Our Fire Survives the Storm: A Cherokee Literary History*. Minneapolis: University of Minnesota Press, 2006.

Kalter, Susan. "John Joseph Mathews' Reverse Ethnography: The Literary Dimensions of Wah'Kon-Tah." *Studies in American Indian Literatures* 14.1 (Spring 2002): 26–50.

Kelsey, Penelope Myrtle. *Tribal Theory in Native American Literature: Dakota and Haudenosaunee Writing and Indigenous Worldviews*. Lincoln: University of Nebraska Press, 2008.

Kerouac, Jack. *On the Road*. 1957. New York: Penguin, 1999.

Kerr, Justin. "A Precolumbian Portfolio: An Archive of Photographs Created by Justin Kerr." Accessed June 20, 2011, http://research.mayavase.com/kerr portfolio.html.

Keys, Lucy Lowrey Hoyt. "Historical Sketches of the Cherokees, Together with Some of Their Customs, Traditions, and Superstitions (1889)." In *Native American Women's Writing, 1800–1924*, edited by Karen L. Kilcup, 71–89. Oxford: Blackwell, 2000.

King, Thomas. Introduction to *All My Relations: An Anthology of Contemporary Canadian Native Fiction*, ix–xvi. Toronto: McClelland and Stewart, 1990.

Kirk, Betty. "A Meeting on Indians: An Inter-American Conference Is Held on Shore of Lake Patzcuaro in Mexico." *New York Times*, April 14, 1940: 139.

Knight, Alan. "Racism, Revolution, and Indigenismo: Mexico, 1910–1940." In *The Idea of Race in Latin America, 1870–1940*, edited by Richard Graham, 71–113. Austin: University of Texas Press, 1990.

Konkle, Maureen. *Writing Indian Nations: Native Intellectuals and the Politics of Historiography, 1827–1863*. Chapel Hill: University of North Carolina Press, 2004.

Kraft, James. *Who Is Witter Bynner?: A Biography*. Albuquerque: University of New Mexico Press, 1995.

Krupat, Arnold. *For Those Who Come After: A Study of Native American Autobiography*. Berkeley: University of California Press, 1985.

———. *The Voice in the Margin: Native American Literature and the Canon*. Berkeley: University of California Press, 1989.

Lambert, Valerie. *Choctaw Nation: A Story of American Indian Resurgence*. Lincoln: University of Nebraska Press, 2007.

Larson, Charles. *American Indian Fiction*. Albuquerque: University of New Mexico Press, 1978.

Latorre, Felipe A., and Dolores L. Latorre. *The Mexican Kickapoo Indians*. Austin: University of Texas Press, 1976.

Leal, Luis. "Rev. of *The Mexican Earth*, by Todd Downing." *Nahua Newsletter* 22 (1996): 27–30.

Lee, Felicia R. "Scholars Say Chronicler of Black Life Passed for White." *New York Times*, December 26, 2010. Accessed March 14, 2012, http://www.nytimes.com/2010/12/27/books/27cane.html?pagewanted=all.

Leonard, Joe M. *Bah, Bah, Black Sheep*. Coral Springs, Fla.: Llumina Press, 2004.

León-Portilla, Miguel. *The Broken Spears: The Aztec Account of the Conquest of Mexico*. 1962. Boston: Beacon Press, 1992.

Lewis, Stephen E. "The Nation, Education, and the 'Indian Problem' in Mexico, 1920–1940." In *The Eagle and the Virgin: Nation and Cultural Revolution in Mexico, 1920–1940*, edited by Mary Kay Vaughan and Stephen E. Lewis, 176–95. Durham: Duke University Press, 2006.

Lincoln, Kenneth. *Native American Renaissance*. Berkeley: University of California Press, 1983.

Littlefield, Daniel F., Jr. "Utopian Dreams of the Cherokee Fullbloods: 1890–1934." *Journal of the West* 10.3 (July 1971): 404–27.

Littlefield, Daniel F., Jr., and James Parins, ed. *Native American Writing in the Southeast: An Anthology*. Jackson: University Press of Mississippi, 1995.

Little Thunder, Julie. "Mixedbloods and Bloodlust in *Cherokee Night*." *Midwest Quarterly: A Journal of Contemporary Thought* 43.4 (Summer 2002): 355–65.

López, Rick A. "The Noche Mexicana and the Exhibition of Popular Arts: Two Ways of Exalting Indianness." In *The Eagle and the Virgin: Nation and Cultural Revolution in Mexico, 1920–1940*, edited by Mary Kay Vaughan and Stephen E. Lewis, 23–42. Durham: Duke University Press, 2006.

Lyons, Scott Richard. *X-Marks: Native Signatures of Assent*. Minneapolis: University of Minnesota Press, 2010.

Maddox, Lucy. *Citizen Indians: Native American Intellectuals, Race & Reform*. Ithaca: Cornell University Press, 2005.

Mathews, John Joseph. Letter to Oliver La Farge. June 27, 1960. Oliver La Farge Collection. Harry Ransom Center, The University of Texas at Austin, Austin, Texas.

———. "John Joseph Mathews' Mexico Diary." April 20, 1940. John Joseph Mathews Collection. University of Oklahoma Libraries, Western History Collections, Norman, Oklahoma.

———. *Life and Death of an Oilman: The Career of E. W. Marland*. Norman: University of Oklahoma Press, 1951.

———. *Sundown*. 1934. Norman: University of Oklahoma Press, 1988.

———. *Talking to the Moon*. Chicago: University of Chicago Press, 1945.

———. *Wah'Kon-Tah: The Osage and the White Man's Road*. Norman:University of Oklahoma Press, 1981.

McKenzie-Jones, Paul. "'We Are among the Poor, the Powerless, the Inexperienced and the Inarticulate': Clyde Warrior's Campaign for a 'Greater Indian America.'" *American Indian Quarterly* 34.2 (Spring 2010): 224–57.

McNickle, D'Arcy. *Native American Tribalism: Indian Survivals and Renewals*. New York: Oxford University Press, 1973.

———. *Runner in the Sun: A Story of Indian Maize*. 1954. Albuquerque: University of New Mexico Press, 1987.

———. *The Surrounded*. 1936. Albuquerque: University of New Mexico Press, 1978.

———. *They Came Here First: The Epic of the American Indian*. Philadelphia: Lippincott, 1949.

———. *Wind from an Enemy Sky*. 1978. Albuquerque: University of New Mexico Press, 1988.

Means, Philip Ainsworth. "Mexico, Its Land and Its People: A Notable History From Earliest Times with a Sympathetic and Convincing Analysis of the Problems of Today." *New York Times*, March 31, 1940: 89.

Menchaca, Martha. *Recovering History, Constructing Race: The Indian, Black, and White Roots of Mexican Americans*. Austin: University of Texas Press, 2001.

Meyer, Michael C., and William L. Sherman. *The Course of Mexican History*. 5th ed. New York: Oxford University Press, 1995.

Momaday, N. Scott. *House Made of Dawn*. New York: Harper and Row, 1968.

Mooney, James. *Myths of the Cherokee*. Washington, D.C.: Government Printing Office, 1900.

Mould, Tom. *Choctaw Tales*. Jackson, Miss.: University Press of Mississippi, 2004.

Mourning Dove. *Cogewea, the Half-Blood: A Depiction of the Great Montana Cattle Range*. 1927. Lincoln: University of Nebraska Press, 1981.

———. *A Salishan Autobiography*. Lincoln: University of Nebraska Press, 1990.

"Murder in May." *Time*, June 9, 1941. Accessed May 24, 2007, http://www.time.com/time/ magazine/article/0,9171,795384,00.html.

Muthyala, John. "*Almanac of the Dead*: The Dream of the Fifth World in the Borderlands." *LIT: Literature Interpretation Theory* 14.4 (2003): 357–85.

"Napoleon's Letters." *New York Times*, November 4, 1934: BR17.

Nichols, John, and Earl Nyholm. *A Concise Dictionary of Minnesota Ojibwe*. Minneapolis: University of Minnesota Press, 1995.

O'Bryan, Aileen. *The Diné: Origin Myths of the Navaho Indians*. Washington, D.C.: Government Printing Office, 1956.

"Oklahoma Deputy Kills 2 Mexican Students, One Kin of Ortiz Rubio; Hoover Sends Regret." *New York Times*, June 9, 1931: 1.

Ortiz, Alfonso. Afterword to *The Surrounded*, 235–49. 1936. Albuquerque: University of New Mexico Press, 1978.

Ortiz, Simon J. "Towards a National Indian Literature: Cultural Authenticity in Nationalism." *MELUS* 8.2 (Summer 1981): 7–12.

"Osages before Oil." *Time*, November 7, 1932. Accessed March 14, 2012, http://www. time.com/time/magazine/article/0,9171,744704,00.html.

"Osage Lore Left By Hoover's Uncle." *New York Times*, November 1, 1932: 19.

Oskison, John Milton. *Black Jack Davy*. New York: D. Appleton, 1926.

———. *Brothers Three*. New York: Macmillan, 1935.

———. *The Singing Bird: A Cherokee Novel*. Norman: University of Oklahoma Press, 2007.

———. "A Tale of the Old I.T." Unpublished manuscript. Western History Collection, University of Oklahoma Libraries, Norman, Oklahoma.

———. *Tecumseh and His Times: The Story of a Great Indian*. New York: G. P. Putnam's Sons, 1938.

———. *Wild Harvest: A Novel of Transition Days in Oklahoma*. New York: D. Appleton, 1925.

Owens, Louis. *Other Destinies: Understanding the American Indian Novel*. Norman: University of Oklahoma Press, 1992.

Owens, Ron. *Oklahoma Heroes: The Oklahoma Peace Officers Memorial*. Paducah, Ky.: Turner Publishing, 2000.

Paredes, Américo. *A Texas-Mexican Cancionero: Folksongs of the Lower Border*. Austin: University of Texas Press, 1995.

Parker, Dorothy R. "D'Arcy McNickle: An Annotated Bibliography of His Published Articles and Book Reviews in a Biographical Context." In *The Legacy of D'Arcy McNickle: Writer, Historian, Activist*, edited by John Purdy, 3–29. Norman: University of Oklahoma Press, 1996.

———. "D'Arcy McNickle's *Runner in the Sun*: Content and Context." In *The Legacy of D'Arcy McNickle: Writer, Historian, Activist*, edited by John Purdy, 117–35. Norman: University of Oklahoma Press, 1996.

———. *Singing an Indian Song: A Biography of D'Arcy McNickle*. Lincoln: University of Nebraska Press, 1992.

Parker, Robert Dale. *The Invention of Native American Literature*. Ithaca, N.Y.: Cornell University Press, 2003.

Parman, Frank. "Downing, George Todd (1902–1974)." *Oklahoma Historical Society's Encyclopedia of Oklahoma History & Culture*. Accessed June 20, 2011, http:// digital.library.okstate.edu/encyclopedia/entries/D/DO013.html.

Perlman, Barbara H. *Allan Houser (Ha-o-zous)*. Boston: David R. Godine, 1987.

Peyer, Bernd C. *American Indian Nonfiction: An Anthology of Writings, 1760s–1930s*. Norman: University of Oklahoma Press, 2007.

Pérez-Torres, Rafael. *Mestizaje: Critical Uses of Race in Chicano Culture*. Minneapolis: University of Minnesota Press, 2006.

Posey, Alexander. *The Fus Fixico Letters: A Creek Humorist in Early Oklahoma*, edited by Daniel F. Littlefield Jr. and Carol A. Hunter. Norman: University of Oklahoma Press, 2002.

Powell, Malea. "Blood and Scholarship: One Mixed-Blood's Story." In *Race, Rhetoric, and Composition*, edited by Keith Gilyard, 1–16. Portsmouth, N.H.: Boynton/Cook, 1999.

Powell, Timothy B., and Melinda Smith Mullikin. Introduction to *The Singing Bird*, xix–xlvii. Norman: University of Oklahoma Press, 2007.

Power, Susan C. *Early Art of the Southeastern Indians: Feathered Serpents and Winged Beings*. Athens: University of Georgia Press, 2004.

Pronzini, Bill, and Marcia Muller. *1001 Midnights: The Aficionado's Guide to Mystery and Detective Fiction*. New York: Arbor House, 1986.

Pulitano, Elvira. *Toward a Native American Critical Theory*. Lincoln: University of Nebraska Press, 2003.

Purdy, John Lloyd. *Word Ways: The Novels of D'Arcy McNickle*. Tucson: University of Arizona Press, 1990.

Rebolledo, Tey Diana. *Women Singing in the Snow: A Cultural Analysis of Chicana Literature*. Tucson: University of Arizona Press, 1995.

Reed, John R. "English Imperialism and the Unacknowledged Crime of *The Moonstone*." *Clio* 2.3 (1973): 281–90.

Reed, Nelson. *The Caste War of Yucatán*. Revised edition. Stanford: Stanford University Press, 2001.

Restall, Matthew. *Seven Myths of the Spanish Conquest*. New York: Oxford University Press, 2003.

Riggs, Lynn. *4 Plays*. New York: Samuel French, 1947.

———. *Big Lake*. New York: Samuel French, 1927.

———. "The Cherokee Night." Lynn Riggs Collection, series 1, box 2, folder 1. McFarlin Library, The University of Tulsa, Tulsa, Oklahoma.

———. *The Cherokee Night and Other Plays*. Norman: University of Oklahoma Press, 2003.

———. "Encounter in Guerrero." Lynn Riggs Papers. Beinecke Rare Book and Manuscript Library, Yale University Library, Cambridge, Massachusetts.

———. *Green Grow the Lilacs*. New York: Samuel French, 1931.

———. Letter to Willard "Spud" Johnson. June 28, 1950. Spud Johnson Collection. Harry Ransom Center, The University of Texas at Austin, Austin, Texas.

———. "A Note on the Principal Revisions Made in GREEN GROW THE LILACS." Lynn Riggs Collection, series 2, box 6, folder 10. McFarlin Library, The University of Tulsa, Tulsa, Oklahoma.

———. *Roadside*. New York: Samuel French, 1930.

———. *Russet Mantle and The Cherokee Night*. New York: Samuel French, 1936.

Riley, Carroll L. *Becoming Aztlan: Mesoamerican Influence in the Greater Southwest, AD 1200–1500*. Salt Lake City: University of Utah Press, 2005.

Ripley, Anthony. "Death Sentence against Indian Commuted by Dakota Governor." *New York Times*, October 25, 1969: 68.

Robinson, Cecil. "The Extended Presence: Mexico and Its Culture in North American Writing." *MELUS* 5.3 (Autumn 1978): 3–15.

Rodríguez, Ana Patricia. "The Fiction of Solidarity: Transfronterista Feminisms and Anti-Imperialist Struggles in Central American Transnational Narratives." *Feminist Studies* 34.1/2 (Spring–Summer 2008): 199–226.

Rodriguez, Gregory. *Mongrels, Bastards, Orphans, and Vagabonds: Mexican Immigration and the Future of Race in America*. New York: Vintage, 2008.

———. "Shades of Mexican." *Los Angeles Times*, September 3, 2007. Accessed March 13, 2012, http://www.latimes.com/news/opinion/la-oe-rodriguez 3sep03,0,3733464.column.

Rodriguez, Juana Maria. "Gerald Vizenor's Shadow Plays: Narrative Mediations and Multiplicities of Power." In *Native American Perspectives on Literature and History*, edited by Alan R. Velie, 107–15. Norman: University of Oklahoma Press, 1994.

Rodriguez, Roberto. "The H2opi Run into the Land of Quetzalcoatl." Accessed March 14, 2012, http://latinola.com/story.php?story=3321.

Rogers, Will. *The Autobiography of Will Rogers*, edited by Donald Day. Boston: Houghton Mifflin, 1949.

———. *Letters of a Self-Made Diplomat to His President*. Vol. 1. New York: Albert and Charles Boni, 1926.

———. *Rogers-isms: The Cowboy Philosopher on the Peace Conference*. New York: Harper & Brothers, 1919.

———. *There's Not a Bathing Suit in Russia and Other Bare Facts*. New York: Albert and Charles Boni, 1927.

———. *Will Rogers' Weekly Articles*. Vol. 6, *The Roosevelt Years: 1933–1935*, edited by James M. Smallwood and Steven K. Gragert. Stillwater: Oklahoma State University Press, 1982.

Romero, Channette. "Envisioning a 'Network of Tribal Coalitions': Leslie Marmon Silko's *Almanac of the Dead*." *American Indian Quarterly* 26.4 (Fall 2002): 623–40.

Roppolo, Kimberly. "Samson Occom as Writing Instructor: The Search for an Intertribal Rhetoric." In *Reasoning Together: The Native Critics Collective*, edited by Craig S. Womack, Daniel Heath Justice, and Christopher B. Teuton, 303–24. Norman: University of Oklahoma Press, 2008.

Rosaldo, Renato. *Culture and Truth: The Remaking of Social Analysis*. Boston: Beacon, 1993.

Ruoff, A. LaVonne Brown. "Pre-1968 Fiction." In *The Cambridge Companion to Native American Literature*, edited by Joy Porter and Kenneth M. Roemer, 161–71. New York: Cambridge University Press, 2005.

————. *American Indian Literatures: An Introduction, Bibliographic Review, and Selected Bibliography*. New York: Modern Languages Association, 1990.

Ruppert, James. *Mediation in Contemporary Native American Fiction*. Norman: University of Oklahoma Press, 1995.

Rus, Jan. "The 'Comunidad Revolucionaria Institucional': The Subversion of Native Government in Highland Chiapas, 1936–1968." In *Everyday Forms of State Formation: Revolution and the Negotiation of Rule in Modern Mexico*, edited by Gilbert M. Joseph and Daniel Nugent, 265–300. Durham: Duke University Press, 1994.

Rzepka, Charles J. *Detective Fiction*. Cambridge, U.K.: Polity, 2005.

Sahagún, Fray Bernardino de. *A History of Ancient Mexico: Anthropological, Mythological, and Social, 1547–1577*. 1932. Trans. Fanny R. Bandelier. Detroit: Blaine, 1971.

Said, Edward. *Culture and Imperialism*. New York: Vintage, 1993.

Saldívar, Ramón. *The Borderlands of Culture: Américo Paredes and the Transnational Imaginary*. Durham: Duke University Press, 2006.

Sanjinés, Javier. "Indigenismo and Mestizaje." In *A Historical Companion to Postcolonial Literatures: Continental Europe and Its Empires*, edited by Prem Poddar, Rajeev S. Patke, and Lars Jensen, 557–62. Edinburgh: Edinburgh University Press, 2008.

Schedler, Christopher. *Border Modernism: Intercultural Readings in American Literary Modernism*. New York: Routledge, 2002.

Schmal, John P. "Indigenous Identity in the Mexican Census." Accessed June 20, 2011, http://www.houstonculture.org/hispanic/census/html.

Schroeder, Susan. "Introduction: The Genre of Conquest Studies." *Indian Conquistadors: Indigenous Allies in the Conquest of Mesoamerica*, edited by Laura E. Matthew and Michael R. Oudijk, 5–27. Norman: University of Oklahoma Press, 2007.

Shoemaker, Nancy. *American Indian Population Recovery in the Twentieth Century*. Albuquerque: University of New Mexico Press, 1999.

Silko, Leslie Marmon. *Almanac of the Dead*. New York: Penguin, 1991.

————. "Books: Notes on Mixtec and Maya Screenfolds, Picture Books of Preconquest Mexico." *In Yellow Woman and a Beauty of the Spirit: Essays on Native American Life Today*, 155–65. New York: Simon & Schuster, 1996.

————. *Ceremony*. New York: Penguin, 1977.

————. "Notes on *Almanac of the Dead*." In *Yellow Woman and a Beauty of the Spirit: Essays on Native American Life Today*, 135–45. New York: Simon & Schuster, 1996.

Smith, Paul Chaat, and Robert Allen Warrior. *Like a Hurricane: The Indian Move-ment from Alcatraz to Wounded Knee*. New York: New Press, 1996.

Standing Bear, Chief. *Land of the Spotted Eagle*. Boston: Houghton Mifflin, 1933.

———. *My Indian Boyhood*. Boston: Houghton Mifflin, 1931.

———. *My People the Sioux*. Boston: Houghton Mifflin, 1928.

Starr, Emmet. *History of the Cherokee Indians and Their Legends and Folk Lore*. Oklahoma City: The Warden Company, 1921.

Stephen, Lynn. *Transborder Lives: Indigenous Oaxacans in Mexico, California, and Oregon*. Durham: Duke University Press, 2007.

Stocking, George W., Jr., ed. *The Shaping of American Anthropology, 1883–1911: A Franz Boas Reader*. New York: Basic Books, 1974.

Sturm, Circe. *Blood Politics: Race, Culture, and Identity in the Cherokee Nation of Oklahoma*. Berkeley: University of California Press, 2002.

Szeghi, Tereza M. "'The Injin Is Civilized and Ain't Extinct No More Than a Rab-bit': Transformation and Transnationalism in Alexander Posey's Fus Fixico Letters." *Studies in American Indian Literatures* 21.3 (Fall 2009): 1–35.

Tedlock, Dennis, trans. *Popul Vuh: The Definitive Edition of the Mayan Book of the Dawn of Life and the Glories of Gods and Kings*. New York: Simon & Schuster, 1996.

Teuton, Christopher B. "Theorizing American Indian Literature: Applying Oral Concepts to Written Traditions." In *Reasoning Together: The Native Critics Col-lective*, edited by Craig S. Womack, Daniel Heath Justice, and Christopher B. Teuton, 193–215. Norman: University of Oklahoma Press, 2008.

Teuton, Sean. *Red Land, Red Power: Grounding Knowledge in the American Indian Novel*. Durham: Duke University Press, 2008.

Tindall, Lora B. "George Downing Family." Accessed June 20, 2011, http://www.rootsweb.ancestry.com/~txfannin/downing.html.

Townsend, Richard F. *The Aztecs*. London: Thames and Hudson, 1992.

Truett, Samuel. *Fugitive Landscapes: The Forgotten History of the U.S.–Mexico Bor-derlands*. New Haven: Yale University Press, 2006.

"Two Held for Trial in Mexican Deaths." *New York Times*, June 11, 1931: 16.

Van Dine, S. S. "Twenty Rules for Writing Detective Stories." In *Writing Detective and Mystery Fiction*, edited by A. S. Burack, 196–201. Boston: The Writer, 1945.

Vaughan, Mary Kay, and Stephen E. Lewis, ed. *The Eagle and the Virgin: Nation and Cultural Revolution in Mexico, 1920–1940*. Durham: Duke University Press, 2006.

Vest, Jay Hansford C. "A Legend of Culture: D'Arcy McNickle's *Runner in the Sun*." In *The Legacy of D'Arcy McNickle: Writer, Historian, Activist*, edited by John Purdy, 152–65. Norman: University of Oklahoma Press, 1996.

Vizenor, Gerald. *Anishinabe Nagamon*. Minneapolis: Nodin Press, 1970.

———. *The Heirs of Columbus*. Hanover, N.H.: Wesleyan University Press, 1991.

———. *Interior Landscapes*. Minneapolis: University of Minnesota Press, 1990.

———. *Manifest Manners: Postindian Warriors of Survivance*. Hanover, N.H.: Wesleyan University Press, 1994.

———. *Summer in the Spring: Lyric Poems of the Ojibway*. Minneapolis: Nodin Press, 1965.

———. *Tribal Scenes and Ceremonies*. Minneapolis: Nodin Press, 1976.

———. "Trickster Discourse: Comic Holotropes and Language Games." In *Narrative Chance: Postmodern Discourse on Native American Indian Literatures*, edited by Gerald Vizenor, 187–211. Norman: University of Oklahoma Press, 1993.

Ware, Amy M. "The Cherokee Kid: Will Rogers and the Tribal Genealogies of American Indian Celebrity." PhD diss., University of Texas at Austin, 2008.

———. "Unexpected Cowboy, Unexpected Indian: The Case of Will Rogers." *Ethnohistory* 56.1 (2009): 1–34.

———. "Will Rogers's Radio: Race and Technology in the Cherokee Nation." *American Indian Quarterly* 33.1 (Winter 2009): 62–97.

Warrior, Robert. *The People and the Word: Reading Native Nonfiction*. Minneapolis: University of Minnesota Press, 2005.

———. *Tribal Secrets: Recovering American Indian Intellectual Traditions*. Minneapolis: University of Minnesota Press, 1995.

Weaver, Jace. "A Lantern to See By: Survivance and a Journey into the Dark Heart of Oklahoma." In *Survivance: Narratives of Native Presence*, edited by Gerald Vizenor, 313–31. Lincoln: University of Nebraska Press, 2008.

———. Foreword to *The Singing Bird: A Cherokee Novel*, edited by Timothy B. Powell and Melinda Smith Mullikin, ix–xv. Norman: University of Oklahoma Press, 2007.

———. *Other Words: American Indian Literature, Law, and Culture*. Norman: University of Oklahoma Press, 2001.

———. *That the People Might Live: Native American Literatures and Native American Community*. New York: Oxford University Press, 1997.

Weaver, Jace, Craig S. Womack, and Robert Warrior. *American Indian Literary Nationalism*. Albuquerque: University of New Mexico Press, 2006.

Wertheim, Arthur Frank, and Barbara Bair, ed. *The Papers of Will Rogers*. Vol. 1, *November, 1879–April 1904*. Norman: University of Oklahoma Press, 1996.

Wilson, Terry P. "John Joseph Mathews." In *Handbook of Native American Literature*, edited by Andrew Wiget, 245–49. 1994. New York: Garland, 1996.

Womack, Craig S. *Art as Performance, Story as Criticism: Reflections on Native Literary Aesthetics*. Norman: University of Oklahoma Press, 2009.

———. *Red on Red: Native American Literary Separatism*. Minneapolis: University of Minnesota Press, 1999.

———. "A Single Decade: Book-Length Native Literary Criticism Between 1986 and 1997." In *Reasoning Together: The Native Critics Collective,* edited by Craig S. Womack, Daniel Heath Justice, and Christopher B. Teuton, 3–104. Norman: University of Oklahoma Press, 2008.

———. "Theorizing American Indian Experience." In *Reasoning Together: The Native Critics Collective,* edited by Craig S. Womack, Daniel Heath Justice, and Christopher B. Teuton, 353–410. Norman: University of Oklahoma Press, 2008.

Woolley, John, and Gerhard Peters. "Herbert Hoover: Message to President Pascual Ortiz Rubio of Mexico on the Death of Emilio Cortes Rubio." The American Presidency Project. Accessed February 8, 2008, http://www.presidency.ucsb.edu/ws/index.php?pid=22701.

———. "Herbert Hoover: Message to the Congress Recommending Legislation for the Relief of the Families of Emilio Cortez Rubio and Manuel Gomez." The American Presidency Project. Accessed February 8, 2008, http://www.presidency.ucsb.edu/ws/index.php?pid=23149.

Woolsey, L. H. "The Shooting of Two Mexican Students." *The American Journal of International Law* 25.3 (1931): 514–16.

Wright, Muriel H. *A Guide to the Indian Tribes of Oklahoma.* 1951. Norman: University of Oklahoma Press, 1986.

———. "Lee F. Harkins, Choctaw." Accessed June 20, 2011, http://digital.library.okstate.edu/Chronicles/v037/v037p285.pdf.

Index

People and the Word, The (Warrior), 21, 110–11

Pérez-Torres, Rafael, 39

Perlman, Barbara H., 170

Peyer, Bernd, 111

Philadelphia Inquirer (newspaper), 32, 33

Phinney, Archie, 39

pilume, use of term, 6

plumed serpent. *See* Quetzalcoatl (deity)

Plumed Serpent, The (Lawrence), 22

Pocahontas, 175

politics: blood, 71–72, 97; of literature, 18; and self-determination, 28, 42, 54, 59–60, 151, 161, 204, 218n93

Poor People's Campaign, 108–9

Popul Vuh, 181–82, 186, 193, 194, 207n46

Posey, Alexander, 75

Powell, Malea, 36

Powell, Timothy B., 24, 126, 201

Power, Susan C., 11

Pratt, Richard Henry, 21, 118

Proctor, Henry, 149

Pronzini, Bill, 34

Purdy, John, 59

Queen, Ellery, 31

Querry, Ron, 35

Quetzalcoatl (deity), 136, 145–46, 150, 165, 188–90

Quinn, Anthony, 84

Quintasket, Christine, 57

Real Indians (Garroutte), 3–4, 6

Reasoning Together, 194

Red Land, Red Power (Teuton), 74, 198

Red on Red (Womack), 22, 100, 147

Red Power: literature, 17, 124, 147, 177, 197–99; representation of, 108, 197; rise of, 174; on self-determination, 124; and shame, 103–4

Reed, Nelson A., 91, 93

religious practices, indigenous, 54–61; nagualism, 45–53, 59

Remembered Earth, The (Hobson), 198

Reservation Blues (Alexie), 174, 176

retribution, 18

revolution, indigenous, 13, 14–17, 15, 65–67, 70, 87–101, 103–4, 140–43, 176

Rickard, Clinton, 199, 200

Rickard, Karen, 200

Ridge, John Rollin, 54

Riel, Louis, 14, 175

Riggs, Lynn, 1; Indian Territory plays, 73–87, 101–5; on indigeneity, 14; on indigenous revolution, 13, 15, 65–67, 87–101; on intertribal violence, 76; on land loss, 70; on Oklahoma statehood, 85, 104–5; recovery of, 68; settler-colonialism in plays, 85–86. *See also specific works*

Riley, Carroll L., 9, 11

Rivera, Miguel Primo de, 115–16

Roadside (Riggs), 73, 82–84

Robinson, Cecil, 2

Rodgers, Richard, 15, 77

Rodríguez, Ana Patricia, 22

Rodriguez, Raymond, 18

Rodriguez, Roberto, 194

Rogers, Clement Vann, 77, 113

Rogers, Will, 2, 3, 16, 17, 35, 61, 84, 109, 113–17, 134, 141, 202

Rogers, Will, Jr., 107, 114

Romero, Channette, 183–84

Roosevelt, Franklin, 28

Roosevelt, Theodore, 28

Rosaldo, Renato, 91

Ross, John, 12, 110

Rough Riders, 28

Rubio, Emilio Cortes, 31, 61–62

Warrior, Robert, 2, 124; as activist,
    200; on American Indian critical
    studies, 24, 199; on exceptionalism,
    197; on literary nationalism, 59,
    147–48; on Mathews, 126, 134,
    205n4; on Native nonfiction, 110–
    11; on Surrounded, 58; on Talking
    to the Moon, 131, 133–34. See also
    specific works
Washington Bulletin (NCAI), 108
Waterlily (E. Deloria), 54
Weaver, Jace, 1–2, 18; on critical
    practice, 112; on exceptionalism,
    197; on indigenous literature, 193;
    on literary nationalism, 59, 147; on
    Riggs, 68–70, 72–73, 77–78, 80; on
    Singing Bird, 54
We Eh Sah Ki, 126–27
Welch, James, 74, 104, 197
Wheeler-Howard Act. See Indian
    Reorganization Act (1934)
White, Annie, 170
White Hawk, Thomas James, 174
Wild Harvest (Oskison), 54
Willard, Howard, 171
Wind from an Enemy Sky (McNickle),
    24, 54, 57
Winter in the Blood (Welch), 104, 198
Winters, Yvor, 85
witchcraft. See nagualism
Woehlke, Walter, 154
Womack, Craig, 2, 17, 129, 173;
    on critical practice, 112; on
    exceptionalism, 197; on indigenous
    resistance, 100; on land as identity,

103; on literary nationalism, 59,
    147–48; on Riggs, 68, 70, 81, 98
World Elsewhere, A (Riggs), 1, 67,
    82, 184; as captivity narrative, 91;
    indigenous revolution in, 87–101;
    premier of, 66; setting, 15, 65, 73
World Literature Today (magazine), 30
World's Columbian Exposition
    (Chicago), 38
Wounded Knee massacre (1890), 118,
    119
Wratten, Blossom, 170
Wratten, George, 170
Wright, George, 119
Wright, Muriel, 34
Wright, Willard Huntington. See Van
    Dine, S. S.
Writing Detective and Mystery Fiction,
    34
Wynema (Callahan), 54

Yaquis, 14, 39, 40, 55, 94, 117, 186
Year of Pilár, The (Riggs), 67, 82;
    ejidos in, 141; gay subject matter
    in, 69; incest in, 102; indigenous
    revolution in, 87–101; land
    reform in, 103, 105; Mayans in, 87;
    performance of, 66; setting, 15, 65,
    73, 91; storyline, 95–96; working
    notes, 102
Yoeme language, 117

Zapata, Emiliano, 84, 142
Zapata, Eufemio, 84
Zapotecs, 143

JAMES H. COX is associate professor of English and associate director of Native American and Indigenous studies at the University of Texas
at Austin. He is the author of *Muting White Noise: Native American and
European American Novel Traditions* and the coeditor of the forthcoming
Oxford Handbook of Indigenous American Literatures.